Hyperautomation with Generative AI

Learn how Hyperautomation and Generative AI can help you transform your business and create new value

Navdeep Singh Gill

Dr. Jagreet Kaur

Suryakant

www.bpbonline.com

First published: 2024

Published by BPB Online
WeWork
119 Marylebone Road
London NW1 5PU

UK | UAE | INDIA | SINGAPORE

ISBN 978-93-55518-590

www.bpbonline.com

Dedicated to

Our parents, **Late S. Ajmer Singh** *and* **Mrs. Sarbjeet Kaur,**
Mr. S. Balwinder Singh *and* **Mrs. Kulwinder Kaur**

Our children **Dilnawaz Kaur, Haralam Singh** *and* **Yuvaan**

And to all our team members at **Xenonstack**

About the Authors

- **Navdeep Singh Gill** is a DeepTech Enthusiast, Author, TEDx Speaker, Angel Investor and Technophile. With More than 21 years of experience in Transformation and Data, he is now the Founder and Global CEO of Xenonstack, building a Real-Time Data and AI Company with focus on Automation, Analytics, and AI. As a Product Architect leading Akira.ai for the Generative AI Platform for LLMOps/FMOps, he has dedicated the past 11+ years building AI-first organizations defining enterprise data strategies and Building Local Community Chandigarh, AI for AI and Quantum. Navdeep has worked with renowned companies such as Ericsson, Reliance Communications Ltd., and HFCL Infotel.

  His expertise spans Network Transformation, Platform engineering, and Cloud Data Platforms for IoT and AI. Leading technical and cross-functional teams, Navdeep brings hands-on experience across all project phases, including strategy, conceptual design, proof of concept, and detailed architectural design. Under his guidance, Xenonstack is forming a robust team specializing in Progressive Delivery, Real-Time Analytics, Computer vision, Edge AI and observability. Navdeep also contributes in the journey towards becoming AI-first organizations and adopting Cloud-Native approaches through strategic application of Data Science, artificial intelligence, Platform Strategy, and Enterprise Data and AI Strategy.

- **Dr. Jagreet Kaur** is a distinguished author, Chief AI Officer and Research Scholar, leading research in responsible AI and Quantum at Xenonstack since 2016. Additionally, she leads the Akira.ai and QElixir for Generative AI and Quantum research. As a Research Scholar at Singapore University with over 17 years of experience in academics, industry and research, Dr. Kaur has made significant contributions to various domains, including database security, data warehousing, data science, and AI. She earned her BTech degree from Guru Nanak Dev Engineering College, Ludhiana, and her MTech degree from Punjab Engineering College, Chandigarh. Driven by her research topic on "Artificial Intelligence Based Analytical Platform for Predictive Analysis in Health Care," she successfully completed her Ph.D.

With a decade-long experience in Artificial Intelligence, Generative AI and Responsible AI, Dr. Kaur is focusing on ethical and responsible AI for Generative AI applications and Quantum Research for Akira.ai and QElixir.

- **Suryakant** is a Data Scientist by heart and a solution architect by designation with a strong background in cutting-edge technologies. With five years of valuable experience at Xenonstack, Suryakant has proven his expertise in Machine Learning, Deep Learning, and Artificial Intelligence. He holds MTech degree from NIT Delhi and BTech degree from IMS Engineering College, showcasing his dedication to continuous learning and academic excellence. Suryakant's passion lies in leveraging advanced analytics and AI techniques to extract valuable insights from complex datasets. With his diverse skill set and commitment to innovation, he plays a crucial role in driving data-driven solutions at Xenonstack.

Currently, Suryakant is actively involved in pioneering Generative AI solutions. With his expertise in Machine Learning, Deep Learning, and Artificial Intelligence, he is at the forefront of exploring the potential of Generative AI in creating innovative and creative solutions. Suryakant's dedication to pushing the boundaries of AI technology and his passion for harnessing the power of data make him an invaluable asset in the field of Generative AI. Through his work, he aims to unlock new possibilities and drive advancements in this exciting and rapidly evolving domain.

About the Reviewer

Rahul Bansal's journey showcases a remarkable blend of technical expertise, management skills, and a passion for innovation. He has consistently demonstrated outstanding leadership qualities and a commitment to excellence, which has left a lasting impact on the organizations and communities he serves. He pursued a Bachelor's degree in computer science engineering from Guru Gobind Singh Indraprastha University, where he honed his technical acumen. Later, he further enhanced his knowledge and skills by completing a Post Graduation in Business Administration from the prestigious Indian Institute of Management, Lucknow, which provided him with a solid foundation in management principles.

With over 14 years of experience in the IT industry, Rahul has worked with reputable multinational companies such as Tata Consultancy Services, IBM, and EXL Services. Currently, he holds the position of heading the India delivery team for WonderBotz India Pvt. Ltd. His expertise lies in the field of Hyperautomation and intelligent automation, where he has implemented several projects for Fortune 500 companies. Rahul's proficiency extends across leading intelligent platforms such as UiPath, Blue Prism, Automation Hero, Microsoft Power Platform, and IDP platforms like ABBYY, Hyperscience, Rossum, and SS&C Chorus DA.

Acknowledgements

We express our deepest gratitude to the divine entity for granting us the strength and determination to embark on this book-writing journey. Our heartfelt appreciation goes out to the entire team at BPB Publications for granting us the opportunity to publish our work.

We would like to extend our sincere acknowledgments to the individuals who hold a special place in our hearts – our beloved parents, Late S. Ajmer Singh & Mrs. Sarbjeet Kaur, and S. Balwinder Singh & Mrs. Kulwinder Kaur. Their unwavering trust in us and the freedom they bestowed upon us to pursue our passions have been instrumental in shaping our lives. We offer our utmost respect and gratitude for their selfless love, care, and sacrifices. We are immensely grateful to our family members– Dilnawaz Kaur, Haralam Singh (children of Mr. Navdeep and Dr. Jagreet), Pooja (wife of Mr. Suryakant), Yuvaan (son of Mr. Suryakant and Mrs. Pooja)– for their incredible patience and understanding during the time we devoted to writing this book. Words cannot adequately express our gratitude for their unwavering support.

We also extend our heartfelt thanks to our team members at Xenonstack for their contribution and our friends for engaging in fruitful discussions, offering valuable suggestions, and assisting us in shaping the book's topics, concepts, and question framing.

We would like to express our appreciation to our critics. Their constructive criticism has been invaluable in the development and refinement of this book. Without their insightful feedback, we would not have been able to bring this work to fruition.

Preface

The book introduces readers to the fundamental components of Hyperautomation and Generative AI. It outlines the initial steps an organization can take to establish the necessary talent, skill set, and IT infrastructure for streamlining routine business activities. It presents a wide range of use cases and examples that demonstrate the diverse applications of Hyperautomation in various industries, sectors, or specific departments within a company. The book also serves as a valuable resource for understanding different tools and platforms such as UiPath, Automation Anywhere, and IBM, assisting readers in selecting the most suitable technology for their exceptional digital transformation endeavors.

Moreover, the book highlights how organizations already utilizing AI (including Generative AI) and RPA technologies can leverage them effectively to expand automation across different business verticals rapidly. The book is divided into four sections, the first three sections covering specific aspects related to Hyperautomation and its implementation. The last section mainly focuses on Generative AI and its collaboration with Hyperautomation. By integrating Generative AI into Hyperautomation workflows, organizations can automate not only repetitive tasks but also leverage AI to generate new ideas, designs, and solutions. For example, in content creation, Generative AI can automatically generate personalized marketing content, product descriptions, or even entire articles.

Section I: Automation and Its Necessity

Chapter 1: The Realism of Hyperautomation - The preferred structure for a book would typically involve initially introducing the central subject, which in this case is Hyperautomation, and then delving deeper into the topic. However, there is a slight modification in the approach taken by this book. Chapter 1 begins by presenting an overview of Hyperautomation and exploring its emergence as the starting point. Subsequently, it focuses on outlining a comprehensive strategy for automating business processes through hyperautomation, which forms the most crucial aspect of the book, setting the tone for its entirety.

Chapter 2: Existence of Different Automations - The chapter provides an overview of various types of automation, particularly on Robotic Process Automation (RPA). It discusses the concept of RPA as a widely adopted form of automation in various industries. The chapter covers the differences between robots, bots, and cobots, and explores the coexistence of humans and robots, highlighting why RPA is considered beneficial rather than detrimental. Additionally, it touches on the functionality of RPA, explaining the mechanics of how it works.

Chapter 3: Fundamentals of RPA Tools and Platforms - In this chapter, the focus is on providing an essential overview of the current tools used in Robotic Process Automation (RPA). The chapter primarily examines UiPath, Automation Anywhere (including IQ Bots), and Blue Prism, discussing their respective features and functionalities.

The specific topics covered in this chapter are:

1. **UiPath:** The chapter provides an overview of UiPath as an automation platform, highlighting its capabilities and functions.

2. **Automation Anywhere with IQ Bots:** This section delves into Automation Anywhere, emphasizing its integration with IQ Bots, which are intelligent automation components.

3. **Blue Prism and Intelligent Robotic Process Automation:** The chapter explores Blue Prism as a tool for Intelligent **Robotic Process Automation (RPA)**, shedding light on its key features and benefits.

Chapter 4: Amalgam of Hyperautomation and RPA - In the fourth chapter of the book, the focus is on the importance of Hyperautomation and how it differs from its counterparts, namely Robotic Process Automation (RPA) and Intelligent Automation. The chapter explores why Hyperautomation is necessary for the current business landscape and highlights its distinct features compared to RPA and intelligent automation.

Section II: Evolution of Automation to Hyperautomation via RPA

Chapter 5: Devising Hyperautomation Solutions - In this chapter, the focus is on the process of developing **Hyperautomation (HyA)** solutions and identifying the types of problems that can be effectively solved through HyA. The chapter delves into the key components and ingredients required for successful HyA implementation and outlines the steps involved in developing such solutions. By understanding the potential of HyA and following the prescribed steps, organizations can leverage automation technologies to address complex challenges and streamline their operations for improved efficiency and productivity.

Chapter 6: Amalgam of Hyperautomation and Artificial Intelligence - Artificial Intelligence (AI) has become a prominent and trending topic in today's era of cutting-edge technologies. In the context of Hyperautomation, this chapter explores AI from multiple perspectives. Firstly, it delves into AI as a concept, elucidating its fundamental principles and capabilities in mimicking human intelligence. Secondly, it highlights AI as a future, discussing its potential impact on various industries and society. Lastly, the chapter examines AI as a process, emphasizing the practical application of AI techniques and algorithms to automate complex tasks and enable intelligent decision-making. By comprehending AI from these angles, organizations can harness its power within Hyperautomation to drive innovation and achieve transformative outcomes.

Chapter 7: Bridging AI with Humans - The seventh chapter builds upon the previous chapters to provide a comprehensive exploration of the world of AI. This chapter takes a deep dive into the notion of preparing both AI and humans for the future. It addresses the current ethical issues surrounding AI, examining the challenges and dilemmas in its development and deployment. Furthermore, the chapter explores strategies to increase trust in AI, emphasizing the importance of transparency, accountability, and fairness. It also delves into making AI more responsible, considering ways to mitigate biases and ensure ethical decision-making. By tackling these crucial questions, chapter seven sheds light on the necessary considerations and actions required to navigate the evolving landscape of AI while ensuring its responsible and ethical use.

Chapter 8: Impact of Machine Learning with Hyperautomation - Machine Learning plays a pivotal role in AI and is an integral component of Hyperautomation. In this chapter, machine learning is thoroughly explored, highlighting its significance in the context of Hyperautomation. The chapter dives into the principles, algorithms, and techniques of machine learning, showcasing how it enables systems to learn from data and make intelligent predictions or decisions. By understanding the intricacies of machine learning and its integration within Hyperautomation, organizations can leverage their capabilities to develop sophisticated automation solutions that adapt, optimize, and continuously improve over time. This chapter serves as a comprehensive guide to harnessing the power of machine learning within the framework of Hyperautomation to drive innovation and achieve operational excellence.

Chapter 9: Operationalizing Hyperautomation - shifts the focus from conceptual discussions to the practical aspects of Hyperautomation by addressing the critical aspect of operationalizing the solution. It emphasizes that for any solution to be successful in a business context, scalability is of utmost importance. This chapter delves into scalability in Hyperautomation, exploring the challenges and considerations in scaling up automation initiatives. It provides insights into the strategies, technologies, and best practices that can enable organizations to scale their Hyperautomation solutions effectively. By highlighting the significance of scalability, Chapter 9 equips readers with the knowledge and guidance necessary to ensure that their Hyperautomation efforts can be expanded and sustained to meet the evolving needs of their business operations.

Chapter 10: Successful Use Cases of Hyperautomation - In the final chapter, three compelling use case studies are presented, showcasing Hyperautomation as an industrial solution to address contemporary challenges. These case studies provide real-world examples of how organizations have successfully applied Hyperautomation to tackle problems in the current age. By examining these use cases, readers gain insights into the practical application of Hyperautomation across various industries, such as manufacturing, healthcare, or finance. The chapter delves into the specific problem domains, the tailored Hyperautomation solutions implemented, and the resulting benefits and outcomes. By presenting these use cases, the chapter highlights the versatility and efficacy of Hyperautomation as a powerful tool to drive innovation, enhance operational efficiency, and solve complex problems in the modern era.

Section III: Emergence of Generative AI and Its Collaboration with Hyperautomation

Chapter 11: Generative AI and Hyperautomation - This bonus chapter delves into the emerging field of Generative AI, highlighting its significance in the current era. The chapter begins with an introduction to Generative AI, providing an overview of its principles, methodologies, and applications. It then explores the collaborative potential of Generative AI and Hyperautomation, showcasing how these transformative technologies can synergistically work together to amplify their impact. Furthermore, a compelling case study is presented, demonstrating a practical solution that leverages both Generative AI and Hyperautomation. One case study also involved serves as a tangible example of how the combination of these technologies can drive innovation, improve processes, and deliver tangible outcomes in real-world scenarios. Overall, this bonus chapter provides valuable insights into the potential of Generative AI and its integration with Hyperautomation, paving the way for organizations to explore and harness the benefits of this cutting-edge technology.

Coloured Images

Please follow the link to download the
Coloured Images of the book:

https://rebrand.ly/a64bosh

We have code bundles from our rich catalogue of books and videos available at **https://github.com/bpbpublications**. Check them out!

Errata

We take immense pride in our work at BPB Publications and follow best practices to ensure the accuracy of our content to provide with an indulging reading experience to our subscribers. Our readers are our mirrors, and we use their inputs to reflect and improve upon human errors, if any, that may have occurred during the publishing processes involved. To let us maintain the quality and help us reach out to any readers who might be having difficulties due to any unforeseen errors, please write to us at :

errata@bpbonline.com

Your support, suggestions and feedbacks are highly appreciated by the BPB Publications' Family.

Did you know that BPB offers eBook versions of every book published, with PDF and ePub files available? You can upgrade to the eBook version at www.bpbonline.com and as a print book customer, you are entitled to a discount on the eBook copy. Get in touch with us at :

business@bpbonline.com for more details.

At **www.bpbonline.com**, you can also read a collection of free technical articles, sign up for a range of free newsletters, and receive exclusive discounts and offers on BPB books and eBooks.

Piracy

If you come across any illegal copies of our works in any form on the internet, we would be grateful if you would provide us with the location address or website name. Please contact us at **business@bpbonline.com** with a link to the material.

If you are interested in becoming an author

If there is a topic that you have expertise in, and you are interested in either writing or contributing to a book, please visit **www.bpbonline.com**. We have worked with thousands of developers and tech professionals, just like you, to help them share their insights with the global tech community. You can make a general application, apply for a specific hot topic that we are recruiting an author for, or submit your own idea.

Reviews

Please leave a review. Once you have read and used this book, why not leave a review on the site that you purchased it from? Potential readers can then see and use your unbiased opinion to make purchase decisions. We at BPB can understand what you think about our products, and our authors can see your feedback on their book. Thank you!

For more information about BPB, please visit **www.bpbonline.com**.

Join our book's Discord space

Join the book's Discord Workspace for Latest updates, Offers, Tech happenings around the world, New Release and Sessions with the Authors:

https://discord.bpbonline.com

Table of Contents

SECTION I

Automation and Its Necessity

This section delves into the concept of automation, tracing its history and exploring its significance in modern industries. It discusses the various types of automation prevalent today and lays the groundwork for the core subject of the book, Hyperautomation.

CHAPTER 1
The Realism of Hyperautomation

"Automation applied to an inefficient operation will magnify the inefficiency"

— *Bill Gates*

Introduction

Automation is a fascinating word that directly emphasizes targeting the manual process and reducing manual efforts. *Automation* as a term is not new in its existence. It has already existed in technical glossaries, since the 1950s. Automation originated from automatic, which was subjected to mechanical in its initial days.

Considering the current trends, automation is not limited to mechanical operations. The current trends suggest that the need for automation for digital processes is increasing significantly. The emergence of RPA and intelligent automation comes into the picture, further evolving into Hyperautomation; this journey from automation to Hyperautomation was arduous and event driven.

There are different types of automation that exist nowadays such as fixed automation, flexible automation and programmable automation (which will be discussed in the next chapter in detail).

The main purpose of this chapter is to cover not only the future of automation but also the past of automation. Let us start with automation and understand what automation is first.

Structure

In this chapter, we will cover the following topics:

- What is automation
- What is hyperautomation
- Journey of Hyperautomation
- High-level plan to automate business processes
- Important points about Hyperautomation
- Benefits of Hyperautomation

Objectives

The main objective of this chapter is to provide ideas on what Hyperautomation is and why it is becoming the following prime requirement in automation. We will also be studying various high-level plans to adopt Hyperautomation.

What is Automation

Automation is **the technique of making a process or a system that operates automatically**.

Before moving ahead, here are some questions: does everybody know about robots?

What are robots? What can be the role of robots? These are common questions that may be running in someone's mind now. In simple words, a robot is a machine. A machine? What is surprising about it?

Let us understand it with a brief discussion; it is an automated machine that can execute specific tasks without human intervention or sometimes a little intervention. Without human intervention surely sounds interesting. As it is a machine, it can work with speed and precision, which helps to increase efficiency and productivity.

Figure 1.1 features the journey of Automation:

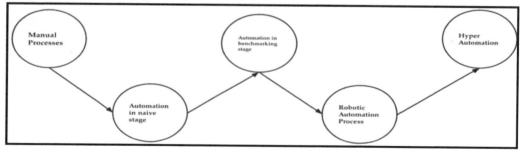

Figure 1.1: *Journey of Automation*

It can be stated that automation has existed throughout the history of humanity, and it will not be hyperbole, as, since the Stone Age, humans have tried to automate things in their senses.

After that, it took several industrial revolutions, many experiments, and inventions to reach the stage of Hyperautomation. The execution of Hyperautomation is entirely not dependent on the concept of automation. It also requires AI and Machine Learning to adapt to hyper-automate any business process.

Here are some facts about the journey of automation:

- In September 1898, *Nikola Tesla* demonstrated his experiment of a remote-control boat at Madison and surprised the world with the blink of automation.
- The industrial revolution started in the 19th century, and it was the point where automation directly impacted human lives.
- The pace of adapting Automation was slow till the end of the 19th century, and the emergence of AI, when the famous incident of defeating *Garry Kasparov* happened, was defeated by the artificial intelligence called Deep Blue.
- In the early 2000s, the focus shifted from automating physicality to digitality. The world started to understand the importance of AI and RPA.

This book leaps forward from here and discusses a cutting-edge technique which has the potential to become the future of Automation, that is, Hyperautomation. What is Hyperautomation? What are its ingredients? What is the necessity? All these sorts of questions have been answered in the book. It will be discussed in this book and the chapter.

What is Hyperautomation

According to the Gartner Glossary, *"Hyperautomation is a business-driven, disciplined approach that organizations use to rapidly identify, vet and automate as many business and IT processes as possible."* Hyperautomation is the next level of automation. It is all about automating the automation. The Hyperautomation takes already running dynamic business processes and tries to automate them. *Figure 1.2* features the various ingredients of Hyperautomation:

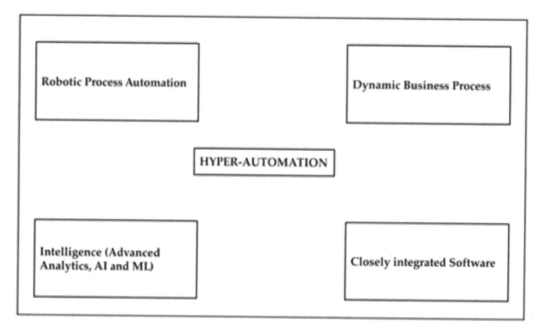

Figure 1.2: Ingredients of Hyperautomation

The essential requirement of implementing Hyperautomation already exists in automated business processes with manual interventions at some stages. Along with the definition, Gartner recommended Hyperautomation as the next level of automation. Gartner predicted that 40% of the already existing business process would be working on planning the implementation of Hyperautomation. RPA has been there for quite a time, automating business to an extent, but imagine a situation which requires decision-making as a process. This decision-making involves further intelligence.

The core principle behind Hyperautomation is to enable more and more intelligence to make decisions, which require manual intervention in an already automated process. By considering this logic, it can be clearly stated that Hyperautomation is the future of automation.

Hyperautomation validates automation and uplifts existing processes with RPA and cutting-edge technology such as Machine Learning, Artificial Intelligence, decision management and **Natural Language Processing (NLP)**. We discussed automation and Hyperautomation briefly, and now the next question that can come to anybody's mind is, what is the difference between these two? How can we distinguish between them? Let us check out the differences between these two technologies in brief.

Table 1.1 demonstrates the difference between Hyperautomation and automation.

Parameters of comparison	Hyperautomation	Automation
Technologies (required)	RPA + Machine Learning + concepts of AI + packaged software.	RPA tools like UiPath, Automation anywhere will be sufficient
Core of implementation	AI-based process automation	Task oriented automation
Dependency on Human interventions	Minimal Level dependency	Moderate level dependency
Output	Intelligent automated process	Automated Process
Range of automation	It can automate a nest of already automated processes which are interlinked	Can only automate processes that include set of defined rules and logics, where no there is no requirement of human intelligence

***Table 1.1:** Difference between automation and Hyperautomation*

Journey of Hyperautomation

Unlike automation, Hyperautomation required the rise of many other technologies to come into existence, because Hyperautomation is not a single technology; in the true sense, it requires a combination of RPA and AI. *Figure 1.3* represents the difference between manual, RPA, and Hyperautomation:

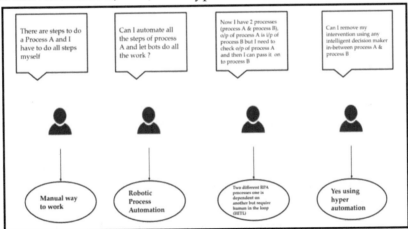

***Figure 1.3:** Manual to Hyperautomation in a Nutshell*

This journey starts with automation, and the history of automation is already discussed previously. There is no point in debating that phase again. Coming to Hyperautomation, we know it is a very naive and the latest technology. The term Hyperautomation was coined by Gartner in 2019 and became a part of their glossary in 2020. Still, it was a theoretical concept. Because Hyperautomation requires robotic intelligence, it can act like a mind, and it creates a dependency on being intelligent. Let us understand this by an example as a high-level flow of the journey of a Hyperautomation solution.

Figure 1.4 demonstrates the journey of Hyperautomation:

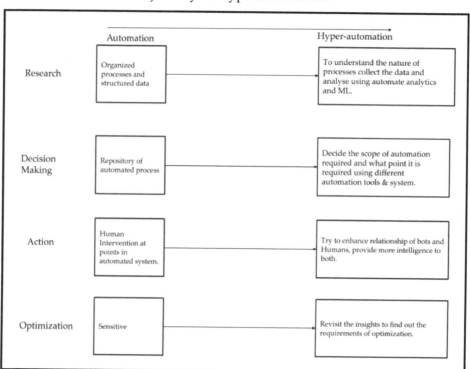

Figure 1.4: *Journey of adopting Hyperautomation of an already automated use-case*

From the above example of the use case, it becomes clear as to which things get improved when an automated process is transformed into a hyper-automated process. This automation journey takes place in four stages:

- **Research:** The difference created at this stage by Hyperautomation is that one can use advanced analytics to get more insights.

- **Decision making:** In the case of Hyperautomation, Artificial Intelligence can be a big help in making decisions, even while deciding the scope of automation.

- **Action:** In Hyperautomation, the prime goal at this stage is to reduce human intervention and improve the relationship between humans and bots.

- **Optimization:** AI and ML-based techniques can be used at this stage to find when and where optimization is required.

High-level plan to automate business processes

Figure 1.5 provides a glimpse of different milestones of Hyperautomation:

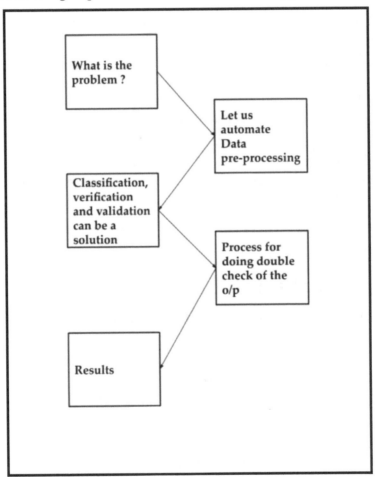

Figure 1.5: Milestones of Hyperautomation

- **Milestone 1 | Identify the problem:** The most basic yet most important step is identifying the problem and its nature. What are the ratio automation and manual steps involved in solving the problem? What is the requirement of intelligence? Identification of the problem should be able to answer these questions. After identifying the problem, the solution should be mapped with business processes.

- **Milestone 2 | Automate the fundamental processes:** Automate the primary processes first, for example, Data Pre-processing. RPA can play a significant role in this milestone. This milestone aims to convert business processes into automated processes using RPA.

- **Milestone 3 | Identify the requirements of AI and ML:** The target of this milestone is to identify the needs of intelligence and to what scope. Intelligence requirements provide a fair idea about how it can be transformed into AI or Machine Learning problems. Try to find these basic answers: what kind of intelligence is required? Is it a classification problem? Or it involves some sort of validation?

- **Milestone 4 | Time to double-check results:** Milestone 4 is about double-checking the output of milestone 3 of whether the outcome can be mapped with the business requirement or whether the results are accurate are coming or not. This can be cross verified using historical data as well.

- **Milestone 5 | Results:** At this milestone, you will have the results. Finely polish the results according to the problem and business requirements. Although human intervention is minimal in Hyperautomation, there is significantly less chance of inaccuracy, and human error is entirely negligible.

Let us discuss some examples of industries where Hyperautomation can provide a solution using the initial plan.

Hyperautomation in Information Technology

Hyperautomation can have a vast amount of uses in Information Technology. Here are some common use cases:

- In the user login management system, automatic OTP generation to secure login, resetting a password, and so on.

- Hyperautomation can provide temporary admin access according to companies' needs, using help from AI for decision-making.

- Server crashes and downtime are a nightmare for every IT department. Hyperautomation can be used to automatically reboot, shut, restart, and reconfigure various types of servers. It helps organizations to reduce IT operational costs and save time.

- With a single click, complex systems can be installed easily, and in a small span of time by using Hyperautomation.

Hyperautomation in banking

Hyperautomation can help banks and accounting departments to automate manual repetitive processes and can use AI for decisions for more critical tasks.

- With the help of Hyperautomation, it can become a quick and straightforward process to open an account.
- **Know Your Customer (KYC)**, and **Anti-Money Laundering (AML)** are processes that can be easily handled with the help of Hyperautomation.
- Hyperautomation can make it easy to track accounts and send automated notifications for the required document submissions.
- To generate audit reports, the manual process takes several hours but can be completed in minutes with the help of Hyperautomation.

Hyperautomation in Human Resources

Here are a few use cases of Hyperautomation in human resources:

- With the help of Hyperautomation, bots compare resumes with the description for a particular job and increase the level of automation.
- It also helps to check and keep track of time-to-time company reviews.
- Bots allow HR to manage the data of employees effectively.
- It also helps to verify the history of an employee.

Hyperautomation use cases in manufacturing

Here are a few use cases of Hyperautomation in manufacturing:

- One of the primary benefits of Hyperautomation in manufacturing is that it can generate accurate reports of production.
- In inventory management, Hyperautomation can be used to automate emails, monitor inventory levels, and paperwork digitization.
- Hyperautomation use cases in manufacturing show how bots can automate bills of material by extracting data and providing accuracy in data, leading to fewer transactional issues and errors.
- **Proofs of Delivery (PODs)** are important documents for the customer service department of manufacturers. These documents contain a high risk for human errors and are highly labor-intensive. These problems can be solved with the help of bots.

Hyperautomation use cases in the retail industry

Here are a few use cases of Hyperautomation in the retail industry:

- Bots can extract data to help businesses categorize products and identify their market share in different regions. This also helps in saving countless hours of work.

- Returning any product involves a lot of formalities and processing. Bots enable checking the record and speeding up the entire process of return.

Important points about Hyperautomation

Before digging deeper into Hyperautomation in the upcoming chapter, here are some things to remember:

- Businesses and their processes are conglomerate systems. While there is a plan to automate different simple manual processes, please note one simple point: those simple processes are parts of a larger ecosystem. Do not just focus on automating simple and segregated processes; also try to make an understanding of what is happening and why it is happening as a whole and redesign your business strategy accordingly.

- Humans will always be a part of the whole process. The primary role of Humans could not be decision-making only; it could be more than that. This could revolve around understanding the succeeding and failing points of systems and processes and developing strategies for making them more robust.

- The most important role which humans can bring to the table is accountability. If a machine makes wrong decisions, who can correct them after detecting them? It is where humans can help machines.

- Understanding business problems should be the first step, and after that, moving to data pre-processing and analytics is the way to go forward.

Benefits of Hyperautomation

Figure 1.6 shows the benefits of Hyperautomation:

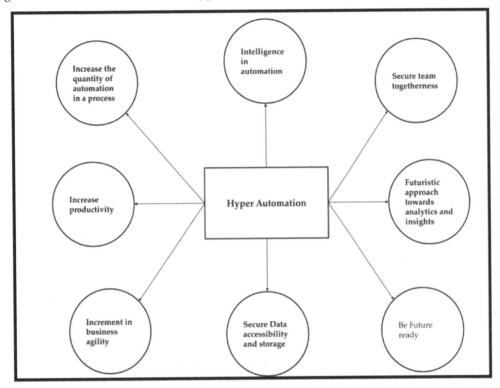

Figure 1.6: *Benefits of Hyperautomation*

Here are the prime benefits of Hyperautomation:

- **Intelligence in automation**: With RPA, the intelligence can be included as using Hyperautomation, and Artificial Intelligence can also be a part of the solution.

- **Increase the quantity of automation in a process**: With the help of Hyperautomation, all the manual processes which were not possible to be automated due to various reasons can be automated, which will increase the quotient of automation in already automated processes.

- **Secure team togetherness**: Hyperautomation can connect everything with everyone and make separate team efforts into a bigger automated and connected process.

- **Increase productivity**: It is simple; if the quotient of automation increases, surely it will affect productivity in a positive way.

- **Futuristic approach towards analytics and insights:** The current approaches do not provide connectivity between analytics and insights. With Hyperautomation, this can be solved.

- **Increment in business agility:** Business agility is directly proportional to scalability, and Hyperautomation can provide scalability to the business, which will directly result in an increment in business agility.

- **Robust data accessibility and storage:** With Hyperautomation, human intervention can be reduced, which makes the whole process less human error-prone and more robust.

- **Be future ready:** Hyperautomation is the future of automation and adopting Hyperautomation can make business future ready.

Conclusion

Hyperautomation is all about handling complex issues and simplifying them using cutting-edge technology, AI and automation. This technology can bring different technology together to acquire the optimum level of automation and intelligence, which can be used to bring humans closer to technology and where both entities can work together. It has already been discussed what Hyperautomation is. How can it be implemented? But its particular use cases have not been discussed. Of course, this knowledge will be addressed in upcoming chapters, but before ending this chapter, the need for Hyperautomation should be clear. With the use of Hyperautomation, processes which require so much computation power and must process a massive amount of data can be automated easily, further reducing repetitive and manual operations. It provides velocity, accuracy, and stability. It results in a reduction in the process running costs and provides an improved customer experience. It is an avant-garde automation that is more swift, accurate and robust while operating different processes. Hyperautomation directly impacts the primary value of business requirements, which is risk management, cost saving and revenue, although with better-processed results.

Key facts

- *Hyperautomation is a business-driven, disciplined approach that organizations use to rapidly identify, vet, and automate as many business and IT processes as possible. - Gartner Glossary.*

- Hyperautomation brings the intelligent quotient to an already running automated process.

- Hyperautomation validates automation and uplift existing processes with the combination of RPA and cutting-edge technology such as Machine Learning, Artificial Intelligence, decision management and **Natural Language Processing (NLP)**.

Key terms

- Artificial Intelligence
- Machine Learning
- Robotic Process of Automation
- Intelligent automation
- Hyperautomation

Questions

1. How can we define the term Hyperautomation?
2. What is the difference between Hyperautomation and automation?
3. What are the essential requirements for implementing a Hyperautomation solution?
4. What are the significant steps in implementing Hyperautomation?

Join our book's Discord space

Join the book's Discord Workspace for Latest updates, Offers, Tech happenings around the world, New Release and Sessions with the Authors:

https://discord.bpbonline.com

CHAPTER 2

Existence of Different Automations

"There's a lot of automation that can happen that isn't a replacement for humans, but of mind-numbing behavior."

— *Stewart Butterfield*

Introduction

Automation allows processes to execute automatically without human intervention. Humans cannot perform different actions simultaneously, but machines have the ability to do so. Cognitive technologies help machines perform possible actions efficiently for industries. Automated manufacturing systems operate a manufacturing process in the industries when making any physical product. They perform operations such as processing, assembly, inspection, and material handling and sometimes accomplish even more than one of these operations in the same system. They are called automated because they perform their operations with a reduced level of human participation compared with the corresponding manual process. In some highly automated systems, there is virtually no human participation in any process. Let us talk about the different types of automation and their functionality.

Structure

In this chapter, we will cover the following topics:

- Different types of Automation
- Global and specific Automations

- Robotic Process Automation
- Robots, bots, and Cobots
- Coexistence of humans and robots
- The functionality of RPA

Objectives

By the end of this chapter, the audience will be able to understand the different types of automation, how they are different from each other, and why automation is beneficial to humans as well. The chapter also provides a glimpse of Robotic Process Automation and how it works, as well as a discussion on bots, robots, and cobots, along with the differences among them.

Different types of automation

Automation systems are classified into three types of automation, as can be seen in *Figure 2.1*:

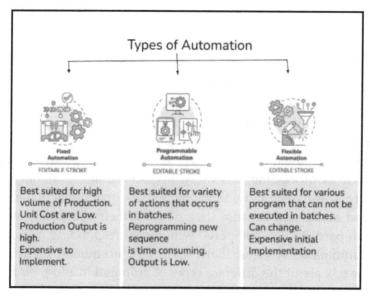

Figure 2.1: Types of Automation

Fixed automation

It is a type of automation that has the capability to automate the processes which have configuration. It follows the sequence of steps for automated processes. Fixed automation is also called **Hard Automation**. It is helpful for many companies with high demand, requiring no change. **World Health Organization (WHO) uses** automation to create food products of one type or other variants. An example of fixed automation is Flow Production.

The characteristics of using Fixed Automation are as follows:

- It is a high investment initially and, therefore expensive to set up initially.
- It produces a large quantity at a high production rate.
- Low cost per unit produced.
- Difficult to accommodate changes.

Programmable automation

It allows the production equipment and automation to be designed with the capability to change the sequence of operations to be processed according to the evolving needs. A program controls the operation sequence, which is a set of instructions code/program so that they can be read and interpreted by the system. It is commonly used in low to medium production, most suitable for batch production, For example, cloth printing machines. This allows them to make thousands of batches of one product at a time.

The characteristics of using Programmable automation are as follows:

- High investment in general-purpose equipment.
- Lower production rates than fixed automation.
- Flexibility to deal with different products and changes in product configuration.
- Used in low and medium-volume production.
- Most suitable for batch production, if required.

Flexible automation

A flexible automated system produces a variety of products. There is no loss in production time while reprogramming the system and altering the physical setup in tools and machine settings. A flexible automation system can produce various combinations of products efficiently. This type of automation tends to have medium production levels and is known as **Soft automation**. These systems will be able to change the physical setup, code, and programs with no loss in time and productivity of the product.

The characteristics of using Flexible automation are as follows:

- High investment for custom machinery/automation cost.
- It has medium production rates and best suited for medium-demand products.
- The flexibility of products to deal with product design variations.
- No time is lost with new changes to production.
- Higher cost per unit.

Global and specific automations

In the previous paragraph, we got familiar with three different types of automated systems fixed, programmable and flexible automation. Here, we will discuss some additional forms of automation, starting with a global, integrative approach and then moving on to other types of automation.

Integrated automation

It is an Integrated Automation of technologies. Integrated automation reduces the complexity of independently automated work processes by streamlining communication between automated processes. Rather than allowing six automated systems to operate separately, integrated automation unifies them under one system. Integrated automation can include technologies such as Flexible Machining Systems, Automated Material Handling, and Computer-Aided Manufacturing.

Computer-Aided Manufacturing

For automated manufacturing processes, **Computer-Aided Manufacturing (CAM)** uses computers and machines. CAM is often integrated with **Computer Aided Design (CAD)** to improve manufacturing processes. Some benefits of CAM include increased material, production consistency, production output, and component quality. CAD designs verified by engineer oversights are then automatically reproduced using CAM.

Robotics Process Automation

Developers write code that automates tasks and the interface at the back end by using **Application Programming Interfaces (APIs)**. Robotic automation interacts with the available IT infrastructure, and there is no requirement for complicated system integration. **Robotic Process Automation (RPA)** is programmed to automate many back-office operations, workflow, and infrastructure. These processes can easily integrate with user portals, websites, and in-house applications. RPA is a set of commands/rules executed by bots and a predefined set of rules. The main aim of RPA is to eliminate the repetitive and time-consuming tasks performed by humans. RPA will also discuss further in the chapter.

Cognitive intelligence

Cognitive intelligence relies on software to automate information-intensive processes. Cognitive intelligence generally uses RPA for automation. It also offers a different range of benefits, which includes reduced operational costs, improved customer satisfaction, and many other benefits, such as bringing precision to complicated business processes based on unstructured data.

Conversational automation

Conversational automation provides a better customer experience than traditional chatbots. It allows for more human-like interactions using NLP. Intelligent bots significantly reduce costs and improve customer experience and journey because of their 24/7 availability and rapid responses.

RPA has been introduced in the bifurcation of automation above. Let us discuss the same in detail.

Robotic Process Automation

Robotic Process Automation (RPA) is a hallmark of **Intelligent Process Automation (IPA)**, which describes logic-driven execution. Pre-programmed rules for primarily used structured data. RPA gets to the heart of Productivity Optimization and takes it to the next level by redefining work and redeploying employees to higher-value jobs. Process bots can perform simple human-like functions such as sending approval requests, downloading attachments from emails, and putting data from one file to another file. Robotic Process Automation has a technical similarity to graphical end-user interface testing mechanisms. *Figure 2.2* shows the various functionalities of a Robot:

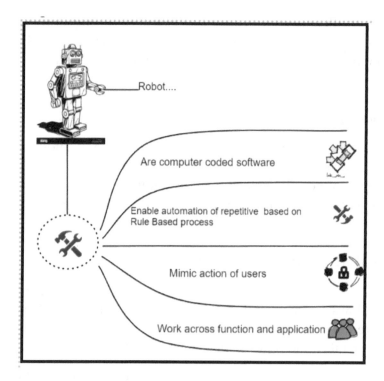

Figure 2.2: Functionalities of Robot

Features of Robotic Process Automation

There are six standard functions of RPA, and they are as follows:

- **Internal System Interface**: This links the data from the legacy system to the front design.

- **Extract data from the internet**: This extracts data for checking stock prices and helps research competitors. It can also be used for updates by removing data using the Internet.

- **External system interface**: Creates an interface for **Electronic Data Interchange (EDI)** that can also run in your web banking system Bank. The system interface to the outside world is also responsible for the data interface between groups. Under this function, data can be extracted from other websites as well.

- **Data check and collection**: Uses data checks to check for unusual results in your data.

- **Data manipulation**: Data stimuli helps merge different data from reports and make changes. For this, we also stimulate data and information.

- **Commercial application**: It can be used in applications where it helps run workflows, send emails, and search Data with specific logic. Applications that can be used for commercials.

Why RPA

Let us discuss this topic with a scenario in the enterprise.

The business scenario is Dynamic. A company must continue developing products, Marketing, and so on to grow.

A typical enterprise operates with several different IT structures. The rate of change in processes remains low. It usually varies due to timing and implementation complexity issues. As a result, business processes do not reflect the processes depicted in the IT structure.

We must hire human employees to keep this technical and organizational debt and check the Gap between systems and processes. For example, an organization that changed sales procedures now requires a 50% upfront payment to confirm product reservations. However, this is not yet encoded in the IT structure. Human workers must dynamically validate billing and payment information and edit sell orders only when a 50% promotion has occurred.

Figure 2.3 illustrates this example scenario of the enterprise:

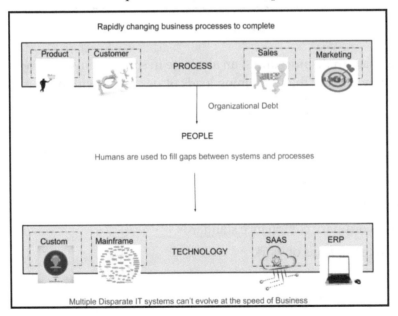

Figure 2.3*: Example scenario of the enterprise*

The problem with humans

With any alteration within the enterprise procedure, a business enterprise might want to rent new personnel and educate current personnel to map IT Shape and enterprise procedure. Both blends are time and money consuming. Moreover, any flourishing enterprise procedure extrude will want retraining.

Figure 2.4 features an example of the business process without RPA:

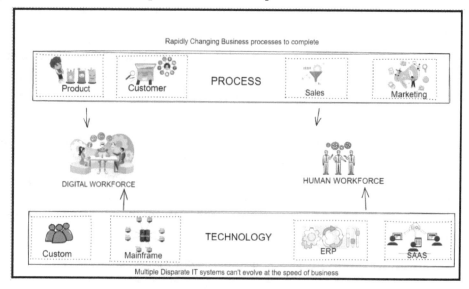

Figure 2.4: *Business process without RPA*

In the case of alternate procedures, an alternate in some strains of software program code is usually quicker than retraining loads of personnel within the company.

Here are a few benefits of using RPA:

- Low technical barrier
- Increased accuracy
- The gadget stays in place
- Increased productivity
- Meets ordinary compliance standards
- No interruptions of work
- Cost saving
- More productive employees

Use cases of RPA

Some of the use cases of RPA are as follows:

- **Imitate human action:** Emulates human fulfillment of the tedious technique of using numerous petitions and structures. Please note that a prime condition for the use case is that no human intelligence is required.

- **Manage excessive volume-repeated tasks:** RPA can hover data from one machine to another. It executes distinct responsibilities such as fact entry, copying, and pasting.

- **Multi-tasking:** Employ more than one complex responsibility throughout more than one structure. This enables the handling of multiple tasks by taking advantage of facts and ship reports.

- **Virtual machine emulsion:** Instead of advancing a brand-new architecture, these automation machines can fetch data among differing and legacy systems by connecting them on a user interface level.

- **Automated remote generated:** Automates data extraction to expand accurate, productive, well-timed reports.

- **Information authenticates and inspects:** Determine and cross-affirm facts among distinct structures to certify and test knowledge to provide authentication and auditing outputs.

- **Technical debt management:** It enables lower technical debt by handling the processes which are running on multiple codes among systems, preventing the advent of custom commission.

- **Quality Assurance (QA):** It can be understood as a process of making a good-quality product into a great-quality product. It is an important step as it directly affects the product which is going to be used by the end user.

- **Data migration:** Allows computerized facts migration via structures which is not always feasible using conventional mediums, such as documents, spreadsheets, or supply facts files.

- **Gap solutions:** Robotic automation fills the gaps with technique deficiencies. It consists of many easy responsibilities, including password resets, System resets, etc.

Challenges Of RPA

While RPA software programs can assist an organization in growth, there are a few obstacles, including the organizational way of life, technical issues, and scaling.

- **Organizational culture**: While RPA will lessen the want for specific task roles, it will add pressure to increase new positions to address extra complicated tasks, allowing personnel to focus on higher-degree approaches and innovative problem-solving. The adaptability of a body of workers might be essential for hit consequences in automation and virtual transformation projects. By instructing your workforce and investing in training programs, you may put together groups for ongoing shifts in priorities.

- **Difficulty in scaling**: While RPA can carry out several simultaneous operations, it could be hard to scale because of regulatory updates or internal changes. According to a Forrester report, 52% of clients declare they struggle to raise their RPA program. An enterprise should have one hundred or more active working robots to qualify as a sophisticated program. However, few RPA tasks develop past the primary ten bots.

Robots, bots, and cobots

Let us now discuss robots and what they are doing, cobots and bots, in no order:

Cobots

A collaborative robot, which is also known as a cobot, can learn multiple tasks so that it can assist human beings. A bot is a software program that performs automated, time-consuming, and repetitive tasks. It can mimic human behavior. A robot is a machine that can perform physical tasks.

The benefits of cobots are as follows:

- **Compact**: Small and very compact. It is used anywhere in the process of production because it takes up small spaces.

- **Installing and programming**: It is easy to install and simple to program.

- **Flexible**: It can quickly adopt new things. That is why cobots can work in different places.

- **Reduction of production costs**: Using cobots reduces the production cost.

Figure 2.5 illustrates the various benefits of cobots:

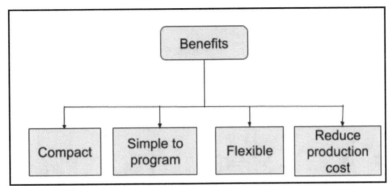

Figure 2.5: *Benefits of Cobots*

Different tools for cobots

Cobots have different kinds of devices. The tools can be divided into categories such as grippers, **End of Arm Tooling (EOAT)**, vision, software, range extenders, and safety and supply systems.

- **Grippers:** These allow the cobot to pick up things and drop that thing somewhere else. There are different kinds of grippers for various tasks, such as finger grippers, vacuum grippers, and magnetic grippers.

- **EOAT: End of Arm Tooling (EOAT)** includes glue dispensers, screw machines, sanders, tool changers, sensors, welding machines and soldering tools. The development of these tools has increased in the present era, meaning, cobots can help the production process more efficiently.

- **Tool changers:** There are different types of tools available in the market for cobots to make them more flexible. This tool allows cobots to perform multiple tasks. For example, in the assembly, one cobot first uses the gripper to pick up and place all the things in the right place. After that, it uses the screwdriver to join the things.

- **Vision systems:** The vision system provides visibility to the cobots. Cobots can identify patterns and objects, and can scan barcodes. This is the great advantage of using cobots. It can supply the products.

Figure 2.6 illustrates the various tools with which cobots can help:

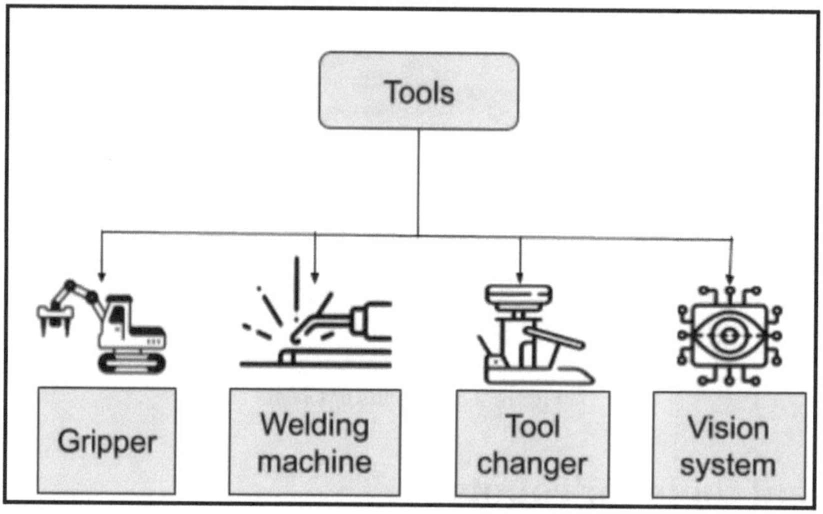

Figure 2.6: *Tools where cobots can help*

Different industries for cobots

There are many industries where cobots are used and successfully integrated.

- **Food Industry:** The demand for cobots in the Food industry has increased in the present situation because of the demand increasing food safety. Automation is more complex than any other industry because it is tough for cobots to manage food products directly. The appearance of cobots and gripper technology has changed it.

- **Plastics industry:** Inside the plastic industry, they produce many products in small quantities. This process needs to be automated, but it is difficult because of the production process changes. In this scenario, cobots have changed it because they are convertible and can learn new things.

- **Packaging industry:** There is a need for cobots in the packaging industry. They can perform packing tasks, like placing products in boxes. Now employees are delighted because cobots can reduce their work and increase productivity.

- **Electronics Industry:** Small products must be handled carefully within the electronics industry. Cobots are built with different types of sensors. That is why they are known as **Sensitive robots**.

Figure 2.7 illustrates the various industries where cobots are used:

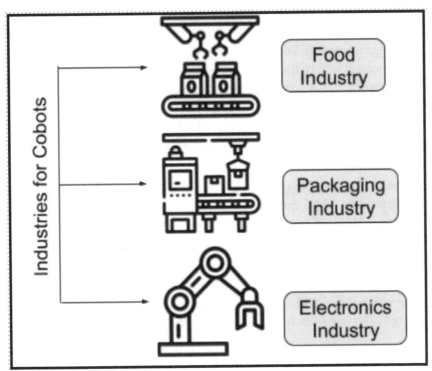

Figure 2.7: *Different industries for cobots*

Robots

A Robot is a machine capable of performing physical tasks without human intervention. There are many different types of Robots to perform different kinds of tasks. They can do better work than humans. Following are the things robots do better than humans:

- Robots can automate manual or repetitive activities in the corporate or industrial sector.
- They work in unpredictable environments to spot hazards such as gas leaks.
- Moreover, they can process and deliver reports for enterprise security.
- Robots can deliver online orders, room service, and food packets when needed.
- Robots help doctors during surgeries.
- Robots can also make music, monitor shorelines for dangerous predators, help search and rescue and even assist with food preparation.

Types of robots

There are as many different types of robots as there are tasks:

- **Pre-Programmed robots:** Pre-programmed robots operate in a controlled environment, where they do simple, monotonous tasks. An example of a pre-programmed robot would be a mechanical arm on an automotive assembly line. The component serves one function to weld a door on, to insert a specific part into the engine, and so on, and its job is to perform that task longer, faster, and more efficiently than a human.

- **Humanoid robots:** Humanoid robots can mimic or copy human behavior. It performs human activities such as jumping, skipping, running, and so on. It is designed just like human beings. Two prominent examples of humanoid robots are Hanson Robotics' Sophia and Boston Dynamics' Atlas.

- **Autonomous robots:** Autonomous robots can do this independently of human operators. These robots are usually designed to carry out tasks without any human intervention. They are different because they use sensors to perceive the world. One example of an autonomous robot is the Roomba vacuum cleaner, which uses sensors to roam freely throughout a home.

- **Teleoperated robots:** Teleoperated robots are semi-autonomous bots which use a wireless network to enable human control from a safe distance. These robots usually work in geographical conditions such as those with adverse weather-related circumstances. For example, teleoperated robots are human-controlled submarines that fix underwater pipe leaks and detect landmines on a battlefield.

- **Augmenting robots:** It is also known as VR robots. The field of robotics for human augmentation is where science fiction could become a reality very soon, with bots that can redefine the definition of humanity by making humans faster and more robust. Some examples of current augmenting robots are robotic prosthetic limbs or exoskeletons used to lift hefty weights.

How do robots function

Based on their functioning, robots are of two types:

- **Independent robots:** Independent robots can work independently without human intervention. These typically require more intense programming but allow robots to take the place of humans when undertaking dangerous, mundane, or otherwise impossible tasks, from bomb diffusion and deep-sea travel to factory automation. Independent robots have proven to be the most undisciplined to society, as they eliminate specific jobs but also present **new** possibilities for growth.

- **Dependent robots:** Dependent robots are non-autonomous robots interacting with humans to enhance their actions. This is a relatively **new** form of technology and expanded into new applications. Still, one form of dependent robot realized is artificial, controlled by the human mind.

Uses of robots

Robots have various types of use cases, which make them ideal. Soon, we will see robots almost everywhere in the future, such as in hospitals, hotels, and even on roads.

- **Robotics in manufacturing:** The manufacturing company is the oldest and most famous user of robots. These robots and co-bots work together to efficiently test and assemble products, such as cars and industrial equipment. It is evaluated that there are more than three million industrial robots in use right now.

- **Logistics robots:** Nowadays, Robots can control shipping and handling. Now we can expect our packages to arrive at blazing speeds; logistics companies use robots in warehouses to help maximize time efficiency. Some robots can take the items off the shelves, transport them across the warehouse floor, and pack them.

- **Robots for home:** Today, Robots are everywhere. We can use them in our homes, also. They can remind us of our routines, and even they can entertain our kids. The most well-known example of a home robot is the autonomous vacuum cleaner Roomba.

- **Travel robots:** The self-driving cars are examples of travel robots. It is a combination of data science and robotics. Companies such as Tesla, Ford, Waymo, Volkswagen, and BMW are all working on self-driving cars. Rideshare companies like Uber and Lyft are also working on autonomous rideshare vehicles which do not require humans to operate the car.

- **Healthcare robotics:** Robots are also used in the healthcare sector. Robots can help or assist surgeons in recovering from injury in physical therapy. For example, Toyota's healthcare assistants help people regain the ability to walk, and TUG is designed to autonomously stroll throughout a hospital and deliver everything from medicines to clean linens.

Bots

A **bot** is a short version of a robot – a software program that performs automated, repetitive, time-consuming tasks. Bots can mimic human behavior. They operate much faster than human users and are more error-free than humans. They can do valuable actions, such as customer service.

How bots work

Nowadays, more than half of the internet traffic can be occupied by bots. In some e-commerce sites, bot traffic can be higher than 90%. The bot can scan content, interact with web pages and social media accounts, or chat with users. Bots, such as search engines, are made of machine learning index content. Bots interact with humans in customer service and answer their queries.

Types of bots

There are different types of bots:

- **Chatbots:** Chatbot refers to those bots that can chat or can respond to human queries by responding to some specific queries. They are programmed with certain responses.

- **Social bots:** These bots can operate on social media platforms. They can generate messages and provide ideas. It is difficult for social bots to make fake accounts because social networks have become sophisticated.

- **Shop bots:** With the help of shopping bots, we can find the best products at the best prices because the bot can observe the user's patterns while navigating the website. After that, the bot customizes the website for the user.

- **Download bots:** We can use bots to automatically download software or any mobile application. They can also be used to attack download sites.

- **Transactional bots:** Transactional bots are used to do transactions on behalf of humans. It allows customers to make a transaction within the context of the conversation.

Advantages of bots

The advantages of bots are as follows:

- Bots are faster than humans at performing repetitive tasks.
- They can save time for customers and clients.

- They reduce labor costs for organizations.
- They are available 24/7.
- We can customize bots as per requirement.
- We can use them for multiple purposes.
- They can offer an improved user experience.

Disadvantages of bots

The disadvantages of bots are as follows:

- Bots cannot be set to perform some exact tasks, and they can misunderstand users – and therefore cause frustration in the process.
- Humans are still necessary to manage the bots and step in if one misinterprets another human.
- Bots can be programmed to be malicious.
- Bots can be used for spam.

Coexistence of humans and robots

In recent times, regarding the feasibility of a safe **Human-Robot Interaction (HRI)**, there has been an exceptional growth of attention by the industrial end-users about the new possibilities opened. Under safety premises, robots and humans share a common workspace without fences on the factory floor and execute various practical tasks in collaboration. HRI features span the several functional aspects of robot action and can be made more different applications; the semi-automatic operation of manipulators for tackling very complex tasks is enhanced thanks to on-the-fly human interaction, teaching, and programming robot action can be more intuitive and friendly. Operators working with robots may closely monitor the quality of products. As a result, collaborative robotics has been considered one of the enabling technologies of the industrial revolution. By the several research results obtained during the last few years within the robotics and automation scientific communities, the realization of these long-standing and great expectations has been made possible.

We have not come that far, so we will have to get used to a life shared with robots. However, within the upcoming few years, we might as well get used to the idea. At this point, technology is at the highest level, and some new technologies are invented and upgraded daily.

The human-robot relationship is becoming a new trend for the current and future automated technology industry. It is now apparent that perfection is possible through human-robotics coexistence. The human sets the rules as the machines accomplish the ruled objectives. The capabilities of a self-driving vehicle are no longer a proposed concept but an evident reality in many market segments. An interdisciplinary research team, however, points out the possibility of a much better work relationship between humans and robots. In an integrated work environment, the same as humans do not have to team apart to realize the same goal; the robots also do not have to team alone towards a common objective. There can be robot-to-human or human-to-robot work processes and not just the robot-to-robot or human-to-human process supervised by humans and robots.

Figure 2.8 features the human-robot coexistence and interaction in open industrial cells:

Figure 2.8: *Human-robot coexistence and interaction in open industrial cells*

The universities of *Duisburg-Essen*, *Trier*, and *Gottingen* take credit for the interdisciplinary research team they summoned to report on the human and robot relationship. The *International Journal of Advanced Manufacturing Technologies* proposes an intermingle process between humans and robots. Thus, if the seclusion gap is minimal between the human-machine work process, the logical errors will reduce, and less time will be needed to accomplish an objective or task.

A simulation process carried out by the research team took place from production logistics. It entailed a supply chain of materials useful in automobiles and industrial engineering. The transportation task participants are a team of humans and a collaborative group of humans and robots.

The transportation tasks were to be accomplished by using assigned vehicles. The simulation began, and the time to achieve each group task was on paper. As it turns out, the results favor the joint team of humans and robots. The collaborative team was more proficient in its delivery. Their coordination process was a success through efficiency, and the least number of accidents or setbacks occurred under the joint section.

The simulation result is bafflingly unexpected, as it was an initial assumption that all odds would favor the wholly automated robotic team. It, therefore, proves the logic that complete system automation does not directly translate to competent efficiency.

Thus, the automation and digitization discussions in line with efficiency have taken a new twist and affirm the importance of teamwork under human-robotic automation. The study's first author from the *University of Gottingen*, Professor *Matthias Klumpp*, supports the concluded findings. He depicts future scenarios in which the superiority of a joint human-to-robotic team will overpower the automated robotic systems. Moreover, the dramatic fear of mass job losses is no longer a threat to the human-centered workforce.

The success of human-machine interaction under robotics needs to consider the highlighted requirements from various disciplines such as sociology, computer science, and business administration. People-driven decision systems are the core of many corporate business scenarios. It is, therefore, safe to conclude that companies' employees have significant input in the technicalities involved in implementing industrial automation.

Why is RPA a boon, and not a curse

Robotic Process Automation is a growing industry in the current software industry. It offers automation technology to adopt the various functions of a software company.

RPA helps the following in the current industry:

- **Boost productivity**: RPA does not tire of performing the same repetitive tasks; it can work 24X7 without any break.
- **Improve efficiency to generate savings**: RPA instantly delivers advanced operational processes at affordable costs, which is impossible with manual operations. Instead of doing manually, which takes a significant amount of time, build a bot, and just run the bot, which cuts out multiple steps of the manual process. Once an RPA project is implemented, without human intervention, because of its ability to complete repetitive tasks, RPA beneficiaries see an immediate reduction in delays and errors. By speeding

up the process, reducing costly mistakes, and increasing employee output, the standard savings fall between 25% to 50%.

Figure 2.9 illustrates the various reasons why RPA is a boon and not a curse:

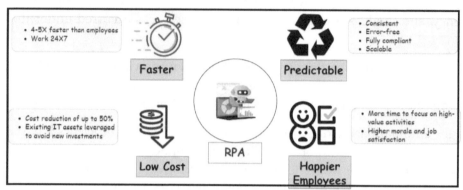

Figure 2.9: *Reasons why RPA is a boon, not a curse*

- **Hit accuracy goals with reliable consistency**: Using RPA, human errors are no longer a factor in most mission-critical workflows within the business. The business may contend with double payments caused by invoices that your team mistakenly duplicated because of a transposed digit in a **Purchase Order (PO)** number; it can be error-free data accuracy with 100% if it will automate with the help of RPA.

- **Improve business data security**: RPA tools concern the business leaders' impact on operational risk. Data breaches and leaks are already familiar and severe problems, and management may have concerns about the RPA system's security. If the RPA management team strictly defines and carefully manages the RPA parameters, the risk of data leaks will be relatively minor. Selecting a well-developed and well-maintained solution can contribute to greater confidence in security. Using RPA allows the opportunity to reduce the number of human touches businesses require to process personal data. When a company reduces contact with sensitive data, a business can achieve compliance and more straightforward implementation of governance practices.

- **Seize opportunities for scale**: Businesses may receive a higher number of orders yearly at a particular time. Without using automation, the company may need to shift employees from other duties or need to onboard temporary hires to handle the information. But robots can scale up and down instantly to handle any volume of work.

- **Create a better customer service experience**: RPA has an increasing foothold in customer service, especially in AI-powered natural language processing.

However, the key benefit is reduced employee involvement in repetitive tasks. Customer service is a high-commitment, high-maintenance process that requires attention and large amounts of time from the employees. By spending less time on administrative tasks, employees can give their attention to customers.

Since RPA has the above advantages, it can be a curse also for us. It all depends on the situation. In hazardous environments, automation and machines serve a good deal since automation is dangerous for working labor. Instead, Automation takes away some jobs but also creates many more. As RPA introduces business, new options will open, and new skill sets will be in demand. Now we need to learn new skills; as employees, we must look toward the future and see if we are adequately prepared.

The functionality of RPA

In RPA, engineers change manual processes into digital ones. With the help of RPA, repetitive and rule-based tasks are easily performable. For example, moving files and folders from one location to another, copying the data, and pasting it to another site.

Companies and organizations are facing problems with the new team member hiring process as this process goes through many steps. RPA has solved it. A new product user can face many challenges, if a new broadband user faces low connectivity, then the user may contact the call center. Using automated systems, companies are dealing with users more efficiently and saving employees time from only responding to customers. They are, therefore, able to dedicate their time to other fields that benefit companies. Let us now discuss a few real-life problems and how RPA solves those problems.

RPA in telecom industry

This industry faces various problems from manual work, such as service completion, billing, and revenue management. It needs manual hours and many employees to complete it successfully, which is a massive expense for a company. Automated robotic processes save companies from such crises.

- RPA allows companies to automate the employee billing process, invoices, and record maintenance without making any mistakes.

- Telecom companies should have a clear view of all customers. Now maintaining all customer records manually is more difficult. It requires more manual hours and more employees, which causes enormous expenses for a company.

RPA helps companies increase scalability, customer satisfaction, productivity, and more.

Healthcare

Every day, the number of patients and maintaining all patient records is complex, but RPA makes it more accessible. Most of the time, patients' families are unsatisfied with hospital services. That is why patients and family members complain to management. Any management authority has a more critical job than responding to complaints. But maintaining a good relationship with the patient's family is also essential. To solve this problem, most authorities are using automated technology.

Now everyone is trying to overcome the COVID-19-created problems. Everyone is now more conscious of their health and is doing health checks timely. Doctor appointments also increased in high counts, and appointment registration is impossible if it is to be done completely manually. To solve this problem, the healthcare industry started using RPA. Organizations are appointing bots for patient appointment registration. It decreases expenses and also saves time with minimal error possibility.

Banking and financial services

In banking and financial services, organizations deal with millions of clients similar to data. Manually performing such jobs is difficult. Organizations use automated processes instead of manual systems. According to the situation, bots are used. In the banking sector, automated process existence is mainly observed. Few RPA solutions where RPA used mostly, such as customer research, account opening, inquiry processing, and anti-money laundering. All banks deal with millions of clients' information. Such high-volume data manual entry is impossible. RPA makes these tasks possible.

Retail sector

The retail sector also faces various problems, such as high-volume inventory maintenance, providing fast and efficient service, and many more. Another critical issue is fulfilling processed orders on time to satisfy customers. Before introducing a new product, one must be aware of the current market. That is why working collaboratively with the research and development team is crucial. Instead of spending a long time on substantial retail data analysis, automated systems are used for sales data analysis as the retail market is changing fast. Automated systems will give analysis results so that retailers can make changes accordingly and get better results. Using RPA, the availability of products in stock can easily be known instead of spending time performing that job manually.

Figure 2.10 illustrates automation in the retail sector:

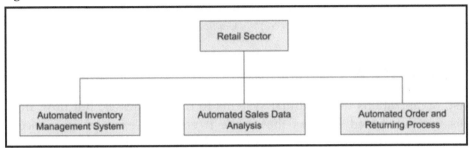

Figure 2.10: *Automation in the Retail Sector*

Supply chain management

Manual maintenance of supply chain management consumes time and workforce to maintain the excellent relationship between customers and suppliers and the selection of product suppliers. RPA can automate different stages of supply chain management. The automated process will make it more efficient.

To establish efficient supply chain management, we first need to automate an email to maintain good relationships between customers, suppliers, shipping agencies, and manufacturers. This ensures that if any product delivery is pending to the customer, the customer will communicate with the supplier. Similar immediate responses from the supplier end are complex for the supplier; that is why suppliers also use automated processes for responding to the customer's mail.

After mail automation, organizations need to automate supply and demand planning. Then, organizations need to automate the supplier selection based on rest delivery product location information from one another. After automation, the supplier selection process needs to automate the order processing and payment system, based on order priority or how much time will take to deliver the order to the customer. We also need to automate the message-sending process of order status. Manually sending messages of order status is difficult and time-consuming. Using automated processes, it can be done quickly. Finally, one needs to automate document processing. In such a way, the whole supply chain process can be automated easily.

Figure 2.11 features the automation of the supply chain management process:

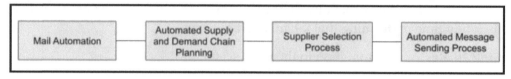

Figure 2.11: *Automation on Supply Chain Management Process*

Benefits of RPA

In the past, organizations used manual systems to run businesses. But now, most companies use automated systems that make it easier to execute any process. Moreover, users have benefitted the maximum. A few advantages are as follows:

- **Boost productivity:** Completing any process manually needs a large amount of labor and time. If a task fails to meet the time, productivity could decrease. Instead of manually, if the organization performs the job using an automated system or robotic process within a minimum time, the job can be completed, which also increases the organization's productivity.

- **Efficiency improvement:** The manual process is more error-prone. In an automated system, once a process is ready, the error or process failure possibility is minimum. Less error and timely job completion will increase the system's efficiency.

- **Time and money saving:** The manual process is time as well as money-consuming. We also need large amounts of labor to meet the goal. However, an automated system needs minimum delivery only for the maintenance of the system. In such a way, it saves money. Moreover, a robotic system will work much faster than a manual process. In such a way, it saves time and money.

- **Improve business security:** With maximum labor, involvement in a process increases the data security breach possibility. But in the case of robotic or automated systems, fewer security problems are observed with data. In such a way, it increases security in the business process.

Conclusion

Automation technology is rapidly adapting to the changing demands of industries and comes with significant benefits to labor costs, revenues, customer satisfaction, brand image, and more. Automation provides benefits across all industries. While automation is not only the solution to industry changes, but also a necessary part of Intelligent digital transformation. After the discussion about different kinds of bots, robots, and cobots, it has been found that cobots do not require any enclosure, and they are simple to set up and program. They are also flexible as we can quickly relocate them.

However, robots require fixed installation, which limits the possibility of relocation. Robots have physical bodies. Bots do not have any physical bodies. Robots are categorized by what they look like, whereas bots are categorized by what they do. Robots are programmable machines that can automatically execute actions, whereas bots are programs that can automatically perform actions.

Overall, RPA holds promising changes for the business world. While it may change the shape of the workforce, we believe its benefits will help businesses increase productivity and overall output quality. But what is next? Let us explore this in the upcoming chapter.

Key facts

- There are different types of automation, some of them are Flexible automation, Programmable automation, Fixed automation, etc.
- Bots can also be differentiated according to functionality, For example, robots and cobots.
- **Robotic Process Automation (RPA)** is a hallmark of **Intelligent Process Automation (IPA)**, which describes logic-driven execution. Pre-programmed rules for primarily used structured data.

Key terms

- **Robotic Process Automation (RPA)**
- Cobots
- **Human-Robot Interaction (HRI)**
- **End of Arm Tooling (EOAT)**
- Flexible automation
- Programmable automation
- Fixed automation
- Hard automation
- Soft automation

Questions

1. What are the different kinds of bots?

2. What are the benefits of RPA?

3. The main dependency of RPA on humans is intelligence. Can it be swapped with Artificial Intelligence?

Join our book's Discord space

Join the book's Discord Workspace for Latest updates, Offers, Tech happenings around the world, New Release and Sessions with the Authors:

https://discord.bpbonline.com

CHAPTER 3

Fundamentals of RPA Tools and Platforms

"Automation is cost-cutting by tightening the corners and not cutting them."

— *Haresh Sippy*

Introduction

In today's digital world, Robotic Process Automation is automating most of the repetitive processes in the business industry. Robotic process automation is slowly becoming one of the top-growing technologies, which is going to be a part of most organizations. RPA is a software technology that helps to build, deploy, and manage the task using bots, and maintain the whole process without or with minimum human interventions. These are, for example, opening a website, logging in with the username and password, navigating to the system, identifying, and extracting information from the site, performing some actions that are defined, and so on. The whole process can be done by humans as well, but bots can do the same process faster and more consistently than people.

There are various tools in the Robotic Process Automation market. In this chapter, three major tools will be explored: UiPath, Automation Anywhere and Blue Prism. Blue Prism is the second largest popular RPA tool. However, in the case of large enterprise businesses, it is Blue Prism that is at the top and it takes over UiPath, because Blue Prism has extra features such as data security, data abstraction, analytics, among others.

Structure

In this chapter, we will cover the following topics:

- UiPath – Automation Platform
- Automation Anywhere with IQ Bots
- Blue Prism and Intelligent Robotic Process Automation

Objectives

The objective of this chapter is to provide knowledge and usage understanding to the reader, for the RPA tools: Blue Prism, Automation anywhere, and UiPath.

UiPath - Automation platform

UiPath is a robotic automation platform for large-scale end-to-end automation. It gives answers for automating habitual workplaces and helps in the process of elevating commercial enterprise change. It makes us loads of strategies to convert tedious responsibilities into automatic processes. The features of UiPath can be seen in *Figure 3.1*:

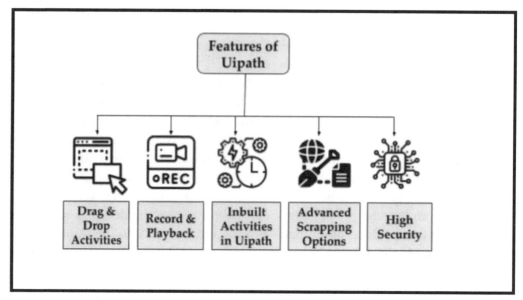

Figure 3.1: Features of UiPath

Features of UiPath

The features of UiPath are as follows:

- **Drag and drop workflow:** The UiPath person will broaden visible system steps via way of means of dragging and dropping associated duties onto the graphical workspace. Then, with person interface properties, they can rework the system's steps into a visible workflow. Users can use the recorder wizard within the UiPath platform, to construct web-based or utility workflows.

- **Record and playback:** The person can use this characteristic to report movements and rework them into an automated systems series. UiPath has the subsequent forms of recording options:

  o **Basic recording:** It makes it a specialty of automating unmarried duties and is usually used to broaden every activity's whole selector.

  o **Desktop recording:** It may be used for lots of moves in addition to utility development.

  o **Web recording:** Web recording is a not an unusual place device for viewing and recording internet web page sports.

  o **Citrix recording:** It may be very extensively used for recording stuff such as pictures and virtualized surrounding automation. UiPath comes with over 300 integrated sports, masking an extensive variety of procedure automation and alertness integration layout duties. You can discover those sports within the Activities pane, which covers maximum layout duties, including records extraction, data entry, and automation.

- **Advanced scraping option:** Scraping records from internet pages and programs are simpler with UiPath Screen Scraping. Furthermore, the data scraping wizard helps in the scraping of data with a repetitive structure. The scraping solution works flawlessly with any program, including .Net, Java, Flash, PDF, Legacy, and SAP.

- **High security and robustness:** You can create super-smart, long-lasting robots with UiPath. With an easily visible canvas, all and sundry within the company can use those bots. UiPath gives the high-safety auto-login capability to run the bots and operates with a locked screen, permitting automatic technique to run in complete privacy.

UiPath components

The components of UiPath are as follows:

- **UiPath studio:** UiPath studio is a user-friendly interface that lets developers visually plan and layout diverse automation approaches via diagrams, and the use of the drag-and-drop functionality. These diagrams are simply a structural mirrored image of precise responsibilities that must be completed.

- **UiPath robot:** After you have constructed your process, the following flow is to position it into movements within the UiPath studio. UiPath Robots are used to translate the techniques into responsibilities, that are then executed. These robots are used to assign diverse responsibilities and convey them out within the equal way as human beings, although without human interference. When a given operation takes place at the computer, they apply UiPath robots to start executing responsibilities automatically.

- **UiPath Orchestrator:** The Orchestrator is a web-primarily based tool in UiPath. It has capabilities for deploying, and monitoring, computerized bots, and approaches. It is a centralized discussion board for coping with and keeping all software program bots.

UiPath architecture

Now that you have understood what UiPath is and what its additives are, it is time to recognize the UiPath architecture. It consists of 2 sections:

- Client and server side
- 3 layers

Figure 3.2 provides a high-level overview of the architecture of UiPath:

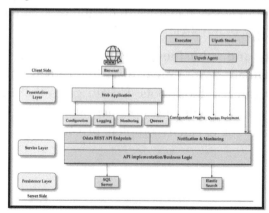

Figure 3.2: *High-level architecture of UiPath*

The client and server side

Let us know more about the client and server side:

- Client-facet UiPath additives are those with whom the user or developer can speak directly. UiPath Studio, Robot, Browser, and UiPath Agent are normally included.

- UiPath's backend operations are taken into consideration at server-side. It saves the responsibilities and workflows that a person produces within the databases.

- The UiPath Orchestrator chooses the important features and software robots to perform the code's tasks.

- The robots' logs and data are saved within the backend. The information is beneficial for studying robotic overall performance and detecting errors.

- UiPath robotic accommodates various elements, such as the follows:

  o **Agent assists for UiPath:** This carrier in UiPath serves as a mediator between the client facet and the server facet of UiPath. All the records and information are conveyed through the handler. It additionally logs messages within the Orchestrator earlier, than being moved to the SQL server. The service can be used to search all the currently available tasks in the device tray. It can also extrude device settings and start/prevent modern-day obligations.

  o **Executor Server for UiPath:** Software robots use this carrier to perform the obligations laid out in the Windows session.

Three layers

Three layers which are part of the architecture are as follows:

- Presentation Layer
- Server Layer
- Persistence Layer

Advance feature of UiPath - AI Fabric

AI Fabric allows you to seamlessly deploy models built by UiPath or UiPath partners. These models can be seamlessly dragged and dropped into RPA workflows, allowing AI to be integrated directly into business applications and processes. You can also improve AI over time and manage your model through an intuitive interface.

About AI fabric

AI Fabric is an application that allows the deployment, management, and continual improve machine learning models to be used in RPA workflows in UiPath Studio. In the latest version 2022.4, UiPath Community changed the name **AI Fabric** to **AI Center**.

AI Center bridges the gap between data science teams and RPA and enables you to instantly apply the limitless cognitive power of AI to any software currently being automated by RPA.

Key features of AI center

The key features of AI Center are as follows:

- **Easily deploy ML models**: Package your own models, upload them directly to Al Center, and make them available for robots to consume within minutes. Alternatively, select UiPath out-of-the-box ML models or pre-trained ML models from UiPath Al technology partners, that work best for your workflows.

- **Drag and drop AI**: Choose a model and drag and drop it into your workflow right in Studio, to accelerate the potential of your automation. Select an ML skill suited to your business needs, from a drop-down option.

- **Model governance**: Gain end-to-end visibility of model versioning and updates. RPA teams will know when models have been updated, and data science teams will know how models are being used in production.

- **Continuous learning**: Continuously improve models by bringing humans to handle exceptions, validate data and send it for retraining.

Components of AI Center

All the components of AI Center are discussed as follows:

- **Projects**

  A project is an isolated set of resources (datasets, pipelines, packages, skills, and logs) that you can use to build a particular ML solution. It is recommended to organize each project to accommodate business automation.

  The Projects page, that is, the first page you see when you access UiPath AI Center, contains a list of available projects. Each project is represented by a card that contains top-level information about the project:

o Project name

o Description

o Active Pipelines

o **Deployed packages** - the number of packages belonging to this project that are deployed as ML skills.

Figure 3.3 gives a glimpse of the project tab of the platform:

Figure 3.3: *Project tab in AI Center, UiPath*

- **Dashboard**

The dashboard page provides a high-level view of the entities (datasets, packages, pipelines) grouped into a particular project. Here, you can find information about who created the project, when it was created, and its description. On the Project page, click the card to go to the dashboard.

Figure 3.4 provides a glimpse of the dashboard under the AI Center:

Figure 3.4: *Dashboard tab in AI centre under UiPath*

- **Datasets**

  A Dataset is a storage folder that contains any number of subfolders and files. This gives your project's machine learning model access to new data points (new files or folders uploaded from your application, or data from UiPath Robots at run time). After selecting a project, the **Datasets** page is accessible from the **Datasets** menu, it enables one to view all the datasets within a project, along with their name, description, and creation time. You can create new datasets and Datasets are editable and deletable.

- **ML Packages**

  An ML Package is a folder containing all the metadata and code needed to train and serve an ML model. An ML Package can have multiple versions, and each version can have an associated change log.

  > **NOTE: To use ML Package within the UiPath workflow, we first need to deploy them as skills in associate tenant**

  After selecting a project, the **ML packages** page is accessible from the **ML Packages** menu.

  Figure 3.5 features the ML packages tab in AI Center, UiPath:

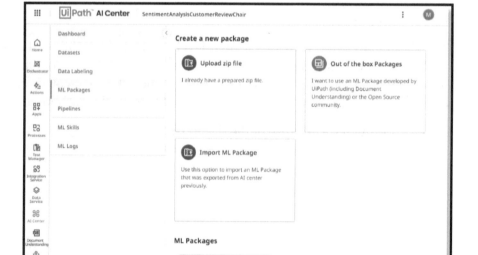

Figure 3.5: ML Packages tab in AI Center, UiPath

Usage guide of UiPath

Download UiPath Studio and Setup Orchestrator and UiPath Assistant and follow the given steps:

1. Go to the link **https://cloud.uipath.com/** and complete the signup process.

2. Sign in to link **https://cloud.uipath.com/** again.

3. Go to the **Help** section and find options to download Studio (community edition). For the Enterprise edition, payment is required.

4. There are two options: **Preview**, and **Stable.** Click on the **Download** button under the stable section and the download will start.

5. Go to the link **https://cloud.uipath.com/** and click on **Admin | Add Tenant |** Select all the possible options | Provide a Tenant name | Save.

6. Click on **Orchestrator | Tenant | Folders | Create a folder | Machines |.**

7. Then, **Add machine | Machine template | Provide template name | Select Production(unattended)= 1 | Testing = 1 | Provision.**

8. Copy the **Machine Key.**

9. Go to **Tenant | Folder | Previously created folder | Machines | Manage Machines in Folder | Select the machine | Update | Users. Hit the three dots and then press on Edit | Choose all the roles | Next | Enable Attended Robot | Enable Unattended Robot | Machine login credentials | Provide the credentials | Next | Update.**

10. Open **UiPath assistant | Profile | Preferences | Orchestrator Settings | Connection Type | Machine Key | Provide Orchestrator URL | Paste the Machine Key (Previously Copied) | Connect.** The connection is **made** now.

11. All the setups are done now. You are ready to build your first automation workflow.

Building a workflow in UiPath Studio

The process to build a workflow in UiPath Studio is as follows:

1. Open UiPath Studio. To create a new process, click on **Process** and give it a name. Click on **Create.** There will be a new workspace open for you to start learning in UiPath. Click on **Open Main Workflow.** This is the place where you can design your workflow.

2. Install the packages according to your project requirements from the **Manage Packages** option under the **Design** tab.

3. To drag an activity, you can find all the activities from the **Activities** panel on the left-hand side. Choose activities according to your requirements.

4. Set up the properties for the activities which you are using. The properties panel is located on the right-hand side.

5. To run the process and get the desired output, click on the **Debug** button under the **Design** tab. The process will now run. Do not interrupt in between until the execution ends.

Applications of UiPath

Here are some UiPath applications in different fields:

Sales

Some UiPath applications in sales are:

- **Invoice development and delivery**: This is an instance of information replication in action. Both CRM and accounting structures ought to have precise income details. Bots can replace accounting facts and put together and ship invoices from the perfect electronic addresses as opposed to manually replicating data.

- **CRM updating:** A new magnificence of answers is evolving to contain electronic mail, call, and different contact data in CRM. An easy bot will be written to replace your CRM facts with patron touch statistics in case you cannot discover an appropriate answer for the usage of the CRM system.

- **Keeping scorecards up to date:** Companies that do not have HR and CRM structures included, can use RPA bots to make certain that CRM changes are submitted to scorecards in real time, permitting income reps to track their progress.

Banking

Some UiPath applications in banking are:

- **Check KYC:** Although devoted KYC answers are evolving, RPA bots may be used to automate quantities of the KYC method, in case your cooperation does not want to use one. A case may be referred to an employee in the event of an edge case that requires human involvement.

- **Sanction of loans:** Like maximum record processing activities, this approach is suitable for RPA automation since complicated enterprise common sense may be embedded in bots, which could partly automate mortgage selections and the guide technique that follows.

- **Execution of trade:** RPA bots can be beneficial in conditions wherein legacy structures are incapable of storing complicated restriction orders. However, that is greater of a band-useful resource solution; within the lengthy run, switching complicated and equipped buying and selling gadgets workload.

The benefit of UiPath

Figure 3.6 demonstrates different benefits of UiPath:

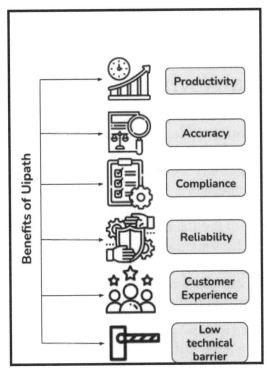

Figure 3.6: Benefits of UiPath

- **Increased productivity:** UiPath automates with a short pace and accessibility. Consider an RPA bot that permits an employee to supply a monthly report in 20 minutes. When accomplished manually, it would take 4 hours. The company's productiveness might boom due to method automation.

- **High efficiency:** RPA software program now no longer want a smash, may function 24 hours a day, seven days a week, and 365 days a year. It additionally no longer takes a smash or grow to be ill. In maximum cases, an unmarried RPA robotics can also additionally update to 5 full-time workers, if not more. Robots can do the equal quality of labor in much less time or with greater paintings than people on equal time.

- **Customer experience:** In an RPA-followed business, routine, repetitive, and interesting responsibilities are assigned to robots, permitting personnel to consciousness greater on patron service. Companies can also additionally meet client desires with the assistance of experts and information personnel.

- **Highly secure:** There is no danger of leakage in data handling because everything is run between machines and there is no human intervention. As a result, records get admission with full robustness, and moreover, it can be monitored and reported precisely.

- **Cost-effective:** UiPath has minimal operating costs and more efficient use of IT resources.

Automation anywhere with IQ Bots

To read semi-structured or unstructured data efficiently and reduce human error, IQ Bots are used. IQ Bot gives the facility of cognitive (intelligent) automation. Automation Anywhere platform helps to create bots with less coding and provides the facility to create a learning instance that helps to know the document type, the language of documents, and a list of data fields to capture and extract from each document. Using IQ Bots, it is possible to train models to preview the results of training. Even using IQ Bot data extraction is also possible. Once an IQ Bot is implemented, it tests to check accuracy. Once its accuracy is high, then production is started. Even users who create and configure automation tasks and deploy TaskBots, create IQ Bot learning instances, deploy the learning instances from staging to production environments, and correct documents with exceptions.

Though Bots implemented with automation anywhere can preprocess the document, the accuracy, however, is low. Automation anywhere has many features such as document preprocessing, and data extraction from documents, pdf files, or images but again, accuracy is low, and extracted data with low accuracy is not beneficiary for any business. When using machine learning, NLP, and computer vision technology, it is observed that the confidence score value is increased. It makes businesses more profitable.

Different types of IQ Bots are Bot Builders, Data Engineers, Admin, Pseudo-user, and Validators. *Figure 3.7* demonstrates how data can be extracted using IQ Bots:

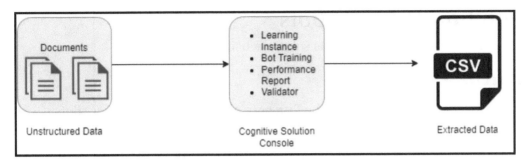

Figure 3.7: Data Extraction with IQ Bots

IQ Bot complement all RPA-based solutions to achieve end-to-end straight-through processing. OCR components are in IQ Bots, to extract data from documents, pdf, or images. IQ Bot OCR accuracy is higher than 75%. IQ Bot is highly enriched with fuzzy logic, and computer vision technology for data recognition. It uses NLP to understand the content of documents, while also using machine learning to extract data from documents, pdfs, or image files.

Benefits of IQ Bots

The benefits of IQ Bots are as follows:

- Compared to OCR technology, the capability of IQ bots OCR is good.
- IQ Bots run faster compared to a normal process.
- It helps to extract data from invoices, documents, image files, and so on. It uses semantic analysis and automated classification techniques to extract data and train the model. IQ Bots make possible auto-detection and different field mapping between files.
- IQ Bots provide pre-trained models that can use a user and easily extract data from desired documents. It also provides a custom model training facility to the user. A user can train the model in automation anywhere on the platform, and extract data according to requirements.
- Exception handling using IQ Bots is easier.
- Document preprocessing.
- Reading text from documents and **Optical Character Recognition (OCR)**
- Document classification into different groups using IQ Bots.
- Complete validation and saving.

Solution using IQ Bots

Let us now read about the various solutions using IQ Bots:

Purchase orders

Figure 3.8 is a high-level view of the Purchase orders uses case using IQ Bots:

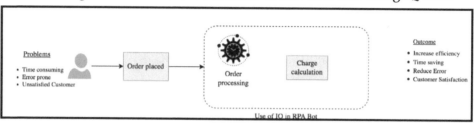

Figure 3.8: *Benefits of IQ Bots uses in Purchase Orders*

The manual sales order process follows many steps, from order receiving to order placing. Maintaining the whole sales order processing system manually is time-consuming and business organizations spend lots of money on employees. After such a high amount of expenses, the whole process runs very slowly, and customers are unsatisfied with the service. Moreover, with time, net profit margins dropped. This problem is currently solved with IQ Bots using automation anywhere platform. The IQ Bot streamlines the whole process end to end very fast. Within a week, the complete system from order receiving, to cash, to order placing is now automated. This does not take months, and there is no need for significant change in the core system or infrastructure.

Insurance

Figure 3.9 provides a high-level overview of the solution under the Insurance domain:

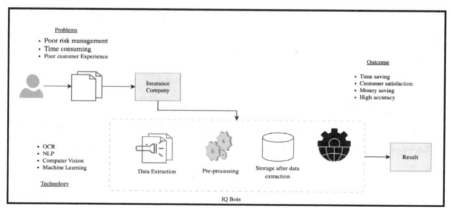

Figure 3.9: *Insurance use case solution*

The insurance industry is another unorganized sector in the business industry. Insurance companies need to process lots of customer documents, and due to manual processing of all documents error possibilities increase, creating poor customer experiences. IQ Bot helps to solve this problem. Document processing with IQ Bots is easier. It can process highly unstructured insurance data from documents and emails. Bots have the capabilities that they can be augmented with highly rich computer vision, **Natural Language Processing** (**NLP**), and **machine learning** (**ML**) technologies. Insurance Processes use AI-powered, intelligent automation to boost insurance claims velocity, increase price transparency, and deliver exceptional customer experience.

Life sciences

Collect and process more data effectively and efficiently for a deeper understanding of results. The core of the life science industry is the vast amount of data; it could be structured or unstructured. This high volume of data helps in advanced research and development, supply chain management, and compliance. Managing this high volume of data manually is time-consuming, as well as uses up a high amount of expenses.

Healthcare

Improve patient experience and operational processes with automated document processing. The Healthcare industry deals with different types of unstructured data. Processing all those data manually is time-consuming and costly. This industry needs to work fast and thus, IQ Bots is a solution. IT efficiently preprocesses unstructured data sets. IQ Bots increase customer experiences.

IQ Bots

The features of IQ Bots are as follows:

- Extract complex data from documents and integrate it with an automated process to automate the entire process and improve business growth.
- Help to improve the document quality with noise reduction, de-skewing and binarization features.
- Easily differentiating documents into different categories also helps to easily identify the relevant documents from the lists of documents.
- It uses ML techniques to extract data from documents.
- After pre-processing of data, it uses AI-driven techniques to improve the extraction results.

- IQ Bots use human expatriates using a synthetic model, and pre-trained models in processes.
- Using machine learning, it easily recognizes patterns.

Usage guide of Automation Anywhere

If you want to start your journey with Automation Anywhere, follow the given steps:

Setup Automation Anywhere

Automation 360 provides a web-based, cloud-native RPA platform for users of all types. Review the tasks involved in setting up Automation 360:

1. To set up Automation Anywhere first need to visit **https://www. automationanywhere.com/products/enterprise/community-edition**. It is a community edition.
2. Fill in all details of the user and then click on **Get Free Community Edition**.
3. The user will get an email from Automation Anywhere with the credentials.
4. Then the user can click on the **Control Room** URL that the user received in their email and give the **username** and **password** to login into the control room. (For the first time logging in, users need to change their credentials).
5. Now, users can see the dashboard for the community edition.
6. The user can now create a bot with Automation Anywhere to do the automation task.

Create first bot in Automation Anywhere

To make your first bot with Automation Anywhere, you need to follow the given steps:

1. After logging into Automation Anywhere dashboard, you need to choose either the **Home** option or **Automation** option from the navigation of the dashboard.
2. If you choose the **Home** option, you need to click on **Create a bot** button, which is on the top left of the page. Or, if you choose the **Automation** option, then you need to click on the top right corner option **Create a new** and then choose the option **bot**.
3. Now you have to give the Name (*maximum character= 50*) of your bot and you can give the description of it (but giving the description is optional).

You can edit the folder path of your bot, which will be structured in the **Automation** section. Then you click on **Create and edit** button.

4. The bot development section will arise. Now you can design your bot for your own task.

5. On the left side, you can see the **Variables, Actions,** and **Trigger** panels.

6. Trigger options will help to trigger some bots or processes, when a particular event occurs depending on your bot setup.

7. Since Automation anywhere is a no-coding platform, here you just need to drag and drop different actions as your bot needs.

8. After dragging and dropping any action, you can set up all its properties on the right side of the page.

9. After setting up your all properties of dragging and dropping **Actions** properly, you can check the **Assistant** option if any error occurs, or there is a need to check the properties on the right upper of the development window.

10. If you need to create or see any variable that you need to use in your project, you can click on the **Variable** panel on the left side of your development window.

11. When your bot is ready, click on the **Run** button if you want to run and click on the **Debugger** button if you want to debug your bot, which is in the top right corner.

Now you can see the output that your bot has done for you!

Use case of IQ Bots

Some of the use cases of IQ Bots are as follows:

Recruitment process

IQ Bot is mainly used to extract data from documents. IQ Bots use computer vision and NLP with OCR, which gives better results. Any business needs to hire new employees and employees submit physical documents. Manual reading of documents and manual data entry is inefficient and time-consuming. General document reading bots fail to extract documents with low visibility. The IQ Bot uses artificial intelligence to extract data from documents and returns a confidence score about the extracted data. It makes it easier for document reading for the HR team.

Invoice processing

Most organizations are spent countless times comparing invoices and extracting data from invoices. IQ Bot helps to complete all data extracting and comparison between invoices within a minimum time. It also works efficiently. It extracts data 90% faster than normal bots. Moreover, it helps organizations minimize their expenses. IQ Bots use machine learning that also help companies reduce expenses in invoice processing.

Inventory reconciliation process

The inventory reconciliation process business organization matches the count of their stock. Organizations are facing different problems in managing stock. Manually managing this process is difficult and error prone. Companies are taking the help of IQ Bot for processing documents efficiently within a minimum time.

In the end, the most important quality of IQ Bots is that they help to automate processes with intelligent automation. It helps to improve the business. IQ Bots with automation anywhere platform is facilitated with less coding features. There is no need to hire highly trained engineers to develop the system. Even those who have some knowledge of technology, after taking knowledge of the platform, can implement processes. It will take less time and implementation and execution of the process with minimum cost. Moreover, it will reduce error possibility.

Blue Prism and Intelligent Robotic Process Automation

In today's digital world, Robotic Process Automation is going to grab most of the repetitive processes in the business industry. Robotic process automation is now one of the topmost growing technologies which is going to implement within most organizations. RPA is a software technology that helps to build, deploy, and manage the task by the software robots and maintain the whole process with or without minimum human interventions, such as opening the website, logging in with the username and password, navigating to the system, identifying, extracting information from the site, and performing some actions that are defined. The whole process can be done by humans as well, but software robots can do the same process faster and more consistently than humans.

There are various tools in the Robotic Process Automation market. Blue Prism is the second largest popular RPA tool. But, in the case of large enterprise businesses, Blue Prism is at the top. It takes over UiPath. Because Blue Prism has extra features such as Data Security, Data Abstraction, Analytics, and many more.

What is Blue Prism

Blue Prism is one of the popular Robotic Process Automation tools with the capability of a virtual workforce powered by software robots. Blue Prism helps enterprises automate the processes of business in an easy-to-develop and deploy in a cost-effective manner. The tools have a no-coding facility, but simply drag and drop functionality. Blue Prism is developed in Java Programming Language.

Blue Prism is developed in 2001, and this tool follows a top-down approach. Moreover, this tool offers a visual designer with no scripts, or any recorder.

Please check *Figure 3.10* for different features of Blue Prism:

Figure 3.10: *Features of Blue Prism*

RPA Blue Prism: Blue Prism components

Blue Prism RPA offers a highly scalable digital workforce to deploy projects on-premises and cloud environment. This RPA tool is now used by more than 1000 enterprises worldwide. This platform also enables high ability, intense performance, failover, and disaster recovery states and addresses potentially significant variations in operational demand.

The architecture of Blue Prism has four main software components:

- Object studio
- Process studio
- Application modeller
- Control room

Object Studio

This enables you to create a reusable **Visual Business Object (VBO)** for your business process. Almost all enterprises need to have communication with external applications to automate tasks. Object Studio is used to automate these tasks. These objects are nothing but diagrammatical programs interacting with external applications, which perform operations.

One Business Object provides an interface with only one external application. Moreover, let each Object Studio does not have the Main Page, but it does have two default pages organized as a flat group.

Process Studio

Enables you to design, create, edit as well as test business processes, developed from reusable VBO. Process Studio is the area in which the Process Diagrams are created. This component of Blue Prism offers features such as business logic, object call, control loops, and variables. Each process created has the Main Page which gets executed first.

Application Modeller

Application Modeller is the functionality to create application models with Object Studio. This exposes the UI Elements of a target application to the Blue Prism program.

Control room

Control Room allows IT services or businesses to perform, schedule, and control the processes. Blue Prism control room offers the interface to administrators for monitoring and reviewing the status in the production environment of the connected runtime resources. The interface also allows for automated schedule settings, extensive management information and manual process start and stop into Blue Prism task queues.

Features of Blue Prism

The features of Blue Prism for RPA are as follows:

Plug and play access

Blue Prism RPA technology ecosystem offers plug-and-play access without knowing any code or development to any business functions such as document management, process mining, analytics, workflow, chat, OCR/ICR, and cognitive natural language processing. Thereby it delivers the best digital system which can easily automate your business processes.

Secure

This is one of the key features of the Blue Prism Tool. It offers an accurate and secure result for any number of business processes, there is no limit. To prevent any types of issues that can affect the workforce, we can use the **Defense in Depth** approach. This approach prescribes that customers have layers of security for their software, applications, and infrastructure. This involves detecting unexpected behavior, monitoring and restricting traffic, and blocking and investigating unexpected behavior.

Work queues

Blue Prism tool dynamically controls the number of robots with the queue-centric approach, functioning on a given queue at a certain time. On the business demands, it provides the maximum flexibility to regulate the number of robots assigned, as it can help to find out the requirements of the bots to function in the queue.

Robust and scalable

Blue Prism provides robust features such as data encryption, load balancing, and end-to-end auditing. It also allows for scalability with central management. So, as needed, all the processes can be automated and can be monitored centrally.

Multi-team environment

A multi-team environment enables us to control the process of business units and digital workers within a single environment. This unique feature of Blue-Prism RPA allows one to mix and match the different processes, resources, and objects for a large extension of RPA in any organization incorporating a true digital transformation approach. This feature significantly enables a new level of security and scalability.

Execution intelligence

Robots connect to systems and react dynamically to the responses in the data in multiple environments. The tool is designed to work intelligently without a person physically monitoring every action occurring on the screen.

Tesseract OCR

Blue Prism V6 is equipped with Tesseract OCR V3.05.01. This option offers complicated language-based text recognition and pattern matching. It is dedicated to a situation, to contact with the on-screen text where it is unsuitable to apply the native character recognition engine.

Usage guide of Blue Prism

To create processes on Blue Prism, we first need to install its application in our local system. Follow the given steps:

1. Go to the Blue Prism login portal and log in with your credentials:

   a. Register if you do not have an account yet.

   b. After creating an account, you will receive an email with a link, click on that link.

   c. This will take you to the Blue Prism portal and here you can log in.

2. Inside the portal, click on a **product** menu. There are two editions are available:

   a. Trial edition (get inside **Blue Prism Enterprise**)

   b. Learning edition

3. Click on **Learning edition**, and the Download (x64) 64-bit option will be available.

4. Click on **Download** (x64) 64-bit, and the application download will start.

   a. When the software gets Download, you will get an email with the **License key** (as a file format).

   b. Check Spam if not found in your Inbox.

   c. Download and save the **License Key** file for future use.

5. Now, **install the downloaded software**, by clicking on the downloaded file:

   a. The installation page will open. Click on Get started and click on Next on the License agreement page by agreeing with the license.

   b. Then select the path, where you want to install and click on Install.

   c. After the installation is done, click on Finish and launch Blue Prism.

   d. Create your password page will open. Here, create your password and click on Save and continue.

   e. Then the Install Database page will open and click on Next. After completing Building Database, click on Next.

   f. Then the **Sign into Blue Prism** page will open. Provide your credentials and click on **Sign in using Blue Prism credentials**.

    g. Here the Activate Blue Prism page will open to activate the License.

       i. Click on the **Browse** button and select the **License Key** file from the system (that was already downloaded in **Step-4-c).**

       ii. Then click on **Next,** and the **License Activated** page will appear if the license is activated successfully.

       iii. That is all for installation. After successful installation, Blue Prism Home page will open.

6. Inside the application, mainly **6 options** available:

    a. **Home:** It includes many charts that provide information on the blue prism database.

    b. **Studio:** In the studio, we can automate a process, build a process using flow, and add logic, calculations, and intelligence.

    c. **Control Room:** This is the key administrative point, where it handles the control, monitoring, execution, and scheduling of process executions on dispersed bots.

    d. **Analytics:** It is a module that allows you to see data graphically in the form of charts such as pie, bars, columns, and lines.

    e. **Release:** This is used to manage configuration package import and export between multiple blue prism settings.

    f. **System:** Administrators use the system tab to manage users.

7. To create a process, go to the **Studio** tab:

    a. This screen shows a tree on the left-hand side, containing Processes and Objects.

    b. Right-click on **Processes**.

    c. Choose to create process.

    d. A new process dialogue appears. Give the process name and click on **Next**. Enter a description (optional) and click on **Finish.**

    e. Click on the newly created process from the left side tree; this will open the editing option to create a process.

    f. Select flows according to the task from the left panel and save the process.

    g. To **Run** the process, go to the toolbar, and click on **run.**

Advantages of Blue Prism

The advantages of Blue Prism are as follows:

- Blue Prism features help businesses develop and maintain software robots, that can perform intelligently and automate business processes.
- Blue Prism offers great optimization efficiency.
- Businesses are focused on strategy-making and implementation. Blue Prism RPA complements the implementation of efficient strategies, so that your business scales the kind of heights you dream of.
- When workflows and processes in the business are automated, customers get instant responses from your side. With more efficient customer support, you can really achieve the trust of the customer.
- Intelligent Robotic process automation with blue prism cuts down on the amount of money you spent on employees. As a result, you can achieve cost-cutting in an efficient way. Moreover, there is not just one but many cost benefits that business owners can receive with the adoption of the blue prism.
- The best part is that blue prism software is user-friendly for developers with no coding knowledge.

Case study of Coca-cola

Coca-cola is one of the largest companies in the world. In 200 countries, the company has more than 500 brands, with 1.9 billion products bought by 200 million customers daily.

Company objectives

The company objectives are as follows:

- Perform HR operational processes with constant improvement.
- Execute HR processes and strategies smoothly.
- Resolve employee queries with good quality.

To address these goals, the company has started to automate the processes using Blue Prism within the finance division. After that, they started processes to automate with Blue Prism for other divisions such as HR.

For automating the processes, their first step was to identify the relevant processes for automation. The main criteria they considered were the process volume, frequency of process and the workforce required for the process. After identifying the relevant processes, they found 150 processes had to be automated.

Problems faced by company

Before Coca-Cola started the implementation using Blue Prism, the HR service team had to audit the data. As the company was running reports, it took a lot of time to audit and then format to analyze exceptions.

Solution

To audit SAP, Coca-Cola started using Blue Prism's Digital Workforce. To save time and drive focus on the resulting data, all their processes were divided into multiple SAP systems. After generating the reports from these automated processes, they went to the respective teams to manually handle the exceptions. Moreover, the reports could be tracked without the need for an extra manual workforce to track them.

Business impact

After using Blue Prism's Digital Workforce, the company started delivering better operational efficiencies with the production capacity into be extended to 24X7.

Other Business impacts are as follows:

- End-to-end auditing performed.
- Improvement of customer experience with high interaction.
- No additional headcount.

Conclusion

This is the time to use the digital workforce. However, organizations need to prepare to ride this change, by investing the apt technology platforms/products, formulating the right business strategy, defining appropriate operating models, and preparing the human workforce to embrace this time. Now the digital workforce is here to take the robot out of the human, not to merely replace human employees but to empower the employees to reach higher orbits.

In the next chapter, we will learn about the fusion of Hyperautomation and RPA.

Key facts

- UiPath is a robotic technique automation platform for large-scale end-to-end automation. It gives answers for automating habitual workplace sports for elevated commercial enterprise change.

- UiPath architecture has been consisted of two main components: the client and server side and the 3 layers, which are, presentation layer, server layer and persistence layer.

- IQ Bots is a feature provided by Automation Anywhere; it is a service that provide learning enabled bots which can uses Machine learning to provide new learning and trainings.

- Blue Prism is developed in 2001, and this tool follows a top-down approach. Moreover, this tool offers a visual designer with no scripts, or any recorder.

Key terms

- IQ Bots

- **Visual Business Object (VBO)**

- Defense in depth approach

- Inventory reconciliation process

- Execution intelligence

Questions

1. What are different components of UiPath?

2. What are different benefits of using UiPath?

3. If there is a solution that requires continuous learning, which solution will be appropriate for it?

4. What are different components of Blue Prism tools?

Join our book's Discord space

Join the book's Discord Workspace for Latest updates, Offers, Tech happenings around the world, New Release and Sessions with the Authors:

https://discord.bpbonline.com

CHAPTER 4

Amalgam of Hyperautomation and RPA

"You're either the one that creates the automation or you're getting automated."

— *Tom Preston-Werner*

Introduction

There are some technologies and tools available in the market which are used to do automation and businesses are trying to use those. However, there is a need to use automation technologies to automate processes intelligently, and for that reason, Intelligent Automation is evolving so quickly. On the other hand, for using automated technologies such as RPA and Intelligent Automation, organizations need to take some business approach to automate the process. Hyperautomation is a technology that requires a more effective system-based approach to growing automation initiatives.

In the next decade, Hyperautomation will be the most demanding technological trend which will have the greatest impact. It helps in repetitive manual tasks which are carried out by human beings. It is the combination of **Robotic Process Automation (RPA)** and some advanced technologies such as **Artificial Intelligence (AI)** and Machine Learning.

Structure

In this chapter, we will cover the following topics:

- Hyperautomation
- Hyperautomation vs RPA.
- Hyperautomation vs Intelligent automation

Objectives

In the previous chapters, the book shed some light on topics such as what Hyperautomation is, what its ingredients are, and shed light on the knowledge of its ingredients. This chapter targets focus on Hyperautomation and its equation with RPA.

Hyperautomation

Hyperautomation is the framework and set of innovative technologies (RPA, AI, Machine Learning, **Intelligent Business Process Management (IBPM)**). It is becoming an important technology in digital transformation because it reduces human involvement. Due to this reason, we can utilize the capabilities of Hyperautomation instead of using just one technology. Hyperautomation helps businesses to automate the entire process. *Figure 4.1* demonstrates Hyperautomation in a nutshell:

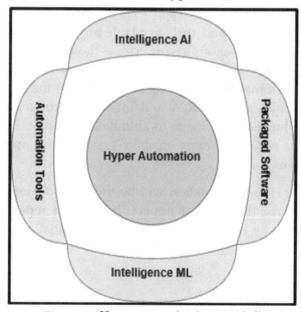

Figure 4.1: Hyperautomation in a nutshell

Key units of Hyperautomation

Hyperautomation does not depend on only one technology. It includes the following technologies:

- **Robotics Process Automation:** It is possible for RPA to configure software robots, which allows them to do time-consuming, repetitive tasks in the system.
- **Machine Learning:** It is the key technology which uses algorithms and data to give learning to the machines. After that, machines can perform complex tasks by themselves without any programming by humans.
- **Artificial Intelligence:** AI is used to create machines that can make decisions and has the capability to solve problems.
- **Big data:** Big data is used to store, analyze and manage large amounts of data, which is produced by devices to recognize patterns and provide solutions.
- **Cobots:** Cobots are an example of collaborative robots. Robots share tasks with human beings.
- **Chatbots:** Chatbots are built based on ML, AI and **Natural Language Processing (NLP)**. Chatbots can hold a conversation in real-time with humans, either using text or speech.

How does Hyperautomation work

Hyperautomation is a combination of different technologies like AI, ML and RPA. Let us understand its working with following points:

- RPA is enhanced by AI and ML, which becomes the core that makes Hyperautomation possible.

- We can combine these technologies, and power and elasticity can be added in places where they were not possible previously. The tasks which could not be automated previously, are now made automatic.

- It can be implemented on top of technologies that companies already have. RPA is the main platform, but there is also IBPMS, **Integration Platforms as a service (IPAAS)** and information engines. It can help in **Digital Twin Organization (DTO)** which is a virtual representation of a product.

Advantages of Hyperautomation

Hyperautomation has many advantages, such as:

- The integration of innovative technologies such as AL, ML, NLP and RPA, which allows performing quickly and efficiently and also can reduce errors.

- It increases employee satisfaction because they do smart work and they do not waste their time on high-volume tasks, which adds no value, and it only increases the ability to enhance productivity.

- In today's digital world, organizations can transform digitally. Organizations align their business processes, and they are investing in technology.

- Hyperautomation reduces the operational costs of organizations. According to Gartner Report, by 2024 combined Hyperautomation with redesigned operating processes will reduce costs by 30%.

- AI and big data can extract information from data effectively.

Challenges in Hyperautomation

It is still a native concept. Some of the biggest challenges include the following:

- Hyperautomation is a combination of multiple technologies hence no single tool will do it. Therefore, vendors are coming up with platforms to have multiple tools or capabilities to provide Hyperautomation solutions. That is why automation vendors are enlarging their capabilities of Hyperautomation.

- Organizations should not make the mistake of assuming that automation technology is for all the solutions. It should be strategic and realistic.

- Hyperautomation depends on archiving architecture. If an organization does not have a digital strategy, Hyperautomation will be a burden instead of an asset.

Why should businesses implement Hyperautomation

The following are some benefits of Hyperautomation for businesses that implement it:

- **Reduces automation restrictions:** Every technology has its own limitations and restrictions. With Hyperautomation, businesses do not have to face challenges because it is efficient. Hyperautomation can utilize the combined capabilities of different technologies.

- **Eases the integrations:** Business will have multiple devices or applications, which are interconnected with each other and transfer data between the devices. Each application is maintained by a specific department and managed by employees. Hyperautomation can simplify data sharing across multiple devices with the help of integrations. *Figure 4.2* features some benefits associated with Hyperautomation:

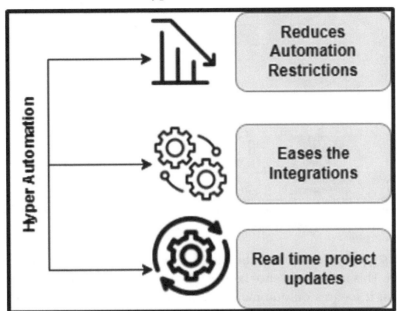

Figure 4.2: Benefits associated with Hyperautomation

- **Real-time project updates:** For a successful business, there should be pipelines that can be used to manage, update, and complete tasks quickly without any delay. Hyperautomation allows businesses to quickly understand pending tasks and notify the organization authorities if there is any delay.

Why is Hyperautomation important

Hyperautomation is very important because of the following reasons:

- Hyperautomation helps organizations by providing a framework to expand, integrates and optimize the automation.
- RPA is growing rapidly compared to other automation technologies. RPA notices how humans interact with applications, developers can automate all their parts of work by recording how they do a task. Bots can copy human behavior. The automated task is measured by speed and accuracy, which are used by organizations to judge the performance of employees on the same task.

Figure 4.3 discusses some different importance of Hyperautomation:

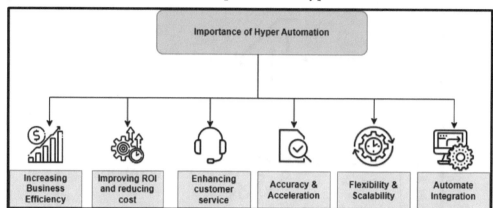

Figure 4.3: *Importance of Hyperautomation*

In Gartner's report, the concentration is on how enterprises can build a process for automation. This is the difference between Hyperautomation and other automation frameworks. It focuses on automation tools such as **Digital Process Automation (DPA)**, **Intelligent Process Automation (IPA)** and Cognitive Automation.

- Hyperautomation helps to accelerate the process of identifying automation offers and then generates the artifacts, bots, scripts, and workflows, which can use DPA, and IPA components.

Hyperautomation use cases

A few Hyperautomation use cases are as follows:

- **Hyperautomation in banking and financial services:** Smart automation system which is made of AI algorithms can productively screen the exchanges and recognize fraudulent and malicious activities. Using an AI-based ML model, we can minimize or eliminate the risks. Today **Anti Money Laundering (AML)** systems use Hyperautomation innovation for forecast and prevention.

- **Hyperautomation in Insurance:** Hyperautomation can help insurance companies in several ways. For example, to process insurance claims, the insurance company can take the help of intelligent automation. There is a great number of stakeholders, providing data to the agencies physically. This data should be additionally verified and checked against client certifications while processing an insurance claim.

Figure 4.4 demonstrates different sectors in which Hyperautomation can have use cases:

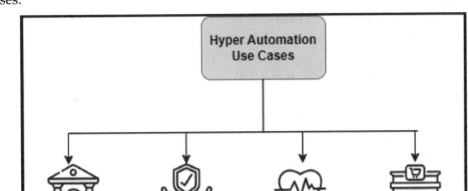

Figure 4.4: *Different use cases under Hyperautomation*

- **Hyperautomation in medical and healthcare:** The healthcare industry has been productive since the pandemic. A few clinics have already started utilizing Digital nurses to pose important inquiries about their well-being and try to understand symptoms of different diseases to help them appropriately with further diagnosis and tell them to reach appropriate medical centers. Automation can do smart billing by examining bills. This can save time by generating quicker bills and payments. Computer-based intelligence can recognize policy and a bot can take up the task of submitting bills with proper documentation.

- **Hyperautomation in retail:** Hyperautomation can help mechanize a few things such as order management, payments, transportation, warehousing and inventory, supplier management, risk management, procurement, and data monitoring, among others.

- **Hyperautomation in BPO and customer service center industry:** This is a critical service for most product or service-based organizations or the BPO business. Experts invest more energy and time in recovering data from different sources and transferring the information physically into the order management system. With a Hyperautomation caller, data can be transferred and handled. AI can be used to observe the call quality and assist CSRs to understand client assumptions in important calls, for example, insurance. AI can help in separating calls to help cut the duration process on client issue goals.

- **Hyperautomation in manufacturing:** Hyperautomation in manufacturing aggregates the human workers. If automation can produce a part, human workers can monitor the workflow with real-time analytics. Enterprise applications can be built using low code for different departments within the unit, to streamline the workflow. Manufacturers can leverage intelligent workflows to achieve their goals.

- **Hyperautomation in construction:** Construction companies can adopt bots to automate repetitive administrative tasks. Cameras are integrated with AI-powered software that enables employers to monitor the equipment and real-time on-site workers. It increases the safety of construction workers. Also, it records **Minutes Of Meetings (MOM)**. In such cases, the virtual assistant of AI integrates with their internal applications. It can act as a useful tool to record meetings and extract relevant information later.

- **Hyperautomation in recruitment:** Recruiting employees is a robust process including processes such as advertising, shortlisting profiles, and onboarding. Hyperautomation eases the workflow and changes the traditional way. AI-enabled intelligent screening software is built with ML capabilities that can understand employee criteria from experience. It can separate the profiles within a short time limit. The talent team can hire chatbots and set up automated email notifications to selected candidates and the relevant interview panelists from the organization who schedule interviews.

Hyperautomation in UiPath

UiPath's platform for Hyperautomation is key to scaling automation across the enterprise with speed and efficiency. It addresses the end-to-end automation lifecycle by using process discovery tools and employee citizen sourcing, to determine what to automate. UiPath is delivering a true end-to-end Hyperautomation platform that combines the core RPA capabilities, including building, managing, and running robots with tools for process discovery, and analytics to report clear business impact. The UiPath Platform for Hyperautomation helps organizations become faster and more supple to face the increased demand and a rapidly changing atmosphere. Here are a couple of its characteristics:

- **Process document data fast and accurately.** UiPath Document Understanding AI helps users extract and interpret data from different documents and ensure end-to-end document processing. The tool works with a wide range of documents from structured to unstructured documents, and it can recognize different objects such as handwriting or checkboxes and can deal with various file formats.

- **Analyze how people completed their work.** UiPath task mining enables the automation team to capture, analyze and prioritize processes in any field.

Hyperautomation vs RPA

The main difference between RPA and Hyperautomation is that RPA focuses mainly on robotically and automating simple processes, while Hyperautomation is the use of advanced technologies, such as **artificial intelligence (AI)**, **machine learning (ML)**, and **robotic process automation (RPA)**, to automate repetitive rule-based tasks that were once completed by humans.

Hyperautomation allows automation to do virtual tasks performed by businesspeople by merging different AI technologies with RPA. Hyperautomation is an expansion of the processes of traditional business-process automation. It allows companies to combine business intelligence systems, undertake complex needs, and increase human expertise and automation experience. Hyperautomation is increasing with the evolution of automation technologies. The advantages of Hyperautomation are lower automation costs, improved IT-business alignment, and improved security and governance.

Hyperautomation involves the use of multiple technologies, tools, or platforms, such as AI, ML, RPA, **business process management (BPM)** and **integration Platform as a Service (iPaaS)**, low-code/no-code tools, packaged software, and other types of decision, process and task automation tools.

Figure 4.5 shows the different components of functionalities of Hyperautomation:

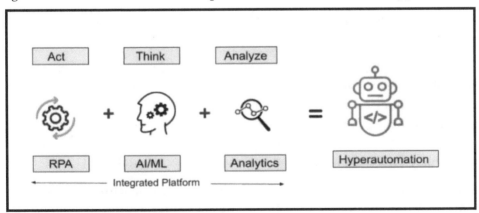

Figure 4.5: *Components functionalities of Hyperautomation*

Nowadays there are a few trends in the IT space, generating more interest right now in RPA. RPA technology provides a huge number of promises by allowing you to automate manual and repetitive tasks that save you time and money. RPA can be broken down into the following:

- **Robotic:** Any entity which can mimic human actions.
- **Process:** Any sequence of steps that lead to a meaningful task.
- **Automation:** When a task is performed automatically without human intervention.

Robotic Process Automation is the use of advanced software technology with AI and machine learning capabilities, to handle high volumes of repetitive tasks. RPA is a trending automation that can help in **repetitive, rule-based, time-consuming** tasks that require more human effort. It is easy to implement and easy to build, deploy, and manage software robots so that they can mimic human actions easily. Software robots can do things like humans do, such as understand what is on a screen, identify and extract data, navigate systems, and perform a wide range of defined actions and tasks. This also includes extracting the data from pdf and saving in an Excel file, extracting data from any website, addressing queries, making calculations, and maintaining some records and performing transactions.

The main goal of implementing RPA technology is to reduce the amount of time and effort required by humans to perform time-consuming and repetitive tasks.

This suggests that when a business uses robotic process automation, it can better use its resources and increase its return on investment.

Following are the comparisons between Hyperautomation and RPA, which have been done with respect to benefits and functionality.

Automation is *the technique of making a process or a system that operates automatically.*

Before going further, there are some general questions we must ask ourselves: do you know about robots? What are those? What are we going to do with robots? These are common questions and may be in your mind now. Some of you may be surprised after listening to the term; some of you may have already heard about it, but it is not well known to you; some of you may be quite familiar with this term, or some of you may find it interesting and curious to know about it.

In simple words, **a robot is a machine.** It is **an automated machine** which means that **it can execute specific tasks without human intervention, or sometimes, a little intervention**. Without human intervention! Sounds interesting. As it is a machine, it can work with speed and precision which help to increase efficiency and productivity. This whole automation got evolved into Robotic Process Automation.

RPA is a type of business process automation that allows defining a set of rules or instructions for a robot to perform. RPA enables businesses to build code sequences that can manage repetitive tasks that do not require human oversight. RPA can help businesses save up to 90% of their workforce's time, increasing operational efficiency and lowering expenses. Robotic Process Automation allows industries to automate tasks across various systems. An industry that implements RPA can automate its entire workflow, infrastructure, and other backend processes, which are mostly labor-intensive and time-consuming. There are several ways to use RPA effectively; let us see the use cases of RPA in different industries.

RPA in different domains

RPA allows all sizes of industries to automate tasks. By implementing RPA, any industry can automate its workflow and backend processes, which are mostly time-consuming and labor-intensive.

RPA in telecommunications

Telecommunication is one of the industries that make use of RPA at another level. Some of the major use cases are:

- Bot that assists on call involve AI/ML and NLP. They are not simple RPA bots.
- Automation can provide comparative price analysis to a telecom company.
- RPA can help so that faults are addressed in real time with negligible human intercession.

Figure 4.6 demonstrates the role of bots in the telecommunication industry:

Figure 4.6: *RPA in telecommunication*

RPA in healthcare

RPA can provide automation processes to the healthcare organization, from operational processes to patient interaction and bill payment.

- Bots can manage and schedule patient appointments.
- RPA can use the document digitization process to prepare documents.
- Bots can track patient records, medical records and so on.

Figure 4.7 demonstrates the role of RPA in healthcare:

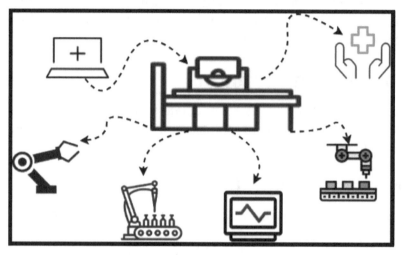

Figure 4.7: *RPA in healthcare*

RPA in insurance

RPA can give operational efficiency to insurance companies. RPA use cases in insurance are as follows:

- Robotic process automation refers to bots doing the repetitive work of human workers, such as information collection of customers, data extraction, and so on.
- Insurers fetch data automatically from registration forms with the help of robotic process automation.
- RPA increases the reliability of data by replacing the manual process and removing human errors.
- Bots can provide their help in a few use cases like the FNOL process (first notification of loss), working on the underwriting process and various types of reconciliations.

Figure 4.8 demonstrates the role of RPA in insurance:

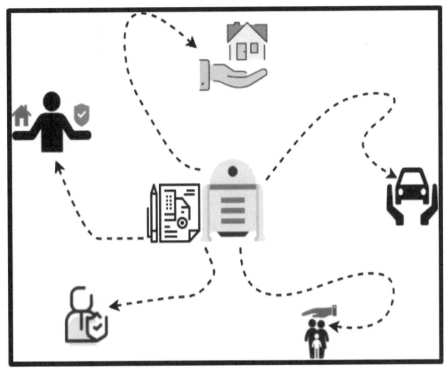

Figure 4.8: *RPA in Insurance*

RPA in Information Technology

RPA has a vast amount of uses in Information Technology. Here are some mostly used solutions:

- In the user login management system, automatically OTP generation to secure login, resetting a password, and so on.
- RPA provides temporary admin access according to companies' needs.
- Server crashes and downtime is a nightmare for every IT department. RPA automatically reboots, shuts, restarts, and reconfigures various types of servers. It helps organizations to reduce IT operational costs and save time.
- With a single click, complex systems can be installed easily and in a small span of time by using RPA.

Figure 4.9 features RPA in information technology:

Figure 4.9: *RPA in information technology*

RPA in banking

RPA helps banks and accounting departments to automate manual repetitive processes. It also allows the employees to do more critical tasks, like:

- With the help of RPA, it becomes a quick and straightforward process to open an account.
- **Know your customer (KYC)** and **Anti-money laundering (AML)** are processes that can be easily handled with the help of RPA.
- RPA makes it easy to track accounts and send automated notifications for the required document submissions.
- To generate audit reports, the manual process takes several hours but can be completed in minutes with the help of RPA bots.

Figure 4.10 features RPA in information technology:

Figure 4.10: *RPA in Banking Sector*

RPA in human resources

RPA in Human resources can be seen in the following use cases:

- RPA bots can compare resumes with the description for a particular job and shortlist those resumes.
- With the help of RPA, offer letters are customized according to the selected candidate.
- It also helps to check and keep track of time-to-time company reviews.
- Bots allow HR to manage the data of employees effectively.
- It also helps to verify the history of an employee.

Figure 4.11 features RPA in human resources:

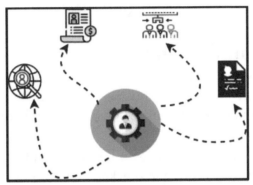

Figure 4.11: *RPA in Human Resources*

RPA use cases in manufacturing

RPA in manufacturing can be seen in the following use cases:

- One of the primary benefits of RPA in manufacturing is that it can generate accurate reports of production.
- In inventory management, RPA can be used to automate emails, and monitor inventory levels, and paperwork digitization.
- RPA use cases in manufacturing show how bots can automate bills of material by extracting data and providing accuracy in data, leading to fewer transactional issues and errors.
- **Proof of Delivery (PODs)** are important documents for the customer service department of manufacturers. These documents contain a high risk for human errors and are highly labor-intensive. These problems can be solved with the help of RPA bots.

Figure 4.12 features RPA in Manufacturing:

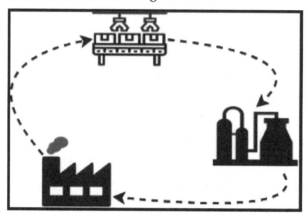

Figure 4.12: *RPA in Manufacturing*

RPA use cases in the retail industry

RPA in the retail industry can be seen in the following use cases:

- Bots can extract data to help businesses categorize products and identify their market share in different regions. This also helps in saving countless hours of work.

- Returning any product involves a lot of formalities and processing. Bots enable checking the record and quickening the entire process of return.

Figure 4.13 features RPA in Manufacturing:

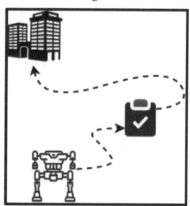

Figure 4.13: *RPA in retains industries*

Before moving ahead, cognitive automation should be discussed as it is a part of automation as well. Cognitive Automation simulates the human learning procedure to grasp knowledge from the dataset and extort the patterns. It can use all the data sources such as images, video, audio and text for decision-making and business intelligence, and this quality makes it independent from the nature of the data.

Working on cognitive computing

Cognitive computing is highly dependent upon deep learning and machine learning. Deep learning uses artificial neural networks; these neural networks can mimic the working of a neuron which is the central processing unit of the human brain. The Artificial Neural Network consists of multiple layers of neurons. Learning will take place when the weights are updated between the interconnection of weights.

Learning is composed of three phases:

- Using Natural Language Processing for understanding human language and interactions.
- Developing and validating the evidence-dependent hypothesis.
- Conforming and learning from user selections and responses.

Why RPA and why cognitive automation

Until now, the *What* and *How* parts of the RPA and Cognitive automation are described. Now let us understand the *Why* part of RPA as well as Cognitive automation, why RPA is necessary and why Cognitive automation is essential, through the following points:

- A task should be all about two things, *Thinking* and *Doing*, but RPA is all about doing. It lacks the thinking part. At the same time, Cognitive automation is powered by both thinking and doing, which is processed sequentially – first thinking and then doing in a looping manner.
- RPA rises the bar of the work by removing the manual part of the work to some extent. However, RPA accomplishes that without any thought process for example button pushing, Information capture and Data entry. These tasks can be handled by using simple programming capabilities and do not require any intelligence.
- To bring intelligence into the game, cognitive automation is required. Cognitive automation combined with RPA's qualities, imports an extra mile of composure via contextual adaptation. It can accommodate new rules and make the workflow dynamic in nature.

Benefits of cognitive automation

These techniques are not similar, but they have some universal benefits. Some of these are as follows:

- Engagement of the customer:
  o Improving customer service
  o Personalizing customer/user experience
  o Increasing customer engagement
  o Enabling the flow of faster responses to customer/market needs
- Efficiency and productivity:
  o Improving productivity and efficiency
  o Improving decision-making and planning
  o Enhancing security and compliance, reduced protection
  o Reducing costs
  o Enhancing the learning experience
- Business growth:
  o Expanding ecosystem
  o Expanding business into new markets
  o Accelerating the rate of innovation of new products/services

Evolving from Robotic Process Automation to Cognitive automation

Though **Robotic Process Automation** is considered as a game changer in the modern era industries, after the rise of Artificial Intelligence, it became necessary to change the mode from doing to thinking. This is to evolve the RPA processes into Cognitive automation. Let us understand why it is required and how we can do that.

Why is it necessary

Let us now investigate the following points:

- The integration of robots and cognitive automation technologies will give an edge to the robots to perform in standard scenarios, as well as in complex situations in which human intelligence (to make decisions and judgments) is required.

- Cognitive automation will give power to the robots to export, understand and decipher the knowledge from various resources, to do pattern recognition and take decisions and make predictions.
- With the involvement of cognitive automation in RPA, RPA can use unstructured data as well as various processes and tasks.

Comparison based on benefits

Table 4.1 features the various comparisons based on benefits:

Hyperautomation	Robotic Process Automation
<ul><li>Fast (automated) identification of automatable processes.</li><li>Efficient automation using artificial intelligence components.</li><li>Enabling the entire organization to automate.</li><li>End-to-end automation of complex processes as completely as possible.</li><li>Management of the complete lifecycle of automation.</li></ul>	<ul><li>Cost Savings.</li><li>RPA reduces the rate of errors and provides a lower level of operational risk.</li><li>RPA can leverage your existing systems, the same way a human employee can.</li></ul>

Table 4.1: *Comparison based on benefits*

Comparison based on functionality

Table 4.2 features the various comparisons based on benefits:

Hyperautomation	Robotic Process Automation
<ul><li>Performed by multiple machine learning, packaged software (No code/low code platforms, analytics) and automation tools.</li><li>AI-based process automation with cognitive ability and can loop humans into the processes.</li><li>Smart and efficient operations.</li><li>Everything that can be automated will be automated.</li></ul>	<ul><li>Performed by the RPA automation tool.</li><li>Easy and fast to implement.</li><li>Efficient operations.</li><li>Rule-based, routine repeat mundane tasks.</li></ul>

Table 4.2: *Comparison based on functionality*

Case studies of Hyperautomation

Some case studies of Hyperautomation are as follows:

- Based on a report published by Deloitte in 2019, AI, ML, and intelligent automation are amongst the top 10 Industry 4.0 technologies that have the most profound impact on major organizations globally.

- As per Gartner's prediction report:

- *By 2022, 65% of organizations that deploy **robotic process automation (RPA)** will introduce **artificial intelligence (AI)**, including **machine learning (ML)**and **natural language processing (NLP)** algorithms.*

- The global market for advanced technologies that will drive the next wave in the IT space-Hyperautomation is projected to be nearly $600 billion in 2022.

- Recently, we had an opportunity to help one of the leading banks in Indonesia to solve a problem they faced in the cheque clearance process. The process involves verification of the authenticity of the signature on the cheque quickly, which is a time-consuming process and often overlooked by the clerks. Simple mistakes in signature verification could result in transaction delays and friction in the bank's operations and customer experience. It is possible with the help of Hyperautomation to build a solution for solving this challenge.

- The benefits offered by Hyperautomation are huge. According to Coherent Market Insights, the international Hyperautomation market is expected to develop at a CAGR of 18.9% during 2020-27, with the widespread digitalization of outdated manufacturing plants being the key contributor to the numbers.

- According to research, it was established that Hyperautomation was valued at approximately **USD 9** billion in 2021 and is projected to reach roughly **USD 26.5** billion by 2028.

- The Hyperautomation market is expected to grow annually at a CAGR of around **23.5 %** by 2022-2028.

- The industry is increasing because of increasing demand for automation industries robots and the constant development in the field of technologies are boosting the market growth. 41.6% of growth will come from North America.

- Gartner expects that by 2024, organizations will lower operational costs by 30% by combining Hyperautomation technologies with redesigned operational processes.

Case studies of RPA

Let us now investigate a few case studies of RPA in various domains:

RPA in finance and accounting

Organizations have been using RPA for finance and accounting processes. From automatically auditing financial statements to speeding up the rate at which accounts receivable and payable complete the tasks. Advanced technology is evolving quickly and can handle huge amounts of data more efficiently than humans while saving huge costs. Such intelligent automation will make your business processes more transparent and accurate. Here are a few cases:

- **Invoice processing:** Invoice processing is a repetitive and tedious task, especially if the invoices are received or generated in various formats. RPA can handle the time-consuming task easily while ensuring the correctness and forwarding the invoices to the approving authority in less time. Overall accounts payables and accounts receivables can be automated with an RPA in the finance industry. The maker and checker process can be almost eliminated as the machine can perform the tasks that match the invoices with the relevant POs automatically.

- **Automatically bill generation:** RPA helps the finance team in generating automatic bills and manage them. It helps in entering timely and accurate billing details in the system, which helps the team to save time significantly without any errors. It is easy to deploy and causes minimal disruption to the system.

- **Inventory management:** This business process is all about control. It needs to be known about inventory levels to maintain a constant product supply. RPA bots can do all the heavy lifting tasks and help leverage the dead stock and stock-outs, improve lead times, and optimize storage costs.

Adoption of RPA in industries

Let us investigate the following points:

- 81% of companies are investing in RPA technology to achieve their financial goals.

- The RPA adoption rates are increasing from 12% in 2019 to 20% in 2021 as mentioned by Computer Economics 2020.

- RPA for finance will grow around 12.7 times its current adoption rate in the next 2-3 years. RPA for Human Resources will grow over 3.7x times, RPA in procurement will increase by 4.3 times its current size while GBS will increase by 5.2 times in the next 2-3 years.

• By 2025, the market for collaborative robotics is expected to reach $12 billion.

Future of Hyperautomation

Hyperautomation is an upcoming technology transformation that will continue to impact companies in almost every industry. People may concentrate on those with a more excellent value for the business, free from repetitive, rule-based and low-value/low-code jobs. Automation and human participation combine to give enterprises, an enhanced client experience and reduce operating costs and increase profitability.

Hyperautomation vs Intelligent Automation

In the current scenario, every business wants to change their working way and they want every task to happen automatically without the help of any manpower. There are some technologies and tools available in the market which are used to do automation and businesses are trying to use those. However, there is a need to use automation technologies to automate processes intelligently, and for that reason, Intelligent Automation is evolving so quickly. On the other hand, for using automation technologies such as RPA and Intelligent Automation, organizations need to take some business approach to automate the process of thinking strategically about how to get the most value out of the entire tapestry of the organization, that is Hyperautomation, which is adopting a more effective system-based approach to growing automation initiatives.

Figure 4.14 demonstrates the spectrum of Hyperautomation.

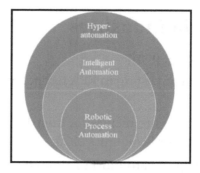

Figure 4.14: *Spectrum of Hyperautomation*

What is Intelligent Automation

Intelligent Automation (IA) is the use of different types of automation technologies by which we can automate our repetitive tasks with the help of RPA with AI, ML and BPM.

Intelligent Automation also allows end-to-end process automation through intelligent bots with decision-making capabilities. Intelligent bots can handle complex and unstructured inputs and learn and improve their own processes.

Intelligent Automation is a technique imposing a new generation of software-based automation. It is the combination of automation technologies with different types of methods, to execute business processes automatically on behalf of knowledge workers. Automation helps to save time and they can work on their skill-based activities (for example, execution, vision, language, and thinking and learning). The goal of using Intelligent Automation is to redesign automated processes to achieve a business outcome, with no or minimal human intervention. As a result, Intelligent Automation can reduce costs, boost process speed, enhance compliance and quality, increase process resilience, and optimize decision outcomes. Ultimately, it boosts revenues and improves customer and employee satisfaction.

Versatile technologies associated with Intelligent Automation

Intelligent automation combines software with RPA, which helps to automate a rule-based, labor-intensive task that does not require human intervention or judgment - with intelligence technologies such as:

- **Artificial intelligence:** The computer systems that simulate human intelligence, AI analyzes data faster than people and can learn from past choices.

- **Machine learning:** A type of AI software with algorithms that identify patterns in structured data and make accurate predictions using historical data as input to future outcomes.

- **Computer vision:** A technology tool, such as OCR, that can convert scanned documents or photos into texts.

- **Natural Language Processing (NLP):** A software that enables a computer to understand, manipulate and interpret spoken or written human languages.

Why do we need Intelligent Automation

Intelligent Automation helps employees to do work faster and better, but it also helps to save time and focus on what really needs human intervention. For example, comments, insights, relationships, and managing their teams because intelligent automation is working for them on the most repetitive and transactional activities. Now, we have more time to focus on qualitative work instead of quantitative.

Waiting to see a bank agent, waiting in a queue to get a train ticket – all these kinds of problems can be solved by intelligent automation. Nearly 90% of customers never bother to complain, and 90% of them will never return. So, it is impossible to understand what makes a client satisfied and how to get their loyalty – and intelligent automation is in the middle of this.

Figure 4.15 shows different types of advantages of Hyperautomation:

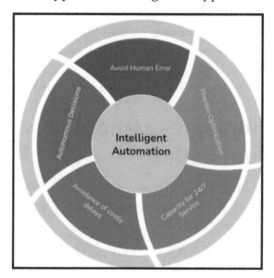

Figure 4.15: *Advantages of Intelligent Automation*

Some of the advantages to the use of Intelligent Automation are as follows:

- **Improving customer experience:** With the help of Intelligent Automation technologies, organizations can improve their customer experience because customers get an immediate response to their questions within a few minutes, whereas manually, those responses would take more than one or two weeks.

- **Increasing process efficiency:** Intelligent Automation can help businesses to increase process efficiency, by which, businesses can satisfy their customers and can get more profit, by cutting down revenue leakage by bringing in efficiency in the process.

- **Optimizing the workforce productivity:** Reducing the workload from employees and automating the process is also an aim of Intelligent Automation. Because of that, employees can increase their workforce productivity and can focus on a high level of tasks where human thinking power is needed.

- **Optimizing back-office operations:** Intelligent Automation can deal with more complex problems with the help of AI, ML, RPA, and other automation technologies. It can optimize most of the back-office operations such as regulatory compliance, record maintenance, accounting and so on.

- **Reducing cost and risk:** At the time of doing repetitive tasks manually, employees get frustrated and make mistakes. With the help of automation, it reduces human error and saves time and costs.

- **Product and service innovation:** Intelligent Automation also helps to innovate which types of products and services will help organizations.

- **More effective and monitoring fraud detection:** Intelligent Automation can also monitor Fraud Detection with the help of RPA and different types of ML models and packages which should be time-to-time updated depending on the demands.

Top barriers to efficient adoption of Intelligent Automation

IPA projects are failing nowadays because people are trying to apply automation to their work without even knowing what their process needs and how much automation is required in it.

Everyone who is working in technology knows that things are always changing, and the band moves quickly. But when it comes to automation, we should not jump. The leaders must understand the how's and whys behind Automation. Automations need to be revisited to check how relevant they are after some time, if there is any further scope of automation in upstream & downstream processes, whether the process has become obsolete and requires a complete rework etc. Organizations should be realistic about the complexity of their processes. If the process is complex and requires human intervention, then human in the loop concept can be brought in. Attended bots can be developed which do part of the process, and the rest of the process is done by a human user.

Automation projects tend to fail in two scenarios: *"Either the process which has been automated, is not a robotic process as it was thought, or the automation is running in such a way that needs to be more dynamic than previously identified"*.

Before using Automation, we must think of what process needs automation and if it needs to be more dynamic or not.

Reasons behind the failure of Automation projects

The reasons why the Automation projects may fail are as follows:

- **The poor selection of the process:** The research has told us that the poor choice of process is the main cause of failure. While we are choosing a project, we have to think about its consequences also. The process is not stable. Inputs are not structured. In such cases, those are not the right processes to automate. If we can automate a process with the help of RPA, AI, and ML, that does not mean that we should automate it. A good process is where the work is:
  - o Repetitive
  - o Performed independently and cognitively in nature
  - o A stable and well-defined process
  - o Rule-based
  - o Logical based Data-drive

- **Strategy:** The project may fail if the business case is not well defined or not well propagated. The prioritization has not been given to the right process at the right time. The main purpose in implementing the Automation project is to operate businesses more fluidly and efficiently. So, we need a strategy to look at how RPA is going to be deployed and utilized. If we have a clear vision, the use of RPA ensures that the right software is chosen to meet the needs of many. One more factor that can lead to RPA failing is not having awareness from stakeholders, or the support from stakeholders such as the CEO, at the early stage of the project. RPA projects are managed by business teams. No robot can operate without a PC, a user account, or access to an application. Without their support, you may find it more challenging to get an RPA project running.

- **People (internal and external):** The insufficient involvement of the stakeholders. RPA partners do not have many skills for automation or less experience may lead to failure. PA works well where the processes are repetitive, and the requirement of human judgment is not required. Even the process which passes the criteria is the best candidate for automation. The RPA is good at following instructions, but it is not good at learning on its own or responding to unexpected events. Taking the human user completely out of the equation through the implementation of RPA will likely lead to operational challenges later. There is still a need for human intervention to manage exceptions. Human users must be on hand to help address these exceptions. They must have a good knowledge of RPA and must be adaptive to change according to the demand.

- **Technology (the incorrect selection of process)**: The scalability should not be limited to hosting but more importantly, to maintaining, managing, and controlling processes. The organizations scale their programs and maintaining and managing the processes creates a new dynamic that the organization will not have experienced in the past. The issue of scalability is complex and requires a concerted effort from across the business to assess. An alternative for the RPA must be explored first. The processes which are likely to use customer data, the implications to privacy as well as the security of sensitive information can become very evident. The failure to invest in the right tool can directly impact the outcome of an organization's automation journey. It will lead to a wastage of time and effort which you have invested in that project. The proper process should be done before selecting the appropriate tool for automation.

How intelligent automation empowers enterprises to transform business processes

RPA developers develop RPA bots for processes that are repetitive and require less human intervention. Intelligent Automation spans the **complete** automation journey—discovery, automation, optimization—automating any front- or back-**workplace enterprise** process, and orchestrating **paintings throughout mixed** human-bot teams. Real-world use cases where RPA can be implemented are HR processes, hospitality, hotel booking, and some finance processes. At the front end, the RPA bot interacts with the UI as humans do and in the back end, it performs logical calculations to perform the tasks.

- **Finance processes**: In finance, reconciliation of reports can be done through an RPA bot by matching balances as humans do, but when a human matches the balance one by one and a robot does it, there is a difference in time. A bot will do the reconciliation faster and more accurately than a human.

- **HR process**: HR processes such as employee leave analytics, employee pay analyses, fulfilling employee document requests, employee data upload on portal or database, and so on, can be easily automated and performed through RPA BOT.

- **Hotel bookings**: Hotel bookings in RPA can be done faster, just as reverting to the customer on time. Moreover, RPA bot can get the email of the booking request, fill in the information, check the booking availability, if the booking is available. then it will proceed for the further step of booking; the bot will book the room and revert the customer for booking confirmation, and so on.

Best practices to build enterprise automation strategy

Some of the best practices to build enterprise automation strategy are as follows:

- **Best practices of RPA with AI and ML**: Every enterprise's main motive is customer satisfaction, and RPA with AI and ML performing smartly can achieve that but only the best practices of these technologies can ensure that.

- **Create process design documents: Process Design Document (PDD)** makes the processes clear and provides a better understanding of the business process to be automated, which includes a flow diagram, steps of the process, discrepancies of the process, time estimation, all scenarios which can occur in the process, and so on.

- **Use reusable component:** There are so many common processes such as login and logout to the web portals, Data Scraping, sending an email and receiving emails and so on. Reuse these components in every process, which will save time-consuming and make the development of the process swift.

- **Developed flow should be readable and not time-consuming:** Using logs in the tool activities to make the developed code understood by other people easily and the developer ensured that the code should not be complex and time-consuming. The RPA process will be worth it only if the RPA code does the process faster than human.

- **Build error handling:** An efficient flow always contains error handling that makes the process execution trouble-free and easy-going at production and saves the process execution from unknown error stoppages.

- **Break process:** RPA BOT works on the business processes which includes subprocesses. Break process flows into a small process that makes the process flow more understandable and after flow division integrates all the flows in the main project.

Need for Hyperautomation

The need for Hyperautomation is to include everybody in an organization, to automate more knowledge labor. It combines several process automation merging tools and components, and technologies to enhance labor automation. Hyperautomation is the merging of Artificial Intelligence, Machine Learning, and automation tools to undertake tasks. That increases the number of people that can use these sophisticated technologies. Hyperautomation refers not only to the sophistication or stages in automation but also refers to a spectrum of instruments. It is equally important for Hyperautomation to choose the right technology that will speak well with staff. Today, most teams are composed of people with different talents and experiences, and it is extremely important to find a tool that everyone can interact with and use effortlessly. Being a mixture of automation technologies, Hyperautomation has the ability to overcome some constraints of a single automation device method. Hyperautomation also helps companies to cross beyond the limits of each process and automate most of the complex and scalable operations.

Hyperautomation has the ability to unify corporate strategy; the aim is to create and optimize end-to-end business processes that create new innovative business proposals. Organizations boost their moral standards by decreasing human interventions in time-consuming and repetitive operations. Hyperautomation also boosts an organization's productivity and efficiency. Organizations need to understand the function of the current workflow of digital technologies. The choice of the developing and ever-growing product market is also a significant problem. In the crowded market, there is a series of mergers and purchases for every organization, which are expected to reduce redundancies throughout their products and enhance customers' experience. Hyperautomation can also help to improve the healthcare business, which provides a better experience for patients, more robust results, and more reliable data.

Intelligent Automation vs. Hyperautomation

Using Intelligent Automation and Hyperautomation interchangeably makes sense since both involve combining automation tools and technologies to achieve a high level of automation for any business.

Intelligent automation is combined of different types of automation technologies such RPA with AI & ML, NLP and so on. However, Hyperautomation is a business-driven, disciplined approach, which is used to rapidly identify, vet and automate as many processes as possible for organizations. The aim of Hyperautomation is to enable remote operation, scalability, and business model disruption.

Hyperautomation is the power of digital destination for businesses of getting hyper-digital to the top-notch seamless customer and employee satisfaction while delivering at scale an optimized enterprise business model under your control. Simply put, "Workload automation is a blueprint of Hyperautomation for an organization". On the other hand, Intelligent Automation helps to put business processes in control by creating a hyper-automated client-centric organization. Depending on the need, it leads businesses to redefine business processes that have an end–to–end automation infrastructure to enhance productivity, reliability, and returns.

As seen in the preceding definitions, the two terms can be differentiated as follows: intelligent automation is a group of specific automation technologies that are used within Hyperautomation initiatives, whereas Hyperautomation is a business approach which uses Intelligent Automation for automated business processes.

To deal with more complex business problems and simplify business processes, AI and other intelligent technologies are emerging with Hyperautomation technology. Hyperautomation enables a working environment as humans with technology together. With Hyperautomation increases collaboration so humans as the key decision makers but they can use technology to interpret big data and apply the insights to their business.

Table 4.3 features the differences between Intelligent Automation and Hyperautomation:

	Intelligent Automation	**Hyperautomation**
Main Use Case	Cognitive automation of multi-step tasks and standard operational workflows.	Cognitive automation of multi-step tasks and standard operational workflows.
Core technologies	<ul><li>AI/ML use cases including OCR, ICR, and NLP.</li><li>Intelligent business process management suites (iBPMS)</li><li>Low-code/no-code tools</li><li>Other types of task automation tools</li><li>Event-driven software architecture</li><li>Integration platform as a service (iPaaS)</li><li>Low-code/no-code tools packaged software</li><li>Robotic process automation (RPA)</li></ul>	<ul><li>Workforce performance augmentation cross-processes</li><li>Wider scope of supported tasks/use cases</li><li>Extra analytical insights</li><li>Suitable for customer-facing processes</li><li>Higher predictability and quality of task execution</li><li>Seamless scalability across other use cases</li></ul>

Implementation Difficulty	Moderate. IA tools require unconstrained access to data, as well as a suitable target environment for deployment. May not be applicable to legacy systems. Slower time to market, but higher ROI.	**High**. Requires a certain degree of digital infrastructure maturity, as well as a meticulous cross-system orchestration to deliver the most gain. Longest time-to-market, but the highest ROI in the long-term perspective.
Remark	In Intelligent Automation, AI and ML can be used to make bots intelligent and these intelligent bots can be further	Under Hyperautomation AI and ML provide different solution and the main role is to minimize human intelligence part.

Table 4.3: Differences between Intelligent Automation and Hyperautomation

Conclusion

Hyperautomation helps IT organizations to be aware of task automation, workload automation, and job scheduling and get better **Return on Investment** (**ROI**). Using **Intelligent Automation** (**IA**), Hyperautomation can enable faster deployment of new features and capabilities without compromising any level of security standards while ensuring compliance at every step along the way.

Any organization can be benefited from the use of Hyperautomation, which uses Intelligent Automation, helps to eliminate repetitive tasks, and automates manual ones, and it also increases productivity and speeds up response times, more accurate results, and most important user experience. Hyperautomation has also enabled an organization to complete tasks with high accuracy and consistency, reduce cost as well as speed up the process. Hyperautomation is plagued with inconsistent product quality and inefficient processes or one that is in a competitive environment, where getting ahead with higher-quality products and more valuable market interactions, equates to gaining market share and improving revenue.

The future of Hyperautomation is very bright, and it will provide an intense effect on businesses and employees. Hyperautomation optimizes digital transformation by enabling it to stay in this competitive environment. With Hyperautomation we can automate several processes and provide insights to the companies which results in N 80% reduction in achieving the same results.

Key facts

- Hyperautomation is the next generation of RPA, which focuses on automating processes, not just specific sub-part to it.
- Hyperautomation is a combination of multiple technologies consisting of RPA, AI, Machine Learning and NLP.
- Due to the preceding fact, it is very important to have in-depth knowledge of these technologies first.

Key terms

- Hyperautomation
- **Robotic Process Automation (RPA)**
- **Artificial Intelligence (AI)**
- Intelligent Automation
- Computer Vision
- **Integration Platforms as a service (IPAAS)**
- **Business Process Management (BPM)**
- **Intelligent Business Process Management Suites (IBPMS)**

Questions

1. What are the main components of Hyperautomation?
2. What are the differences between Hyperautomation and Intelligent automation?
3. What are the differences between Hyperautomation and RPA?

Join our book's Discord space

Join the book's Discord Workspace for Latest updates, Offers, Tech happenings around the world, New Release and Sessions with the Authors:

https://discord.bpbonline.com

Evolution of Automation to Hyperautomation via RPA

Building upon the understanding of automation, this section traces the evolution from traditional automation to hyperautomation, passing through the realm of RPA. It addresses the essential technologies required to develop hyperautomation solutions, including AI, machine learning, deep learning, and their roles in driving hyperautomation. Additionally, it offers a high-level plan for using hyperautomation to solve diverse business problems.

CHAPTER 5

Devising Hyperautomation Solutions

Automation is no longer just a problem for those working in manufacturing. Physical labor was replaced by robots; mental labor is going to be replaced by AI and software.

— Andrew Yang

Introduction

Hyperautomation is increasing automation in business processes by introducing **artificial intelligence (AI)**, **machine learning (ML)**, and **robotic process automation (RPA)**. Almost any repetitive tasks in the business need to identify and need to automate, in order to perform repetitive tasks. Hyperautomation is the key factor in digital transformation. It helps to decrease human involvement in low-value processes. Hyperautomation helps organizations rapidly adapt to changes in the business process. Digital transformation and automation initiatives over the past year acted as differentiated business ecosystems, that were further operating in a decentralized and semi-centralized way. Hyperautomation reduces the burden of organizations and employees from repetitive processes and aging infrastructure to its resources. The transformation that Hyperautomation enables organizations to operate more efficiently, often reduces costs and increases competitiveness. AI and RPA are different things because RPA is process-driven, while AI is data-driven. Moreover, they have lots in common. The combination of AI and RPA technologies results in intelligent automation, which enables virtual end-to-end processes that can be automated. In the next decade, Hyperautomation will be the most demanding technological trend with the greatest impact. It helps in repetitive manual tasks which are carried out by human beings. It combines RPA and advanced technologies such as AI and Machine Learning.

AI is a method of making intelligent computers, computer-controlled robots, or software that can think intelligently like humans. Artificial intelligence is accomplished with the patterns of the human brain by analyzing the cognitive process. The result of these studies develops intelligent software and systems. Gartner predicts that by 2022, 55% of enterprise architecture programs will be supported by AI-enabled software. RPA does not refer to a physical robot or an AI robot. Software, virtual, or bot can automate repetitive tasks and processes. It can eliminate human error and increases productivity and efficiency. RPA bots can automate all rule-based tasks. They can copy or cut and paste data, move files and folders, scrape data from web browsers, fill the form, and extract data from documents. Let us understand in detail about Hyperautomation solutions with the help of this chapter.

Structure

In this chapter, we will cover the following topics:

- Ingredients of the recipe
- The blueprint for Hyperautomation
- Steps of the Recipe
- Problems and Hyperautomation as its solution
- Use Cases – Hyperautomation tech as a solution
- Challenges of implementing Hyperautomation

Objectives

This chapter discusses Hyperautomation in-depth; it explores the **how** part of Hyperautomation solutions. By the end of the chapter, the reader will learn how to implement Hyperautomation as the solution to different problems, and the steps to adopt it. The reader will also learn how to implement Hyperautomation itself.

Ingredients of the recipe

The section discusses the different types of preliminaries required for implementing Hyperautomation as a solution to a problem. These are the top five ingredients which are mentioned in this section. Let us understand all ingredient one by one.

First ingredient: Know the problem statement

The first ingredient, not just for Hyperautomation, but for every solution, should be identifying the problem and the requirements completely with utmost clarity. No doubts and uncertainties should exist regarding the problem and requirements, for which, the solution will be implemented using Hyperautomation. Some checklist points for ensuring the first ingredients are as follows:

- **Keep it simple**: Identify the problem and describe it as simply as possible.
- **Choose vertical**: Define the vertical of the problem clearly.
- **Define the use case**: Define the use case clearly; it should be clear and easy for the implementation team to understand.
- **Go in-depth**: Define how to solve it and explore every possible depth.
- **Strong planning**: After defining all the above things, it is time to do the planning and spend the proper required time on it.

These are the checklists that can be used to ensure the first ingredient. It will take some time to ensure the first ingredient. However, it is very important to give it proper time as this is the base of the whole solution using Hyperautomation.

Second ingredient: Group of manual or semi-automated processes

As the saying goes, *Necessity is the mother of all inventions*. So before considering Hyperautomation, one should identify its need. This need comes from already running processes that are manual or already semi-automated. Also, in these processes, there could be a need for intelligence (human or artificial). However, if the process flow does not depend on any kind of intelligence, then there is no need for Hyperautomation; it can be handled by RPA only. One must understand that one problem can have multiple solutions, and success relies on choosing the optimal solution. If there is no need for intelligence to handle the processes, then Hyperautomation can be avoided as it requires a cost of implementation, which can make the solution non-optimal.

Third ingredient: A dedicated team

The right set of passionate and dedicated people for the solution is the most difficult and most crucial ingredient in the list of ingredients. Of course, the Hyperautomation solution will require people with distinguished expertise. The expertise selection depends on the technology's rooster, which will be part of Hyperautomation. For that, please check the fifth ingredient for the details.

Fourth ingredient: Infrastructure

This ingredient will provide the playground for the solution, whether there is a requirement for new infrastructure or for the updating of existing infrastructure (in most cases). It also requires a specialized skillset and role to decide the optimal infrastructure. Infrastructure planning should be at a high level with prime stakeholders. A dedicated team is also required to manage Infrastructure.

Fifth ingredient: Technologies

Figure 5.1 reflects the variety of versatile technologies associated with the concept of Hyperautomation. It includes process mining and task mining, robotic process automation, artificial intelligence, machine learning practices, **Digital Twin of the Organization (DTO)**, **Optical Character Recognition (OCR)**, and **Natural Language Processing (NLP)**.

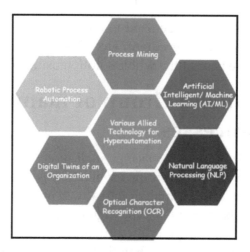

Figure 5.1: Various allied technology for Hyperautomation

The design of a Hyperautomation tool focuses on procedures that require automation and focuses on strategic objectives. It boosts the production and quality control of a given item. With Hyperautomation, automation techniques are used to carry out low-value work. The appropriate design allows autonomous manufacturing to work efficiently with minimum human involvement. People with Hyperautomation may establish a flexible, dynamic workplace, using data for fast and efficient decisions. A company requires a strong automation foundation to get a Hyperautomation plan off the ground. Automation of fundamental operations, automation tools for data storage, and a handful of additional automation solutions are essential to accommodate different teams and departments.

Hyperautomation is a technique that uses the advanced automation technology ecosystem to increase human expertise in the organization. Its objective is to gradually automate corporate processes to enhance education and agility, by building information and knowledge, to make decision-making more efficient. Hyperautomation is an inevitable market situation in which enterprises rapidly identify and automate all business operations. Organizations that invested in automation will probably recognize the advantages of optimizing robotic activities and processes. ML is a discipline that automatically employs computer techniques to develop systems over time and is often used synonymously with AI. To find data trends, organizations utilize both supervised and unchecked algorithms. Supervised algorithms develop inputs and outputs before they can predict themselves. Unmonitored algorithms monitor structured input and create pattern recognition insights. The strategic deployment of AI and ML is necessary for Hyperautomation.

Instantly, Hyperautomation incorporates more intelligence and a more comprehensive range of tools, instead of referring to an out-of-the-box invention. It includes various tools to push enterprises to take fundamental ways of determining and automating, improving, finding, planning, quantifying, and monitoring workflows and processes throughout the company. Process mining and task mining tools find automation possibilities and prioritize them. Automation tools can reduce building automation effort and costs. Various tools for corporate logic to make automation easier to adapt and reuse, is smart management of business processes, policy, and management. AI and automated learning techniques expand automation capabilities. **Natural Language Processing (NLP)**, optical identification of characters, virtual agents, and chatbots are all available instruments in this field.

Eco-system of Hyperautomation

The Hyperautomation ecosystem consists of the following elements:

- **Chatbots:** Features like chatbots are used to interact and engage with customers. Chatbots are integrated with intelligent **Business Process Management (BPM)** suites and **Integrated Platform as Service (iPaas)** platforms, to improve customer experience and responsiveness.

- **RPA and advanced analytics: Robotic Process Automation (RPA)** tools are used in Hyperautomation ecosystems to automate data extraction, entry, and processing workflows. RPA enables employees to be more productive by freeing up time by eliminating repetitive tasks. Advanced analytics is performed on the data collected by bots, to generate profitable insights for businesses to better marketing solutions.

- **Artificial Intelligence:** Artificial Intelligence is combined with Deep Learning to augment various business processes and refine bots' capabilities. OCR technology with AI helps businesses automate data extraction and enter ERP systems. RPA, with a blend of NLP and OCR, can recognize text from unstructured documents, organize it, and sort through it. It can process high volumes of customer and transaction data daily, leading to improved business efficiency.

The blueprint of Hyperautomation

Figure 5.2 demonstrates the blueprint of Hyperautomation at a very high level:

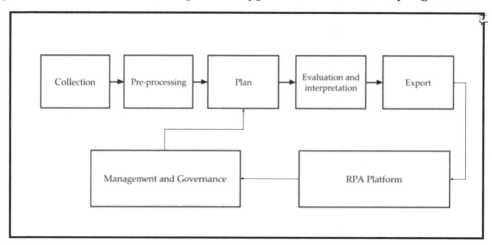

Figure 5.2: *Blueprint of Hyperautomation*

The blocks that are part of the blueprint of Hyperautomation are as follows:

- **Collection:** Collection here refers to acquiring business requirements, problem statements, knowledge of existing systems, and subject data of already existing system.

- **Pre-processing:** This block represents the acquisition of prerequisites, tools, and all the necessary things required to kick the implementation. It should also include the determination of ROI of automation and process assessment.

- **The plan:** At this stage, the high-level planning should be completed, and all the prerequisites should be ready at the starting line. The block is concerned with developing the implementation, which is subjected to deciding milestones | epics | user stories | sprints | tasks.

- **Evaluation and interpretation:** The block is subjected to evaluate and interpret what is developed as the solution and the output of the solution.

- **Export:** Export the output and results; this is the block where the export pipeline should be placed.
- **Management and governance:** The main function of this block is to make the whole solution robust and sustainable. It provided agility to the whole solution, which means checking if everything is working fine. If not, go to plan block, do some tweaks here and there, and make it correct again.
- **RPA Platform:** The block is concerned with deciding the right RPA platform (please refer to *Chapter 3, Fundamentals of RPA Tools & Platform* for more details on choosing the correct RPA platform). This block is going to be the worker block of the whole solution.

Steps of the recipe

It has been previously discussed that Hyperautomation is not based on a single technology. It is the integration of different technologies. Let us first discuss the workflow of the process for Hyperautomation with the help of the following *Figure 5.3*.

Road to Hyperautomation

Figure 5.3 provides a glimpse of road to Hyperautomation from Simple automation:

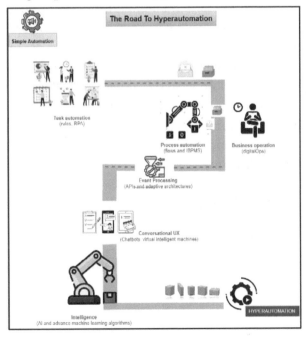

Figure 5.3: Road map of Hyperautomation

Refer to the following steps to understand the road map of Hyperautomation:

- **Milestone 1- Need to understand the need of Hyperautomation:** Artificial Intelligence, Machine Learning, Robotic Process Automation, Natural Language Processing, and other advanced and intelligent technologies combinedly describe Hyperautomation.

- **Milestone 2- Make automated business processes:** Hyperautomation is important in increasing efficiency and augmenting human work. Hyperautomation encompasses a range of tools that can be automated, especially the more sophisticated aspects of automation, including discovery, analysis, measuring, design, monitoring, and reassessing.

- **Milestone 3- Check the reliability of the systems:** Since systems rely on a single automation tool by leveraging various automation technologies, Hyperautomation overcomes some constraints of those systems. It enables businesses to go beyond specific procedures and partially automate scalable and time-consuming operations.

- **Milestone 4- Decide the focus:** Organizations' focus should be on how digital technologies integrate into existing workflows and their roles in new processes. Simply adding automation into a business process without knowing how to play its function, can have significant ramifications at the organizational level.

- **Milestone 5- Try to decrease the manuality:** It is a paradigm for deploying several automation technologies strategically. Hyperautomation is not taking over all the tasks from the human employees; instead, automation frees workers from repetitive tasks and low-value duties, allowing them to focus on more valuable tasks, and making the businesses more profitable.

- **Milestone 6- Focus on providing better customer experience:** Hyper automation may create better customer experiences while lowering the costs of business processes and increasing productivity, by combining automation and human participation.

Dedicated workflow process for Hyperautomation

Figure 5.4 exemplifies the workflow of the Hyperautomation methodology:

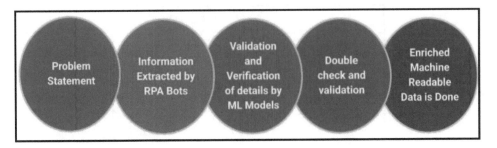

Figure 5.4: *Workflow progressive steps for Hyperautomation*

This starts with the problem statement step, which then proceeds toward the information extracted by RPA bots, further followed by validation and verification of details by ML models. The step of double check and validation has been considered, and in the end, the enriched machine-readable data is completed and validated. Hyperautomation provides the capacity to bridge organizational boundaries, with more extensive automation opportunities. It contributes to the automation of many areas of company decision-making. These include rapid automation of processes, advanced analytical applications, increased team member happiness and motivation, value-added workforce work, more accurate insights, better compliance, decreased risk, improved productivity, and enhanced teamwork. As companies seek to use a broader range of automation solutions to alleviate functional and process barriers, the focus is on achieving end-to-end automation of processes. Hyperautomation is excellent for the client and the team members, who are eventually directly proportionate to the employer. A process modeling tool is employed for the process to be recorded, stored, and optimized by business and IT stakeholders, and prioritized in all areas for improvement. Decision-modeling software may also be utilized to automate the checks manually by managers or finance teams until the possible process is automated. AI is a primary catalyst for improved process automation, human enhancement, and commitment. A comprehensive toolset for intelligent automation allows better, smarter, quicker results focusing on each process stage. Various emerging technologies work together with hyper-automatic technology to assist enterprises in developing as much end-to-end business.

Major steps of Hyperautomation

Hyperautomation is not based on only one technology; it is an amalgamation of different technologies and processes. *Figure 5.5* demonstrates the major steps of Hyperautomation in a nutshell:

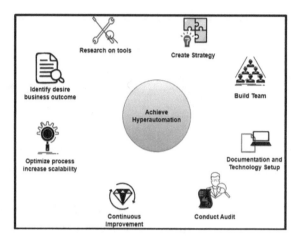

Figure 5.5: *Steps of Hyperautomation*

The different steps of Hyperautomation are further explained as follows:

Identify desired business outcomes

It is important to start by identifying the reason for any process implementation. It is also discussed in the ingredients section. Reasonless process implementation can cause a project to fail because of a goalless journey. To make a rock-solid plan for the project's success, it is important to determine the specific goals that the organization aims to achieve through Hyperautomation. Developers should take the time to establish how Hyperautomation can benefit the entire organization instead of a specific team or process set.

Optimizing the process for scalability

Hyperautomation involves a wide-scale adoption of automation strategies. It is important to consider every opportunity through the lens of scalability. Solutions developed should be scalable to meet the future demand and resilient to failures. Hyperautomation requires a holistic approach. It is important to find ways to future-proof each step along the way.

Research for tools

Ignore the temptation of buzzworthy technologies and ensure each chosen tool aligns with the desired business outcomes. The best Hyperautomation strategies are meant to supplant humans only partially. It frees high-value workers from the productivity handcuffs of rote tasks. Workers will be available to spend time on high-value projects.

For example, an automated robotic process and machine learning tools produce insights from data, by evaluating user behaviors and sentiments. However, a marketing team still needs to turn these findings into creative promotions to capture new business. Similarly, in customer service, artificial intelligence can prioritize incoming customer service calls, and all low-priority calls will forward to chatbots and virtual assistants.

Create a strategy

Developing a data strategy is vital. It is the first step to achieving Hyperautomation. It revolves around what Hyperautomation should look like for the business and what the organization wants to achieve through the initiative. Moreover, it is the key to getting people on board and allocating resources wherever needed.

Build a team

Build teams with individuals who are properly connected across the organization. Team members should be equipped with the right skill set. Business analysts and data experts need to work together to combine both technical and strategic knowledge and need to ensure the best possible outcomes.

Document everything

All business processes and decisions should be documented. It will help chart the project's history and allow the organization to measure progress. Moreover, improvement is required with time.

Conduct an audit

Analyze the level of digitization that the organization already has across the business as well as the need to identify the processes that still need automating. There might be some that are already well covered, including data collection and KPIs, for example, but others might be completely *manual* and in need of migrating to an automated process. Decide what is most important for the business and plan accordingly.

Set up the right tech stack

It is to ensure that the business has the capability to integrate various data in real-time. Choose flexible and scalable solutions to provide access to different sources, such as data analysts, data warehouses, and structured data.

Continuous improvement

There is continuous improvement by getting an end-to-end business overview, to fuel more transparency, encourage information sharing, and prompt the right discussion between departments. The level of communication and collaboration will ultimately lead to better decisions and stronger business performance.

Key gains using Hyperautomation

Hyperautomation builds a connection between systems and operations with structured and unstructured data, simplifying data analysis and enabling faster decision-making. Let us now see the key gains of using Hyperautomation in detail:

Data sharing

Hyperautomation increases data integration across business lines, systems, and applications and ensures faster and more efficient data access. Organizations can benefit from linking data across hiring, onboarding, and salary payments of the whole department's operations.

Real-time information access

Organizations can understand what is happening in cross-enterprise projects; for example, seeing what has been requested, who it has been assigned to, who made a mistake, and how to correct it.

Productivity

Hyperautomation allows organizations to spend more time on value-added activities. Hyperautomation helps in data entry and scanning customer information. It eliminates the manual interaction of emails between departments such as HR and IT, to ensure a better overall team member experience. It digitizes processes across departments to enable end-to-end automation processes like procure-to-pay.

Increase work automation

RPA only allows users to automate a set of rule-based, repetitive tasks that makes the user's work easier. However, with Hyperautomation tools, a user can do much more. Hyperautomation combines many components and technologies to extend the level of automation applied to the business, allowing users to do more work efficiently.

Automated processes

Whether it is a repetitive process or requires knowledge, strategy, and reasoning, Hyperautomation brings high intelligence to RPA, automating many processes and reducing manual labor. It also minimizes the user's work. Employees can free up their time to focus on more important and innovative tasks and let the collective power of Hyperautomation do the rest.

Fosters team collaboration

Hyperautomation connects everyone and everything. From finance teams to IT, connect data, processes, and operations to engage everyone in the transformation. A combination of RPA, intelligent tools, and software robots interact with and facilitate user collaboration across all key organizational processes.

Increase productivity

Empowering the user workforce with a rich toolset that includes the latest technology and advanced automation, implies that users can do more with less. By removing bottlenecks across the operational chain, streamlining processes, and eliminating time-consuming manual tasks, Hyperautomation increases team member productivity, engagement, and motivation, resulting in a more proactive and innovative approach to work, so that the user can work on it.

Advanced analytics and insights

Many organizations often do not understand where employees are inefficient and what they need to improve, constantly optimizing processes for better returns. However, to do this, business leaders need deep insight into data that is only possible by setting up advanced analytics capabilities. Hyperautomation unlocks the potential of data to transform organizations by gaining insights, that allow organizations to understand current business trends, predict future outcomes, make appropriate course corrections and improvements, and can transform.

Increases business agility

Business agility means the feasibility of an organization to grow and change as needed. Hyperautomation tools ensure unlimited scalability for the business. Intelligent automation tools that are layered or interdependent, make it easier for organizations to quickly adapt to changing dynamics, discover new opportunities, and evolve when needed.

Increased employee engagement and satisfaction

Hyperautomation improves work quality, leverages cutting-edge technology to reduce manual work, and increases team members' happiness and satisfaction. It also encourages employees, from program developers to business analysts, to contribute to digital transformation, increasing team member engagement and creating a more competitive and collaborative environment.

Improved data accessibility and storage

Built on the premise of software and process integration, Hyperautomation enables seamless interaction between data storage and on-premises infrastructure. As multi-cloud/hybrid cloud becomes the new normal, system integration will become an integral part of the transformation. It allows all systems to communicate easily and allows all core systems to access data from the same central repository. Additionally, adding AI and machine learning to Hyperautomation tools enables the creation of *digital twins*, essentially virtual models of physical assets or processes.

Augments ROI

The goal of any new initiative or transformational program is to improve the current state and achieve better results. For example, consider automating invoice processing. Instead of having bots read and extract information, Hyperautomation goes further by automating the multi-tiered end-to-end invoice processing process to benefit the process, resulting in better outcomes and successful returns.

Be future ready

Hyperautomation goes beyond RPA, under which a bot has the ability to perform a sequence of steps in a single task. On the other hand, Hyperautomation is forward-looking as it enables machines to read business processes, understand how they work, improve them, and then persistently keep improving them. It means that companies can be years ahead without risking user technology infrastructure becoming obsolete, as Hyperautomation evolves and grows with the business.

Hyperautomation is used in various industries, helping organizations improve business on a bigger scale. It can help banks in many ways, including regulatory compliance, marketing, sales, and distribution. The robotic process manages lower-level tasks so that teams can improve strategic decision-making availability. It helps banks improve the **Know Your Customer (KYC)** processes and compliance. It can create intelligent billing processes by collecting and consolidating billing details without human intervention. Intelligent chatbots can support and automate bill submissions. It also helps voice recognition and enables speech transcription into text. It improves the back-office and customer-facing operations in healthcare and banking services, enhances the overall customer experience, and grows operational efficiencies. In the real world, RPA is used in call centers to automate manual processes. It helps agents pull information about a client from multiple systems quickly. It helps to extend different services such as CRM, package tracking, and project automation. The bottom line with Hyperautomation is that anything that can be automated should be automated. It ensures that every intelligent tool is optimized to provide the greatest business benefit across the broader organization. Companies across all industries must be ready to make rapid changes and innovate, in order to stay competitive in today's global and digital world.

Problems and Hyperautomation as its solution

Before starting the Hyperautomation and how it can help in business process solutions, let us discuss automation. Automation refers to the use of technologies with minimum human interruption; the process will perform faster, reduce human errors, and more effectively and efficiently manage a work process without taking any break.

In various industries, automation has become a standard business-driven approach, from health to banking. Automation allows businesses to streamline their operations, by reducing costs and risk, and increasing productivity and efficiency.

For example, at the time of testing for various regression, defects on a website would take tedious human effort if done manually, but the same could be done much faster and effectively using test automation.

Hyperautomation is the automation of cutting-edge technologies, including Artificial Intelligence, Machine Learning, and Robotic Process Automation, to automate complex business processes. The robots rapidly perform tasks that would otherwise require laborious human intervention.

One example might include using RPA to automate the **Continuous Integration (CI)** business flow or using machine learning, like in helenium, to improve the stability of Selenium-based automated tests.

There are two types of processes that Hyperautomation can leverage, also demonstrated in *Figure 5.6:*

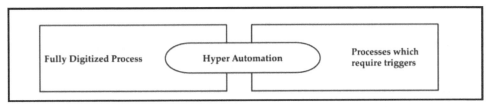

Figure 5.6: Processes that can leverage Hyperautomation

Let us now go over the processes that can leverage Hyperautomation:

Fully digitalized processes

Some processes get triggered with structured data from the company's internal or client processes. These are candidates for an easy automation implementation or should be already automated. The following are the specific process candidates that are for Hyperautomation across standard business functions such as sales, finance, marketing, and customer service, as well as industries like banking and insurance.

Accounts Payable

The **Accounts Payable** (**AP**) process includes receiving, processing, and paying invoices from suppliers that provide services to the company. Manual processing is expensive, leads to longer processing times, and increases the risk of errors. Additionally, with data extraction technologies such as **Optical Character Recognition** (**OCR**) with RPA and Machine Learning, businesses can automate most of the tasks of the AP process.

Claims handling

Claim process handling is a broad category in various settings. We will mainly focus on insurance claims and workplace claims.

Insurance claims: Insurers can automate the entire process of claim processing without any human intervention. The automated claim process contains the following:

- **Claims intake**: Extracting data from documents.
- **Claims assessment:** Understanding and analyzing the claims to identify whether they align with the customers' policy.
- **Claims settlement**: Automating transactions for valid claims.

Customer service operations

Hyperautomation can give efficient customer service with the help of three technologies for end-to-end automation of serving simple customer requests:

- With the help of NLP, Hyperautomation helps to understand the Customer inputs (for example, query, document, email).
- RPA software bots or scripts for output (for example, sending response emails or messages).

- Machine Learning algorithms are used to classify customer requests and match them to potential actions.

Banking customer onboarding

The customer onboarding process in the banking system is document-heavy due to KYC regulations. The processes involve:

- Identity verification
- Screening
- Scoring
- Customer due diligence
- Account activation
- Reporting

Automation of customer onboarding is provided by:

- **Pre-trained bots** are used to extract information from documents, input data into their systems, and build risk profiles via machine learning.
- Historical data train intelligent bots to improve their accuracy.
- Machine Learning Models and human-in-the-loop enable verification and validation of information.

Anti-Money laundering

Companies can either provide end-to-end AML solutions or combine RPA bots to provide automation for preventing fraud in transactions in the following ways:

- Fraud detection models identify usual patterns through ML algorithms.
- RPA bots collect related data and processes to validate customer records.

Redaction for privacy preservation

Redaction is necessary to protect personal data. For example, in the US, courts subpoena insurers for their customers' medical records, and insurers must ensure that those records include only the requested data and nothing more. For example, **Nonpublic Personal Information (NPI)** such as social security numbers or telephone information needs to be removed from these documents.

ML-based solutions can automatically identify NPI and remove it from documents.

Processes triggered by incoming documents or email

In these processes:

- An RPA bot or script collects incoming emails or documents. This email or document may contain semi-structured or unstructured data.

- Emails or documents are processed using a machine-learning model which extracts machine-readable data from the document.

- Either ML models or rules validate machine-readable data. For example, invoices could be validated for VAT compliance or to ensure they are not fraudulent.

- Using humans in the software loop, a human can review the output when the machine learning model confidence score is low.

Use cases: Hyperautomation tech as a solution

Some industry use cases of Hyperautomation as a solution could include the following:

- Enhancing automation workflows through the use of artificial intelligence.

- Document understanding such as verification of images or pdf content using OCR.

- Using NLP to determine incoming emails' sentiments by classifying depends on keywords.

A few more use cases of Hyperautomation in the fields or finance, healthcare, e-commerce industry, and so on, are explained as follows.

Hyperautomation in finance

Finance is an industry where for delightful customer experience, cost reduction and attaining efficiency are the utmost priority. Hyperautomation can provide streamlined tasks dealing with large volumes of financial and high-quality data and make those processes quicker to execute.

For example, Hyperautomation allows the use of technology such as OCR and computer vision to read PDF invoices and expense receipts for better data extractions. It helps to free the staff bandwidth to perform higher-value tasks.

Hyperautomation in healthcare

In the healthcare industry, managing drug inventories, hospital billing cycles, and streamlining patient health record data management is much more complex and time-consuming. However, we can build up a reliable and accurate healthcare system for the public with the help of Hyperautomation. It can automate the processes.

Hyperautomation in the E-commerce industry

In the E-commerce industry, customer satisfaction is the top priority, and one of the major points is an instant reply to the customer. Although it is nearly impossible to send customer query feedback 24X7 actively, AI-based Hyperautomation can streamline front-end and back-end processes, including targeted marketing through emails, social media, supplier, and inventory management, enabling accurate decision-making, and driving business revenue.

Hyperautomation in QA industry

Hyperautomation in QA automation means from test case-based automation to an optimized process without human intervention and automating the entire process using advanced technologies. Hyperautomation mainly focuses on the following:

- Faster application releases.
- Minimal time to execute testing tasks.
- Testing should be more product focused.

Hyperautomation in continuous testing

It is one step more in the QA industry to automate the testing dependencies and requirements such as:

- **Application testing**: This is what you test for the development code. The only thing we can automate here is code availability under test. CI/CD pipeline comes in handy in ensuring the availability of code/application by automating the packaging and deployment of an application to the right environment for testing.

- **Test data and environments**: In the application code for testing, Test data is the combination of various inputs and parameters needed. Hyperautomation can leverage existing APIs to automate the data generation, by creating runtime scripts to trigger upon test run. Moreover, automation in the test environment, that is, device and OS configuration, can be achieved using containerization that pre-configures the environment.

- **Test execution agents**: The process of choosing the right automation platform for executing the tests.
- **Test window**: The test window is where you decide which tests to run. This can be automated using the CI/CD pipeline by, for example, running smoke tests whenever the build moves from the dev to the test environment.

Hyperautomation helps IT organizations be aware of task automation, workload automation, and job scheduling, and get better **Return on Investment (ROI)**. Using **Intelligent Automation (IA)**, Hyperautomation can enable faster deployment of new features and capabilities without compromising any level of security standards, while ensuring compliance at every step along the way.

Any organization can be benefited from the use of Hyperautomation, which uses Intelligent Automation, helps to eliminate repetitive tasks, and automates manual ones. It also increases productivity and speeds up response times, more accurate results, and, most important, user experience. Hyperautomation has also enabled an organization to complete tasks with high accuracy and consistency, reduce cost, and speed up the process. Hyperautomation is plagued with inconsistent product quality and inefficient processes, or one that is in a competitive environment where getting ahead with higher-quality products and more valuable market interactions equates to gaining market share and improving revenue.

The future of Hyperautomation is very bright, and it will have an intense effect on businesses and employees. Hyperautomation optimizes digital transformation by enabling it to stay in this competitive environment. With Hyperautomation, we can automate several processes and provide insights to the companies, which results in 80% reduction in achieving the same results.

Challenges of implementing Hyperautomation

Every implementation has its own challenges. In the same way, hyperautomation also has some challenges, which are discussed as follows:

- Decide **Key Performance Indicators (KPIs)** of the success of Hyperautomation solutions according to the business requirements.
- Based on KPIs, develop a way to calculate the return on investment.
- It has been discussed in the previous section that infrastructure provides a playground to the whole solution, which directly emphasis on understanding the infrastructure challenges.
- Lack of information on existing infrastructure is another challenge that should be addressed during implementing Hyperautomation.

- Maintaining customer experience and satisfaction is another challenge during implementation.

- Fear of loss of job within employees that results in not sharing process details.

- Right selection of tool for the need.

- Organizations and their short-sightedness will lead to them looking for large benefits within short span of time while not thinking and preparing for a longer term. Due to this most programs fail.

- Lack of support from IT or senior leader leading to failure of such projects.

Conclusion

Hyperautomation is used in various industries, helping organizations improve business on a bigger scale. It can help banks in many ways, including regulatory compliance, marketing, sales, and distribution. The robotic process manages lower-level tasks, so that teams can improve strategic decision-making availability. It helps banks improve the KYC processes and compliance. It can create intelligent billing processes by collecting and consolidating billing details without human intervention. Intelligent chatbots can support and automate bill submissions. It also helps voice recognition and enables speech transcription into text. It improves the back-office and customer-facing operations in healthcare service and in banking services, enhances the overall customer experience, and grows operational efficiencies. In the real world, RPA is used in call centers to automate manual processes. It helps agents pull information about a client from multiple systems quickly. It helps to extend different services such as CRM, package tracking, and project automation.

The bottom line with Hyperautomation is that anything that can be automated should be automated. It ensures that every intelligent tool is optimized to provide the greatest business benefit across the broader organization. Companies across all industries must be ready to make rapid changes and innovate, to stay competitive in today's global and digital world. The bottom line is that anything that can be automated is called Hyperautomation. When we combine intelligent and advanced technologies such as AI, Machine Learning, NLP, and RPA, the sky's is the limit with how much benefit any company can drive. To provide the greatest business benefits across the broader organization, Hyperautomation ensures that every intelligent tool is optimized. Companies across all industries worldwide, are now ready to make rapid changes and innovate to stay competitive. Simplilearn's post-graduate program in digital transformation, in partnership with *Purdue University*, is perfect for professionals who are looking to drive strategic initiatives and lead their respective organizations to success.

Companies across all industries must be ready to make rapid changes and innovate, to stay competitive in today's global and digital world.

Key facts

- Hyperautomation is not based on any single technology. It is the amalgam of different technologies.

- Hyperautomation goes beyond RPA, only allowing a bot to perform a sequence of steps in a single task. Rather, Hyperautomation is forward-looking as it enables machines to read business processes, understand how they work, improve them, and keep improving them.

- Hyperautomation optimizes digital transformation by enabling it to stay in this competitive environment.

Key terms

- **Digital Twin of the Organization (DTO)**
- **Business Process Management** suites **(BPM)**
- **Know Your Customer (KYC)**
- **Continuous Integration** and **Continuous Deployment (CI/CD)**
- **Optical Character Recognition (OCR)**
- **Anti-Money Laundering (AML)**
- **Nonpublic Personal Information (NPI)**

Questions

1. What could be the first ingredient for Hyperautomation solution?
2. What is the most important ingredient of Hyperautomation?
3. What are the differences between Hyperautomation and RPA?
4. What are two types of processes that Hyperautomation can leverage?

CHAPTER 6

Amalgam of Hyperautomation and Artificial Intelligence

"What is happening with automation and globalization, that's not going away."

— *Campbell Brown*

Introduction

When we begin searching on Google, it assists us in completing a sentence or words. When we search for outfits on Amazon, it recommends products by displaying ads on Google. When we open Netflix, it suggests the best movies to watch. When we get bored, Google assistant tells us jokes or motivational speeches. A technology that has transformed the 21st century would surely be **Artificial Intelligence (AI)**. This technology has become certain in our day-by-day life. But a more pressing question is whether AI has shown signs of surpassing humans.

The recent growth in architecture has changed the face of science and engineering. This growth is so fundamental that it excessively reshapes relationships among people and organizations. This provides for understanding and learning intelligent behavior in living and engineered systems.

The demand for AI has increased in this century due to the requirement of computing power and social networking apps such as Facebook (face recognition to tag friends),

Twitter (trained to remove wounding or reportable content), Instagram (customizes the content for the investigate tab), and YouTube (suggestions and recommendations for the same type of videos) heavily rely on artificial intelligence.

AI and **Robotic Process Automation (RPA)** are different because RPA is process-driven, and AI is data-driven. However, they have lots in common as well. The combination of AI and RPA technologies results in intelligent automation, which enables virtual end-to-end processes that can be automated. In the next decade, Hyperautomation will be the most demanding technological trend with the greatest impact. It helps in repetitive manual tasks which are carried out by human beings. It combines RPA and advanced technologies such as AI and Machine Learning.

Structure

In this chapter, we will cover the following topics:

- Artificial Intelligence
- Working of Artificial Intelligence
- Issues in AI
- Applications of Artificial Intelligence
- Technologies including AI
- Artificial Intelligence as a boon or a curse
- The past, present and future of AI
- Combination of RPA and AI: Hyperautomation

Objectives

This chapter mainly discusses AI, its history, current state, and future. The chapter has been divided into three phases. The first phase discusses AI's advantages and challenges. The second phase discusses the chronology of AI, and the third phase discusses Hyperautomation as a combination of RPA and AI.

Artificial Intelligence

Artificial intelligence is a branch of computer science, and it refers to a technique that enables machines to mimic human behavior. AI can improve past iterations and become smarter and more aware, allowing it to improve its capabilities and knowledge. With AI, machines perform comprehensible tasks such as learning, planning, reasoning, decision-making as well as problem-solving. AI is the simulation of human intelligence by machines, and it could solve big real-world challenges. This is the main reason why we are discussing whether AI is a boon or a curse!

Types of Artificial Intelligence

In the current classification system, there are four primary AI types:

- Reactive AI
- Limited Memory AI
- Theory of Mind AI
- Self-Aware AI

Figure 6.1 demonstrates these different types of AI:

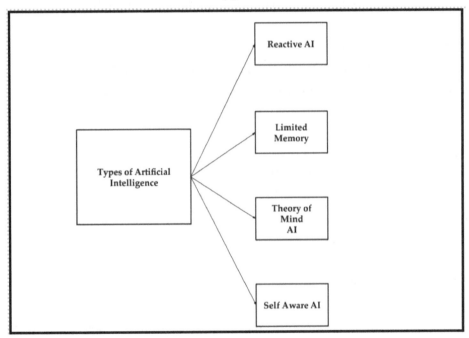

Figure 6.1: *Types of Artificial Intelligence*

Reactive AI

Reactive AI refers to the type of AI system that reacts to current input, based on predefined rules or patterns, and does not have the ability to learn from experience or make predictions about future events. Reactive AI provides a predictable output, based on the input they receive, but it cannot reason about the past or the future.

Reactive AI is often used in applications where a quick and accurate response to a specific stimulus is required, such as in self-driving cars, game-playing AI, and voice assistants. However, reactive AI has limitations in more complex and dynamic environments, where the AI system needs to adapt to changing circumstances and predict future events. These systems are often categorized as **limited memory** or **long-term memory** AI, depending on their ability to retain past experiences and use them to inform future decisions.

This includes spam filters for our email that keep promotions and phishing attempt out of our inboxes, as well as the Netflix recommendation engine.

Reactive AI was an enormous step forward in AI development, but this type of AI cannot function beyond the tasks it was initially designed for. That makes the Reactive AI types inherently limited and tender for improvement.

Limited memory AI

Limited memory AI learns from the past and builds experiential knowledge by observing actions or data, and uses historical, observational data in combination with pre-programmed information to make predictions and perform complex classification tasks.

Autonomous vehicles use limited memory AI to identify other cars' speed and direction, helping them **read the read** and adjust as needed and process for understanding the incoming data, making them safer on the roads.

Using limited memory AI autonomous vehicles' work is fleeting, and it is not saved in the car's long-term memory.

Theory of mind AI

When a robot holds a meaningful conversation with an emotionally intelligent robot that looks and sounds like a real human being and similar types of AI, machines will acquire true decision-making capabilities like humans. AI can understand and remember emotions that adjust behavior based on those emotions as interacting with people.

There are a few hurdles to achieving the theory of mind AI, because the process of shifting behavior based on rapidly shifting emotions is so fluid in human communication. There are ongoing efforts to develop emotionally intelligent machines that can understand and respond to human emotions more nuancedly.

Self-aware AI

The most advanced type of AI is Self-Aware AI, and that is a case where AI have self-awareness as well as awareness of others also. They will have a level of consciousness and intelligence like human beings. This type of AI will have desires, needs, emotions, and mental states. They will be able to make impossible inferences with other types of sophisticated AI.

Working of AI

AI system is a careful process of reverse-engineering human traits and capabilities in a machine, and computational prowess to surpass what we are capable of. In order to understand how AI actually works, we need to deep dive into the various sub-domains of Artificial Intelligence and understand how domains could be applied to the various fields of the industry.

Machine Learning

Machine Learning (ML) is a technology that enables the process of drawing conclusions and making decisions, based on previous data. By identifying patterns and analyzing historical data, ML models can understand the significance of each data point and arrive at a possible conclusion without human intervention. By evaluating data, ML can save time for businesses and lead to better decision-making.

Deep Learning

Deep Learning is an ML technique that teaches machines to process inputs through layers to classify them, infer, and predict the outcome. It can be further classified into:

- **Neural Networks:** Neural Networks work on similar rules to human neural cells. They have many processes and algorithms that capture the relationship between various underlying variables and process the data as a human neural network.

- **Natural Language Processing (NLP):** NLP is the science of reading, understanding, and interpreting a language by a machine, that understands what the user plans to communicate, and responds accordingly.

- **Computer vision:** Computer vision algorithms try to understand any image by breaking down an image and studying various parts of the object, which helps the machine classify and learn from a set of images, and make better decisions based on past knowledge.

- **Cognitive computing:** Cognitive computing algorithms aim to replicate human brain functionality by examining and interpreting text, speech, images, and objects like human cognition to produce the intended results.

Issues in AI

Artificial intelligence is essential across various industries, including healthcare, retail, manufacturing, and government. There are ethical challenges with AI, and as always, we need to stay vigilant about these issues to ensure that AI is not doing more harm than good. Some biggest ethical challenges of artificial intelligence can be seen in *Figure 6.2*:

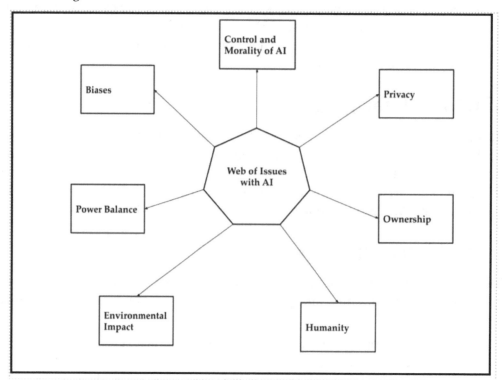

Figure 6.2: Web of Issues with AI

Biases

We require data to train our AI algorithms and need to do everything to eliminate bias in data. When we train our AI algorithm to recognize facial features using a database that does not include the right balance of faces, the algorithm will not work as well on non-white faces, thus creating a built-in bias that can have a colossal collision. It is important that we eliminate as much bias as possible as we train our AI, instead of shrugging our shoulders and assuming that we are training our AI to reflect our society accurately and begins with being aware of the potential for bias in our AI solutions.

Control and morality of AI

We use more and more AI, and we ask machines to make increasingly important decisions. Right now, there is an international convention that dictates the use of autonomous drones that could potentially fire a rocket and kill someone. There needs to be a human in the decision-making process before the missile gets deployed. Some of the critical control problems of AI are embroiled in confusion regarding rules and regulations. AI has to increasingly make split decisions in high-frequency trading, with over 90% of all financial trades driven by algorithms. Thus, there is no chance to put a human being in control of the decisions. The same is true for autonomous cars that react immediately if a child runs out on the road. Thus, it is important that the AI is in control of the situation and creates interesting ethical challenges around AI and control.

Privacy

Privacy for using data has long been an ethical dilemma of AI that need data to train and assume that all the data is coming from adults with full mental capabilities, who make choices for themselves, about the use of their data. Now, there is a Barbie AI-enabled doll that children can speak to, but what does this mean in terms of ethics? There is an algorithm that collects data from children's conversations with this toy, and there are also many companies that collect data and sell it to other companies. These kinds of data collection have rules, and users need to protect their private information.

Power balance

Many companies such as Amazon, Facebook, and Google are using AI to squash their competitors and become virtually unstoppable in the marketplace. Many countries like China also have ambitious AI strategies supported by the government. We ensure that monopolies and generating are distributing wealth equally and that few countries race ahead of the rest of the world using AI applications. Balancing that power is a vital challenge in the world of AI.

Ownership

We can use AI to create text, bots, or even fake videos that can be misleading. Who owns this type of material, and what do we do with this fake news if it spreads across the internet? We also have AI that can create art and music, and so, when AI writes a new piece of music, who owns it? No one.

Environmental impact

Sometimes we do not think about the environmental impact of AI but start using data on a cloud computer to train an algorithm and that data is used to run recommendation engines on our website. We use the power of AI energy for the highest good and use AI to solve some of the world's biggest and most pressing problems. If we only use AI because we can, we might have to reconsider our choices.

Humanity

The final issue is, *how does AI make us feel like humans?* AI is now very fast, powerful, improved, and efficient, and it can leave humans feeling minor. This issue may make us think about what it means to be human. AI is expected to keep automating our jobs, but it will not replace all of them. Instead, it will enhance the jobs. Therefore, we need to become more skilled at working in collaboration with intelligent machines, to make the shift with respect to both technology and people. We must also be cautious when it comes to the use of AI.

Applications of Artificial Intelligence

AI applications are numerous and ensure benefits like improved services, better customer satisfaction, and behavior forecasts. Some of the major applications of artificial intelligence are as shown in the following *Figure 6.3:*

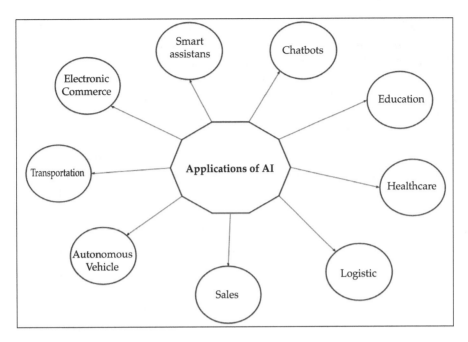

Figure 6.3: *Different applications of artificial intelligence*

Some major applications of Artificial Intelligence are as follows:

- **Smart assistants**: Siri, Google Home, and Amazon Echo are well-known smart assistants and good examples of AI applications. These devices use NLP to interpret the visitor and consumer response and respond either verbally or through the execution of a particular action.

- **Chatbots:** AI in chatbots come in many forms, and the most common are NLP, which powers the language side of the chatbot, to ML, which powers data and algorithms. When we use a web page, we find interactive chatbots that suggest products/restaurants/hotels/services based on our queries. Chatbots are computer programs that replicate and process human conversations. It is one of the clearest examples of artificial intelligence, as are Amazon's Alexa, Apple's, or Microsoft's Cortana, which we find integrated into our everyday devices.

- **Education:** The use of Artificial Intelligence makes it possible to detect and provide the right solutions. For a student, AI helps as an alternative to adapt to the needs of each student, control class attendance, and prevent school dropouts.

- **Healthcare:** More accurate and timely diagnosis is critical for appropriate treatment in the health sector. For example, during the COVID-19 pandemic, AI could give early warnings of the Pandemic, predict isolated infections, analyze information, or carry out pre-diagnosis of the virus through apps.

- **Logistics and transportation:** AI has played a crucial role in the COVID-19 pandemic, with several autonomous cars and drones transporting medical supplies and delivering vaccines in remote locations. Besides, now AI is useful in avoiding smashes and traffic jams, improving traffic behavior, and optimizing traffic light control.

- **Sales:** AI applications also offer sales forecasts to choose the best products to propose to customers. Multinationals such as Amazon, use AI to identify if a product or a launch would be successful or not, even before it is put out on sale. AI helps in minimizing the purchase and distribution processes and avoids any losses or breakages. *Figure 6.4* demonstrates the different roles of AI in Sales:

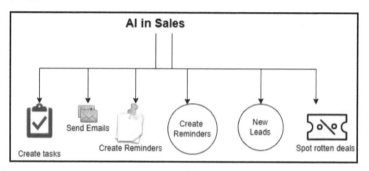

Figure 6.4: AI in sales

- **Autonomous vehicles:** Artificial Intelligence is the most important, powerful, and sophisticated component of autonomous vehicles. These vehicles have sensors, cameras, and smart communications systems that generate extensive data. This data, in combination with AI, can help to mimic human behavior and enable cars and vehicles to perform perfectly.

Some of its functions are:

- Recommend related products to the customer.
- Remind them of the past purchase.
- Predict whether any product will be successful.
- Optimize inventory and avoid out-of-stock and predicted revenues.

Technologies including AI

Becoming familiar with AI and the companies, helped managers discuss Artificial Intelligence more intelligently with their teams. Some technologies including AI are:

- **Machine learning:** ML is part of most commercial organizations' enterprise. Artificial intelligence strategies have great possibilities for ML algorithms, development tools, APIs, model deployment, and more. We took the opportunity from computers to learn without random programming.

- **Deep learning platforms:** Deep learning is a subfield of machine learning inspired by the human brain. **Artificial Neural Networks (ANN)** passes information through these networks, which helps especially when it comes to recognizing patterns and classification.

- **Natural Language Processing (NLP):** NLP is a bridge between humans and machines or computers. Computer programs understand spoken or written human speech. Many software such as Amazon's Alexa, Apple's Siri, Microsoft's Cortana, and Google Assistant use NLP to understand better and respond to users' questions and their behavior. This is used extensively in service, support, and customer transactions, but has massive potential to improve an organization's internal processes.

- **Speech recognition:** This is the different ability of a program to recognize and analyze spoken language words and phrases and convert them into data. An enterprise can apply speech recognition for call routing, voice recognition, and speech-to-text processing. One downside of speech recognition is that words cannot be captured due to variations in pronunciation and background noise.

- **Hardware with integrated AI:** This includes appliances with integrated AI, chips, and **Graphics Processing Units (GPUs)**. Google has embedded AI into its hardware to establish an end-to-end control and give it a push into the future. The impact of integrating AI to end with hardware goes through customer applications, such as generating entertainment and bringing about the next level of gaming. We will be used to proper deep learning.

Artificial Intelligence: A boon or a curse

Our Society does not negatively impact its surroundings; even Artificial Intelligence has many negative outcomes. Whether they are to us, humans, or to other things, AI does certainly come with some costs.

Adopting AI is often characterized as a terrible disaster for the human workplace. AI, also a form of robot or other automated programs, displaces thousands of jobs in multiple different work fields and performs the same human-like tasks; many companies are implementing them.

Data is the main feedstock of AI; it is easily hacked, which creates a huge concern for privacy. As many humans start to hop on the new technological wave and use more smart devices, huge data will be collected, resulting in a more extensive invasion of privacy.

IoT devices are a big contributor to this ongoing privacy issue, mainly because of their increasingly strong ability to connect to one another and create a shared network of devices. This may be very convenient for the human user, and so it is prone to cyber-attacks. Several vulnerable devices gain control and explain how hackers use closely connected IoT devices to change into botnets. Through this scenario, privacy will be lost, as hackers can save, destroy, and share our personal data.

There are more benefits and drawbacks of AI, but the main constant point of society is to resolve the issues that AI brings along, as discussed:

- **Solution = AI + humans**: AI makes its way into and takes over all the major industries, and thus, keeping humans in these areas is also crucial. Mostly, all the problems that AI encounters, such as hacks, malfunctions, and transparency, can be resolved with the help of humans. If humans assist AI, every task can be executed with better efficiency, leading to a better output. In that area, where human input is essential or where AI can be more effective, working together is the solution in all cases. AI should work alongside humans.

- **Hacks:** Humans can supply real-time security, supervision, and solutions.

- **Malfunctions:** Humans can identify, monitor, and perfect an AI application through their expertise.

- **Job displacement:** Humans can work with AI to produce finer results.

Use of AI will further increase in the future and shape our lives. It has its advantages and disadvantages. It has the elements that support it, be it a boon or curse. But still, there is a debate about whether it will be a boon or a curse.

It is well-known that everything in excess can be risky or dangerous; the same concept can be applied to Artificial Intelligence. The emergence of Artificial Intelligence is revolutionizing modern-day technologies.

The impact of artificial intelligence in different fields or sectors such as healthcare, surveillance, and banking has already been discussed. So, artificial intelligence has some boon effects already.

Advantages of Artificial Intelligence

Some advantages of AI are as follows:

- Artificial Intelligence reduces human error.

- Contributes to risky tasks that are not possible for humans to perform, such as exploring the depths of the sea, space expeditions, and so on.
- As compared to human labor, AI can perform tasks to a longer extent with constant human intervention required.
- Companies can depend on AI to safeguard consumer data.

Disadvantages of Artificial Intelligence

Some disadvantages of AI are as follows:

- Higher costs are involved because of machine complexity.
- Since AI automates a lot of tasks, it has made humans dependent on smart devices and become lazy.
- AI can easily perform continuous and heavy tasks; it has already started replacing human labor; for example, process automation in our industries.
- As of now, AI cannot replicate human emotions and connection, an essential attribute to the team working.
- AI and machines are programmed to perform functions, and so it may take some time for them to innovate at performing tasks.

The past, present, and future of AI

AI usually reminds humans of super robots with more knowledge than any human being, like the visions of the MCU. But what is it really? Basically, artificial intelligence lets computers perform human tasks that require intelligence. In some cases, it may exceed the level of human intelligence.

Past of AI

The concept of AI has been around for centuries, but it was in the 1950s that its true potential was explored. Generations of scientists, mathematicians, and philosophers all had the concept of AI, and the British polymath Alan Turing used the information and suggested that if humans use available information and reason to solve problems and make decisions, why cannot machines do the same? Turing outlined methods for testing machines and their intelligence in his 1950 paper, *Computing Machinery and Intelligence*, but his findings still need to advance.

In the 1980s, an expansion of funding and algorithmic tools revived AI research. *John Hopfield* and *David Rumelhart* popularized *deep learning* techniques that allow computers to learn through experience.

On the other hand, *Edward Feigenbaum* introduced an expert system that mimics the decision-making process of human experts. But it was in the 2000s that AI flourished despite achieving many of its groundbreaking goals and needing more government funding and public attention. Let us understand the chronology of AI in brief:

- The year is 1923 when, for the very first time, the word Robot was used in a play named **Rossum's University Robots (RUR)** by *Karel Kapeks*.

- The year was 1945 when the term Robotics came into existence by *Issac Asimov*, an alumnus of Columbia University.

- 1950 was a remarkable year for AI which changed things completely; during this year, *Alan Turing* performed the famous Turing Test.

- The term Artificial Intelligence was used first time in 1956 by *John McCarthy*.

- Just after two years of the preceding event, in 1958, *John McCarthy* summoned LISP programming language for AI.

- In 1964, *Danny Bobrow* published a thesis that proved the understanding of Natural Language by computers and demonstrated that they can solve algebra word problems accurately.

- Stanford Cart, the first-ever automatic vehicle (obviously controlled by the computer), was invented in 1979.

- In 1990, AI demonstrated its potential in different areas, such as Case-based reasoning, Scheduling, Multi-agent planning, Significant demonstrations in Machine learning, and Games.

- *Gerry Kasparov*, the world chess champion of 1997, was beaten in his own game by the Deep Blue Chess Program.

- The year was 2000 when two significant milestones were achieved; Robot pets were made commercially available, and a robot named Kismet, that can express emotions, was displayed by MIT.

- **WABOT1** was invented in Japan in 1972; it was a full-fledged intelligent robot.

- The emergence of expert systems came into existence in the year 1980; these systems can solve complex problems.

- In 2005-2006, AI caught the attention of world tech giants like Twitter, Facebook, Watson AI (from IBM) and Netflix.

Present of AI

With so much artificial intelligence in use and so much potential, it is easier to imagine our future with it, especially regarding business.

Artificial intelligence can collect and organize large amounts of information to generate insights and inferences beyond the manual processing capabilities of humans. It also increases organizational efficiency but reduces the potential for error, detecting irregular patterns such as spam and fraud to alert businesses to suspicious activity in real-time. AI aims to reduce costs in many ways. For example, *train* a machine to handle customer support calls, replacing many jobs in this manner. It is also well known that businesses that do not use AI are likely to fall behind the competition.

AI is so important and advanced that a Japanese venture capital firm made history by becoming the first company to appoint an AI board member for its ability to predict market trends faster than humans.

Artificial intelligence will become ubiquitous in all areas of life, such as future self-driving cars, more accurate weather forecasts, and advanced health checks.

Future of AI

We are on the threshold of the Fourth Industrial Revolution. This revolution is very different from its previous three industrial revolutions. From steam and waterpower, electricity and assembly lines, and computerization to challenging ideas about what it means to be human.

Smarter technology in factories and workplaces, connected machines interacting with each other, visualizing entire production chains, and making decisions autonomously are just some ways the industrial revolution will drive economic progress. One of the greatest promises of the Fourth Industrial Revolution is its potential to improve the quality of life and raise income levels for the world's population. Our workplaces and organizations are becoming **smarter** and more efficient as machines, and people start working together, using connected devices to improve supply chains and warehouses.

According to Gigabit Magazine, there are seven phases to building a smarter world with AI:

1. **Domain specific expertise:** Machines can develop expertise in a particular field beyond human capabilities because they can quickly access information and make decisions.

2. **Rule-based systems:** Domiciliary applications and RPA software surround us everywhere, every day.

3. **Reasoning machines:** These algorithms have a theory of mind and a certain ability to attribute mental states to themselves and others. They have beliefs,

intentions, knowledge, and an awareness of how their logic works. It is, therefore, capable of reasoning, negotiating, and interacting with humans and other machines.

4. **Context awareness and retention:** An algorithm that builds a set of information used and updated by a machine. For example, chatbots and robot-advisors.

5. **Artificial superintelligence:** Developing AI algorithms that can outperform the smartest people in every field.

6. **Self-aware systems:** Those working in the AI field aim to create and develop systems with human-like intelligence. There is no such evidence today, but some say it will be in just five years, while others think we may never reach that level of intelligence.

7. **Singularity and transcendence:** The development path made possible by ASI could lead to a massive expansion of human capabilities, one day extended, and that too, extended to the point where humans can connect their brains to each other and the successor of the current Internet.

Combination of RPA and AI: Hyperautomation

One possibility MIT is exploring is the creation of AI robots with biological brains made up of human neurons, *connecting a human brain with a computer network via an implant*. This is highly unlikely to happen soon and will undoubtedly raise ethical issues. *Elon Musk* is redeveloping an implantable chip called *NeuraLink*. *Elon Musk* said, "I think it is going to blow your minds, like a Fitbit in your skull with tiny wires."

AI and RPA are different things because RPA is process-driven, and AI is data-driven. Moreover, they have lots of common things. The combination of AI and RPA technologies results in intelligent automation, which enables virtual end-to-end processes that can be automated. In the next decade, Hyperautomation will be the most demanding technological trend with the greatest impact. It helps in repetitive manual tasks which are carried out by human beings. It combines RPA and advanced technologies such as AI and Machine Learning.

AI is a method of making intelligent computers, computer-controlled robots, or software that can think intelligently like humans. Artificial intelligence is accomplished with the patterns of the human brain, by analyzing the cognitive process. The result of these studies develops intelligent software and systems. Gartner predicts that by 2022, 55% of enterprise architecture programs will be supported by AI-enabled software.

RPA does not refer to a physical robot or an AI robot. It is a software robot or virtual robot or bot that can automate repetitive tasks and processes. It can eliminate human error and increases productivity and efficiency. RPA bots can automate all rule-based tasks. They can copy or cut and paste data, move files and folders, scrape data from web browsers, fill the form, and extract data from documents.

Applications of AI and RPA

AI and RPA are two different technologies. RPA is efficient but only does what the user or programmer tells it to do, while AI can teach itself. RPA can automate repetitive tasks, and AI can bridge the gap where RPA falls. RPA deals with structured data. AI gathers insights from semi-structured and unstructured data in text, scanned documents, webpages, and PDFs. AI brings value by processing and converting the data to an unstructured form for RPA to understand.

What is Hyperautomation

Hyperautomation is the framework and set of innovative technologies, such as RPA, AI, Machine Learning, **Intelligent Business Process Management (IBPM)**. It is the main factor in digital transformation because it reduces human involvement. That is why we can utilize the capabilities of Hyperautomation instead of using just one technology. Hyperautomation helps businesses to automate entire processes.

Benefits of Hyperautomation

Hyperautomation has many advantages, such as:

- The integration of innovative technologies such as AL, ML, NLP, and RPA allows it to perform quickly and efficiently, and it can also reduce errors.

- It increases team member satisfaction because they do smart work, and they do not have to waste their time on high-volume tasks, which adds no value. It increases the ability to enhance productivity.

- In today's digital world, organizations can transform digitally. Organization aligns their business processes, and they are investing in technology.

- Hyperautomation reduces the operational costs of organizations. According to Gartner Report, by 2024, combined Hyperautomation with redesigned operating processes will reduce costs by 30%.

- AI and Big Data can extract information from data effectively.

Challenges and limitations of Hyperautomation

The challenges and limitations of Hyperautomation are as follows:

- **Integration with existing systems:** Integrating new technologies, such as RPA and AI, with existing systems can be challenging and require significant investment in time and resources.

- **Data privacy and security concerns:** The use of RPA and AI requires access to large amounts of sensitive data, which can raise privacy and security concerns if not properly managed and protected.

- **Lack of skilled workforce:** Implementing RPA and AI requires a specialized skill set, and a shortage of trained professionals may lead to increased costs and longer implementation times.

- **Ethical and legal considerations:** The use of RPA and AI raises ethical and legal questions around issues such as employment and the use of automated systems for decision-making.

- **Resistance to change:** Some employees may resist the implementation of RPA and AI, as they may view it as a threat to their jobs.

- **Technical complexity:** Implementing RPA and AI can be technically complex because it requires a significant investment in technology and infrastructure.

- **Limited scope:** RPA and AI can automate only a limited set of tasks and processes, which may not be suitable for all types of work.

- **Bias and unintended consequences:** AI systems can perpetuate existing biases and lead to unintended consequences if not properly designed and monitored.

Why is Hyperautomation important

Hyperautomation is very important for the following reasons:

- Hyperautomation helps organizations by providing a framework to expand, integrate and optimize automation.

- RPA is proliferating compared to other automation technologies. RPA notices how humans interact with applications, and developers can automate all their parts of work by recording how they do a task. Bots can copy human behavior. The automated task is measured by speed and accuracy, which organizations use to judge the performance of employees on the same task.

- In Gartner's report, the concentration is on how enterprises can build a process for automation. This is the difference between hyperautomation and other automation frameworks. It focuses on automation tools such as **Digital Process Automation (DPA)**, **Intelligent Process Automation (IPA)**, and Cognitive Automation.

- Hyperautomation helps to accelerate the process of identifying automation offers and then generates the artifacts, bots, scripts, and workflows, which can use DPA and IPA components.

How Hyperautomation works

Hyperautomation typically follows a structured approach, which includes the following steps:

- **Process discovery:** The first step in Hyperautomation is to identify the business processes that can be automated. This involves analyzing the business process to understand its inputs, outputs, tasks, and decision points.

- **Process mining:** This step involves using software tools to collect and analyze data from various sources to understand the actual process flow, including process variations and inefficiencies.

- **Process optimization:** Once the process is understood, it can be optimized to improve efficiency and reduce costs. This is a follow-up mail regarding your contribution to the Journal as we have not heard anything from you regarding your submission of the manuscript.

- **Automation:** Once the process has been optimized, the next step is to automate the process using a combination of technologies such as robotic process automation, artificial intelligence, machine learning, and low-code development tools.

- **Monitoring and maintenance:** After the process has been automated, it is important to monitor its performance and ensure that it continues to operate smoothly. Any issues that arise should be addressed promptly to avoid disruption to the business process.

Hyperautomation can help businesses to improve efficiency, reduce costs, and improve the quality of their services. By automating routine and repetitive tasks, businesses can free up resources to focus on higher value-added activities, such as customer service and innovation.

Eco-system of Hyperautomation

The Hyperautomation ecosystem consists of the following elements:

- **Chatbots:** Features like chatbots are used to interact and engage with customers. Chatbots are integrated with IBPMS and IPAAS platforms to improve customer experience and responsiveness.

- **RPA and advanced analytics:** RPA tools are used in Hyperautomation ecosystems to automate data extraction, entry, and processing workflows. RPA enables employees to be more productive by freeing up time by eliminating repetitive tasks. Advanced analytics is performed on the data collected by APIs to generate profitable insights for businesses to better marketing solutions.

- **Artificial Intelligence:** Artificial Intelligence is combined with Deep Learning to augment various business processes and refine bots' capabilities. OCR technology with AI helps businesses to automate data extraction and enter ERP systems. RPA, with a blend of NLP and OCR, can recognize text from unstructured documents, organize it, and sort through it. It can process high volumes of customer and transaction data daily, leading to improved business efficiency.

Conclusion

AI has transformed human lives and we cannot imagine our world without its active role. In the future, we will see more revolutionized AI, with autonomous driving and flying in our daily lives. AI is replacing many human-driven tasks. If humans and AI have line-up interests, both will go hand in hand, and if they do not, it gets inconsistent.

AI technology has clearly seen a resurgence in recent years. AI is ubiquitous in every aspect of life, from self-driving cars to more accurate weather forecasts to early-stage health checks. AI is taught to perform tasks that require human thought and reasoning. Workplaces and organizations are becoming *smarter* and more efficient as machines and people begin to work together. Over time, we use connected devices to improve our warehouses and supply chains.

With more intelligent technology at work, machines interact, visualize the entire production chain and make decisions autonomously. The Industrial Revolution has enabled many business advancements, but there is still a long way to go.

Talking about the combination of AI and RPA and using it as Hyperautomation, the future of Hyperautomation is very bright and will have a huge impact on your business and workforce. Hyperautomation optimizes your digital transformation by enabling you to survive in this competitive environment. Hyperautomation allows you to automate multiple processes and bring insights to your business, allowing you to achieve the same results with 80% less.

Key facts

- The existence zone of AI, whether it is a boon or a curse, depends completely on its usage.
- There is a history associated with the emergence of AI, and it is treated as cutting-edge technology in the present era. But the future of AI is yet to bloom in full-fledged manner.
- Hyperautomation is a naive technology for now in the field of RPA and AI, but it has the potential to help the overall process of decision-making.

Key terms

- **Rossum's University Robots (RUR)**
- LISP programming language
- Deep Blue Chess Program
- WABOT1
- Job Displacement
- Interactive Robot Pets
- Self-Aware Systems

Questions

1. What are the main benefits of AI and its challenges?
2. Describe the incident that happened in 1997, which supported the emergence of AI.
3. What is WABOT1?
4. When was the Stanford cart invented?
5. What are IBPMS and IPAAS?

Join our book's Discord space

Join the book's Discord Workspace for Latest updates, Offers, Tech happenings around the world, New Release and Sessions with the Authors:

https://discord.bpbonline.com

CHAPTER 7

Bridging AI with Humans

"Within a few decades, machine intelligence will surpass human intelligence, leading to The Singularity — technological change so rapid and profound it represents a rupture in the fabric of human history."

— *Ray Kurzweil*

Introduction

In today's world, technology is growing very fast, and humans are exposed to various new technologies every day. One of the fastest-growing computer science technologies is **Artificial Intelligence (AI)**. Artificial intelligence is poised to revolutionize the world by creating intelligent machines. Artificial intelligence is all around us now. We are currently working on various subfields, from general to specific, such as self-driving cars, playing chess, proving theorems, playing music, and painting. AI is one of the fascinating and ubiquitous areas of computer science with a bright future. AI tends to make machines think like humans.

Structure

In this chapter, we will cover the following topics:

- AI and its ethical issues
- Making AI more responsible
- Trust AI and its principles

Objectives

The objective of this chapter is to explore the possibilities of bringing AI as a technology close to humans, considering the functional, emotional, and behavioral aspects. The next revolution will be subjected to AI, and humans must make themselves ready for AI. On the other hand, developers of AI need to think about the basic human traits which are very important, such as ethnicity, trust, and responsibility. This chapter discusses what, why, and how around these traits.

AI and its ethical issues

Machine learning, a subfield of artificial intelligence, has numerous applications that have transformed various aspects of our lives. From predictive analytics to **Natural Language Processing** (**NLP**), machine learning has brought significant benefits to many areas, such as healthcare, education, and finance. However, along with these benefits, machine learning also raises ethical concerns. One of the most significant ethical issues arising from machine learning is the potential for algorithmic bias. This occurs when the data used to train a machine learning algorithm is biased, leading to discriminatory outcomes.

For example, facial recognition algorithms have been shown to be less accurate in recognizing people with darker skin tones, which can lead to biased outcomes in law enforcement or hiring practices. This bias can exacerbate existing social inequalities and injustices. Another ethical issue is the lack of transparency in AI algorithms.

Many AI models are complex and opaque, making it challenging to understand how they arrive at their predictions. This lack of transparency can make it difficult to detect and correct biases or other ethical issues, leading to potentially harmful outcomes. Privacy is also a significant ethical concern in AI. AI algorithms often rely on large amounts of data, including personal information, to make predictions. There is a risk that this data can be used for unauthorized purposes, such as surveillance, or that it can be vulnerable to hacking or other security breaches.

Addressing ethical issues

The use of AI is becoming increasingly widespread and powerful, raising concerns about the need for strict regulation. Despite this, there is little consensus on who should be responsible for regulating AI, and current regulatory bodies lack the necessary expertise to effectively oversee the use of these technologies. As it stands, many companies that develop and use AI systems are primarily self-regulated. They rely on existing laws and regulations, as well as negative reactions from consumers and shareholders, to keep themselves in check.

However, there is a growing concern that this approach is not sufficient and that more oversight is needed to ensure that AI is being used ethically and in ways that benefit society. To address these concerns, some experts have called for greater government regulation of AI. However, there is also recognition that many existing regulatory bodies are not equipped with the technical knowledge necessary to effectively regulate AI. Additionally, there is concern that too much regulation could stifle innovation and limit the potential benefits of these technologies. To strike a balance, some experts suggest that there needs to be more education around tech ethics, to ensure that individuals working in the tech industry and other fields are equipped with the knowledge and skills necessary to ensure that AI is being used in ethical ways. This education could also help to ensure that individuals are better equipped to evaluate the potential risks and benefits of AI, both in their personal lives and as citizens in a democratic society.

Ultimately, AI has the potential to offer numerous benefits, from improving healthcare to helping in reducing carbon emissions. However, it is also clear that ethical concerns must be addressed if these benefits are to be fully realized. By taking a thoughtful and collaborative approach to regulation and education, it may be possible to ensure that AI is used in ways that serve human purposes and promote a more just and equitable society.

The topic of AI ethics is currently one of the most discussed areas in the field of technology philosophy. AI could redefine the way we understand our moral concepts, ethical practices, and moral theories. The development of machines with artificial intelligence that could surpass human capabilities is a challenge to the human perception of ourselves as the only beings with the highest moral standing in the world. Therefore, the future of AI ethics is uncertain, but it holds considerable potential for excitement and surprise.

Making AI more responsible

AI has transformed our world in ways that were unimaginable just a few decades ago. It is used in healthcare, transportation, finance, entertainment, and many other industries. However, as AI becomes more integrated into our daily lives, using it in a responsible manner becomes an emerging need to be ensured. Responsible AI is the ethical and moral use of AI that considers the impact on society, the environment, and individuals. In this blog, we will explore the meaning of responsible AI, why it is necessary, the principles that guide it, and the benefits of implementing it.

The world of AI

AI is rapidly transforming the world we live in. It has revolutionized industries ranging from healthcare and transportation to finance and entertainment. AI is essentially the ability of machines to simulate human intelligence and thought processes, allowing them to perform tasks that would typically require human intelligence. Here is a summary:

- The history of AI dates to the 1950s when the term was first coined by *John McCarthy, Marvin Minsky, Nathaniel Rochester, and Claude Shannon*. In the following decades, AI research and development continued to grow and expand, leading to the development of expert systems, machine learning algorithms, and deep learning.

- Today, AI is used in a wide range of applications, including self-driving cars, virtual assistants, and facial recognition systems. AI is also used in healthcare to diagnose diseases, predict patient outcomes, and develop new treatments. It is used in finance for fraud detection, credit scoring, and investment analysis. In transportation, AI is used to optimise routes, improve safety, and develop autonomous vehicles. In entertainment, AI is used to create personalised content and recommend products to consumers.

- The future potential of AI is vast and has the potential to transform our world in many positive ways. AI can be used to revolutionise healthcare by enabling personalised medicine and developing new treatments. It can be used to personalise education by adapting learning materials to individual students' needs and abilities.

AI can be used to monitor and predict environmental changes, enabling more effective conservation and management of natural resources. It can be used to optimise business operations, improve customer service, and develop new products and services. AI can also be used to develop advanced robots that can perform tasks such as cleaning, cooking, and caregiving.

Interpretation of responsible AI

As AI becomes more integrated into our daily lives, there is an increasing need for responsible AI, that is designed and used in an ethical and transparent manner. Responsible AI refers to the development and use of AI systems that are:

- Transparent
- Explainable
- Configurable

Let us discuss them one by one:

Transparent AI

Transparent AI refers to AI systems that are designed in a way that makes their inner workings and decision-making processes visible and understandable to the users. Transparency enables users to understand how an AI system is making decisions, allowing them to trust the system and its outcomes. In contrast, opaque AI systems, which operate as **black boxes**, can lead to suspicion and mistrust of the system's outcomes. Transparent AI can help ensure that AI systems are not perpetuating biases or discrimination and can allow for easier regulation and governance of AI.

Explainable AI

Explainable AI refers to the ability of AI systems to provide clear and understandable explanations for their decision-making processes. Explainability is particularly important in high-stakes applications such as healthcare, where incorrect decisions can have severe consequences. Explainable AI can help users understand why an AI system made a particular decision and can enable them to verify the system's outcomes. It also allows users to detect any errors or biases in the system's decision-making process.

Configurable AI

Configurable AI refers to the ability of AI systems to be modified and adapted, to meet specific user needs and requirements. Configurability can enable users to customise AI systems to meet their specific needs, leading to more accurate and useful outcomes. Configurable AI can also allow users to adjust the level of automation or human input in the system's decision-making process. Configurability can help to ensure that AI systems are not used in a one-size-fits-all manner and can be adapted to different contexts and scenarios.

The need to make AI responsible

As AI technology continues to rapidly evolve, there is an increasing requirement to make AI systems responsible and accountable. AI systems have the potential to bring significant benefits to society, but they also pose risks and challenges that need to be addressed. Making AI responsible, involves designing and using AI systems in a way that ensures that they are ethical, transparent, and trustworthy.

One reason why there is a need to make AI responsible is that AI systems can perpetuate biases and discrimination. AI systems learn from the data that they are trained on, and if that data is biased, the AI system will also be biased. This can lead to discriminatory outcomes that can negatively impact number of communities.

For example, AI systems used in hiring or loan approval processes can perpetuate biases against certain groups, such as women or people of colour. Making AI responsible involves ensuring that AI systems are trained on unbiased data and that their decision-making processes are transparent and explainable.

Another reason why there is a need to make AI responsible is that AI systems can be used to manipulate or deceive people. For example, deepfakes, which are AI-generated videos or images, can be used to spread false information or manipulate public opinion. Making AI responsible involves ensuring that AI systems are used ethically and that their outcomes are verifiable and transparent.

Finally, making AI responsible is necessary to ensure that AI systems are safe and secure. AI systems can pose risks to individuals and society if they are not designed or used in a responsible manner. For example, AI systems used in autonomous vehicles need to be designed to prioritise safety and to minimise the risk of accidents. Making AI responsible involves designing and testing AI systems to ensure that they are safe and secure.

Principles of responsible AI

There are several principles of responsible AI that can guide the development and use of AI systems. These principles are intended to ensure that AI systems are designed and used in an ethical, transparent, and trustworthy manner. The following are some of the key principles of responsible AI:

- **Fairness:** AI systems should be designed to avoid bias and discrimination, and to promote fairness and equality. This involves ensuring that the data used to train AI systems is unbiased and representative, and that AI systems are designed to avoid perpetuating existing biases and discrimination.

- **Transparency:** AI systems should be designed to be transparent and explainable. This means that the decision-making processes of AI systems should be clear and understandable, and that users should be able to understand how AI systems arrive at their decisions.

- **Accountability:** AI systems should be designed to be accountable, meaning that there should be clear lines of responsibility and accountability for their actions. This involves ensuring that there are mechanisms in place to hold AI systems and their developers accountable for their actions.

- **Safety and security:** AI systems should be designed to be safe and secure, and to minimize the risks that they pose to individuals and society. This involves designing AI systems to prioritize safety and security, and to minimize the risk of accidents or other negative outcomes.

- **Privacy:** AI systems should be designed to respect the privacy and confidentiality of individuals. This involves ensuring that personal data is collected and used in a way that is transparent and ethical, and that individuals have control over their personal data.

- **Robustness:** AI systems should be designed to be robust, meaning that they should be able to function effectively in a variety of different environments and under different conditions. This involves designing AI systems to be adaptable and resilient, and to be able to handle unexpected situations or changes in the environment. By following these principles, AI developers and users can ensure that AI systems are designed and used in a responsible manner that promotes the well-being of individuals and society. These principles can also help to address the ethical and social challenges posed by AI technology, and to ensure that AI systems are aligned with the values and goals of society.

Implementation and design

The implementation and design of responsible AI is essential to ensure that AI systems are developed and used in an ethical and trustworthy manner. There are several key considerations that should be considered when designing and implementing AI systems:

- **Data collection:** The data used to train AI systems should be carefully selected and collected in a way that is ethical and transparent. This involves ensuring that the data is representative and unbiased, and that individuals are aware of how their data is being used.

- **Data processing:** The processing of data by AI systems should be transparent and explainable, and decisions made by AI systems should be understandable and justifiable. This involves designing AI systems to be able to provide clear explanations for their decisions, and to be able to identify and correct biases and errors.

- **Model selection:** The selection of models and algorithms used in AI systems should be based on careful consideration of their ethical implications and should be chosen to minimize bias and discrimination. This involves ensuring that AI systems are designed to be transparent and explainable, and that users can understand how the system is making decisions.

- **Human oversight:** The implementation of AI systems should involve human oversight and input to ensure that decisions made by AI systems are ethical and aligned with human values. This involves designing AI systems to incorporate human input and oversight, and to be able to identify and correct errors made by the system.

- **Ethical considerations:** The design and implementation of AI systems should consider the ethical implications of the technology. This involves considering the potential impacts of AI on individuals and society and designing systems that are aligned with human values and priorities.

- **Testing and evaluation:** AI systems should be rigorously tested and evaluated to ensure that they are functioning as intended, and it should be ensured that they are aligned with ethical and social considerations. This involves testing AI systems in a variety of different scenarios and evaluating their impact on individuals and society.

Benefits

There are numerous potential benefits to making AI more responsible and ethical. Some of the most significant benefits include:

- **Improved accuracy:** When AI systems are designed to minimize bias and discrimination, they can achieve higher levels of accuracy and precision. This can be particularly important in areas such as healthcare and finance, where accurate predictions and decision-making are essential.

- **Increased trust:** When AI systems are transparent and explainable, users are more likely to trust the technology and the decisions it makes. This can lead to greater adoption and use of AI systems, which can drive innovation and growth in the industry.

- **Reduced risk:** By designing AI systems with ethical considerations in mind, developers and users can minimize the potential risks associated with the technology. This can help to protect individuals and society from harm, while also promoting the responsible use of the technology.

- **Improved efficiency:** AI systems can be designed to automate complex and time-consuming tasks, which can help to improve efficiency and productivity in a wide range of industries. By making AI more responsible and ethical, these benefits can be achieved without sacrificing accuracy or fairness.

- **Enhanced decision-making:** By incorporating human oversight and input into AI systems, decisions made by the technology can be aligned with human values and priorities. This can help to ensure that AI is used in a way that is beneficial to society, rather than being driven purely by financial or other incentives.

- **Increased innovation:** By promoting the responsible and ethical use of AI, developers and users can create an environment that encourages innovation and growth in the industry. This can lead to new and exciting applications of the technology, which can benefit individuals and so on.

Use cases for responsible AI

AI has drastically revolutionised the way people interpret workplaces in today's scenario. Following are some use cases of a responsible AI which can be incorporated in the world around us:

- **Accelerating the governance:** One of the recent and in demand use of responsible AI is accelerating governance. Artificial intelligence has been continuously improving and developing due to its dynamic nature. Like technology, government is required to function by the organization rapidly. Responsible AI is used to eliminate risks and errors, thus boosting the company's governance effectively and efficiently.

- **Measuring the work:** The work is now measurable with another amazing use case of responsible AI, or having an ethical framework is key. AI ensures having processes that are measurable in place, for instance, explainability, visibility and having a technical auditable or an ethical framework as a key, as managing responsibility can account for subjectivity at times.

- **Ethically enhanced AI:** Another top use case of responsible AI is the betterment of ethical AI in the workplace. It has been helpful in developing smart tools and frameworks that can not only assess but also plan for the artificial intelligence models in being ethical and fair with respect to the strategy of the company.

- **More preparation of AI models:** Responsible AI is also used to impart a chance to prepare models of AI more, to improve efficiency and boost productivity. The principles of responsible AI can be used by an organization according to the requirements and demands of end-users to prepare AI models.

- **Adapting testing of bias:** Bias testing is being adopted by many companies which will help in eliminating insufficient processes and tools. There are many frameworks with a strong ecosystem support and open-source tools for machine learning. Particularly, in non-regulatory cases, these tools can be used to leverage responsible AI focusing on assessment of bias with mitigation.

Trust AI and its principles

Public trust in AI is essential for continued acceptance of the technology that transforms how we live and work. The benefits and potential of AI for society and business are undeniable. AI helps people make better predictions and informed decisions, enabling innovation and increased productivity, helping in various areas such as detecting credit card fraud, diagnosing disease, and so on.

Problem of trust in AI

The risks and challenges posed by AI, such as the codification and reinforcement of unfair biases and violations of human rights such as privacy, are also undeniable. These issues are of public concern and raise questions about the reliability and regulation of AI systems. If AI systems are not proven to be trustworthy, their widespread adoption will be hampered, and the potentially large social and economic benefits will not be fully realized. Even though trust is paramount, little is known about what public trust in AI is like and what impact it will have across countries.

In 2020, KPMG and the University of Queensland did a survey examining Australians' trust in AI systems. This report builds this research on trust in AI with a comprehensive understanding of citizens' perspectives, in five nations: the United States, Canada, Germany, the United Kingdom, and Australia. Some of the key findings of this report include:

- Citizens have low confidence in AI systems.
- Citizens are happy with some, but not all, use of AI.
- Citizens want to learn more about AI, but there is currently very little awareness and understanding of AI and its uses.
- The more people believe that the effectiveness of AI is uncertain, the less they trust in AI systems.
- Public trust and support for AI depends on the purpose of the AI system.

What does it take to trust AI

To trust a technology, we first must prove that it works and is accurate under all conceivable conditions. Humans live in a society based on high levels of trust. There are many systems that require trust, most of which we do not even think about daily. Today, many products come with safety guarantees, from child seats to batteries.

But how can such guarantees be obtained?

In the case of AI, developers can use mathematical proofs to provide certainty.

Some of the trust issues with AI include:

- The potential negative impact of AI poses a grave threat to humanity. Experts discuss impacts such as job losses from AI:
  - o Humans may soon be replaced by AI in a variety of roles. The prowess of AI is already emerging in various industries such as healthcare, retail, aviation, and manufacturing, as AI-enabled applications transform and streamline various business operations.
  - o That is why established companies are using AI to automate core tasks.

- Another big problem with the development of AI is that it could quickly become smarter than humans and eventually take over humans:

  o Experts suggest AI-powered robots will be smarter than humans by 2045. As such, experts, and tech enthusiasts fear that AI-powered robots will soon take over humanity.

  o Advanced AI-enabled robots can also develop cognitive and behavioral intelligence. Such intelligence allows AIs to have emotions and morals, and to understand right and wrong according to their own definitions that may not match human morality.

  o This phenomenon may be of particular concern as there is no globally accepted code of ethics that can be used to design algorithms for AI.

- AI is prone to unintentional biases that can be problematic for certain groups of people:

  o AI bias is generated due to the data used to train the AI model. If there is human bias in the data used to train, the results produced by AI systems will also be biased.

  o Such AI biases can discriminate against people of certain races, genders, or nationalities.

These concerns have given experts and tech enthusiasts a question of trust in AI. To build trustworthy AI, developers must address these concerns and find practical solutions.

Measuring AI trust

What if AI could produce trustworthy fact sheets, such as nutrition labeling on food or star ratings for electronics on energy efficiency? The ability to make decisions quickly can have far-reaching impact. But what does this framework contain? There are **four** main building blocks that can serve as the pillars of trust in AI: Safety, Reliability, Transparency, and Accountability. This is also important in providing a fair model for all target audiences:

- Misclassifications and prediction errors are always possible. However, clearly stating the nature of the error gives the user confidence. AI models trained with a user-centric approach will perform better when needed. When performance metrics include business KPIs in addition to statistical analysis, model reliability tends to improve as business needs evolve.

- AI models built on the pillars of fairness, transparency, and certainty help ensure transparent and biased models. A user-centric approach combined with extensive testing in multiple scenarios helps build fair models. Even after deployment, the model should be constantly monitored and unbiased to ensure that the model remains safe and unbiased throughout its lifecycle.

- This is a key factor needed to facilitate human augmentation over the lifecycle of an AI model, especially when model fairness is monitored or when model performance degrades over the lifecycle. A mechanism to provide explanation and feedback on the model from a ground truth perspective keeps the model robust and increases transparency throughout its lifecycle.

- It is important to emphasize the benefits and impact of AI within defined boundaries. Also, an ethical framework for AI models is needed to enhance privacy and model security, maximize a safe user experience, and thereby enable digital trust.

Trust in AI is not a mythical idea. Using these **four** key building blocks as part of your AI system will increase your confidence in AI, allowing you to use it in large-scale, important projects without worrying about unintended consequences.

Building trustworthy AI

Trust is something which can be associated with co conciseness. If our conscience allows ourselves to believe in some one, then only Trust can exist. This section is mainly focused on what factors can be added with AI so that it can be trustworthy as well. Tech companies and developers can consider the following factors to build trustworthy AI.

Explainability

AI has a serious black box problem where AI systems give key decisions on machine learning algorithms rather than big data. Therefore, end users and developers may not understand why the AI system made certain decisions. Due to the lack of explanation, the user may doubt the accuracy of the results produced by the AI system.

Therefore, developers must build explainable AI systems. To do that, organizations using AI need to open their black boxes and understand how AI systems make critical decisions and produce results.

After researchers understand exactly how AI systems work, they can educate people about AI and make AI systems more transparent. And companies implementing AI can take additional steps to make their AI systems more transparent.

Integrity

Machine learning integrity is a necessary requirement for developing trustworthy AI systems. The integrity of machine learning helps AI systems generate output according to the developer's pre-defined operational and technical parameters. Machine learning integrity allows developers to ensure that the AI system is working as intended. This is how developers can design trustworthy AI systems that provide accurate results according to predefined conditions.

Reproducibility

Reproducibility ensures that results produced by AI systems can be reproduced. If the results are not reproducible, there is no clear way to understand why the results were produced.

Moreover, the results produced by AI systems can be affected by multiple factors such as algorithms, artifacts, system parameters, different versions of code, and different datasets. Therefore, ensuring reproducibility can be very difficult.

Developing reproducible AI systems requires the maintenance of the provenance of every outcome. This allows developers to understand how each result is generated and easily identify inaccuracies. Therefore, to build trustworthy AI systems, developers should focus on achieving reproducible results.

Conscious development

When developing AI systems, developers must ensure that decisions made by AI are in the interests of humans. To do this, AI systems must be aligned with human principles and values.

Therefore, the goals developed for AI systems should be aligned with human values and focused on improving human life. This mindset allows developers to consciously design applications that benefit humanity.

However, following this approach can be complicated as many developers create AI applications with good intentions, but these applications violate privacy by collecting large amounts of sensitive data.

In such scenarios, developers can design AI applications that are not too invasive and use effective security protocols to protect sensitive data. It enables developers to design secure, highly functional, and trusted AI applications.

The development team should consist of different people who can help design the algorithm and collect different training data. Development teams can use different training data to keep AI systems from producing biased results. Diverse teams can also identify problems that smaller teams might miss, leading to the development of trustworthy AI applications.

Regulations

The European Union has created ethical guidelines for building trustworthy AI. These guidelines are intended to help developers build legal, ethical, and robust AI systems. Similarly, government agencies should create guidelines and regulations for designing trustworthy AI systems. Such guidelines can be designed for achieving the following goals:

- AI system is secure and does not violate user privacy.
- AI systems must not harm the environment or other living things.
- AI systems are designed to empower humans and are driven by humans.
- Avoid unintentional bias when developing AI applications.
- Design mechanisms to ensure accountability and accountability for AI systems and their results.

By considering these points when formulating regulations, governments can guide developers to build trustworthy AI applications.

Bias and fairness

Bias can enter in different ways at different stages of the modeling process. The training data used may have an inherent bias for historical reasons. Alternatively, bias can enter the modeling if data samples are inconsistent across classes or misrepresentative of different groups.

Transparency

Factors such as the release of model details to decision-making systems, information about how they work together to make the final prediction, and insight into how the model performs under different conditions are important.

Sustainability

Developing AI solutions can result in a large carbon footprint due to the processing of large amounts of data, the use of large computing instances, and the energy required to cool such data centers. We need to make optimal use of resources, monitor resource consumption, and optimize AI solutions to reduce our carbon footprint and be sustainable.

Lack of understanding and ways to bridge the gap

Most descriptions of AI model predictions are in numbers, force charts and graphs, features, or heat maps that only data scientists understand, and most are invisible to end users. This leads to a lack of understanding, an inability to act on AI decisions, and an increased reluctance to use AI results.

Generating and communicating counterfactuals

The system's ability to recommend the least feasible and achievable change, allowing it to turn adverse decisions into favorable ones, is also critical in building trust in AI systems. Regarding the prediction of health insurance premiums, the possibility of recommending users to lose 5 to 7 kilograms of weight or quit smoking will significantly reduce the burden of insurance premiums, which will enhance the transparency of the decision-making system.

Bias mitigation

Debiasing techniques such as posterior weighing and sampling allows us to remove biases at the preprocessing stage by conditioning the data, while techniques such as adversarial debiasing, which is a method during processing or training, allows us to identify who is missing. It is good practice to manage biases at all stages of modeling. During data preprocessing and profiling stages, protected attributes can be automatically detected and reweighting and resampling techniques can be applied to overcome historical and representative biases in data. Similarly, modeling biases during testing and assurance phases should be identified prior to deployment.

Uncertainty quantification with explanations

Quantifying uncertainty is important in AI modeling, especially in fields such as financial services, life sciences, and healthcare, where forecast variability and outcome distribution are much more important than point forecasts. Quantifying uncertainty not only indicates model behavior, but also points out data gaps that can increase the variability of model predictions.

Calculating the model uncertainty associated with the key features identified by the explainer provides meaningful insight into the overall behavior of the model, including the variability of model predictions.

Gaining trust in AI decisions

As the use of AI systems gains momentum, companies must recognize the responsibility of their decision-making models when implementing the technology, providing end-users with information on each step and providing the necessary clarifications where appropriate. Context and timing are critical in AI-based decision-making models. The best way for users to gain trust in AI's decisions is to remain transparent and communicate explanations, uncertainties, and biases to users in a human-perceivable way with domain context. Even so, explainable, or interpretable AI is only part of building trust. There are other concepts such as debiasing and performance relevance. AI systems perform as well as the data they were trained on, so they must be continually retrained to remain fair and unbiased. To ensure this, performance measurement must go beyond statistical measures to include actionable business indicators. If continuous retraining is not part of modeling system, model may become irrelevant.

AI principles

Before knowing about AI principles, you must know why AI principles are important.

Companies around the world are waking up to the risks that AI can pose, such as automation bias and potential job losses. At the same time, AI offers many tangible benefits to organizations and society. Many of the risks associated with AI have ethical implications, but clear guidance and **principles** can provide recommended ethical practices and behaviors for individuals and organizations.

From technology providers to the government, new companies seem to announce their AI principles every day. These are general guidelines on how to responsibly design, train, test, and deploy AI systems. On the surface, this is great news. It shows the realization that AI, unleashed into the world without much foresight, could have devastating social and economic consequences. In an enterprise context, this means carefully weighing the risks and benefits of adopting AI. Let us discuss how to apply each of these AI principles to business.

Fairness and bias

This principle is about ensuring that artificial intelligence systems do not harm people or customers through unfair treatment. The report *The Ethics Of AI* describes how AI systems inherit bias and provides guidance for avoiding bias from an organizational and technical perspective. AI algorithms and datasets can reflect, reinforce, or mitigate unfair bias. To recognize that distinguishing difference between fair and unfair bias is not always easy and varies from culture to society. We need to avoid undue influence on people, especially those related to sensitive characteristics such as race, ethnicity, gender, national origin, income, sexual orientation, ability, political or religious beliefs.

Trust and transparency

Since many AI systems are black boxes or otherwise incomprehensible to humans, explainability/interpretability is often required. For the public to trust AI, it must be transparent. Tech companies need clarity on who is training their AI systems, what data was used in that training, and most importantly what was used to make the algorithm's recommendations. If you use AI to make important decisions, it must be explainable.

Accountability

AI systems are often the result of complex supply chains that can involve data providers, data laborers, technology providers and system integrators. Who is to blame when AI systems go wrong? How do we stop things from going wrong in the first place? These things need to be taken care of.

Social benefit

The proliferation of new technologies is having an increasing impact on society. Advances in AI will transform a wide range of fields, including healthcare, security, energy, transportation, manufacturing, and entertainment. To proceed, consider a wide range of social and economic factors when considering the potential development and use of AI technology, where the overall expected benefits appear to materially outweigh the foreseeable risks and harms.

AI also improves our ability to make sense of content at scale. We need to continue to respect the cultural, social, and legal norms of the countries in which we operate, while working to make high-quality, accurate information readily available using AI. We also need to continue to carefully evaluate the availability of our technology on a non-commercial basis. Many technology providers and countries have policies stipulating the use of AI for the benefit of society. This is happening today as companies try to use AI to develop COVID-19 vaccines.

Privacy and security

The data that feeds the AI model can be personal or impersonal in nature. Regardless of how it is defined, companies need to make sure the rules are in place and as AI systems are trained and then deployed to provide differentiated treatment, they must respect individual privacy. Incorporate privacy principles into the development and use of AI technology. Provide notice and consent opportunities, encourage privacy-preserving architectures, and provide appropriate transparency and control over data use.

Built and tested for safety

This should be done to develop and employ rigorous security practices to avoid unintended consequences that lead to the risk of harm. Carefully design AI systems accordingly and attempt to develop them in line with the best practices in AI security research. Optionally, test AI technology in constrained environments and monitor its behavior after deployment.

Maintain high standards of scientific excellence

Innovation is rooted in a scientific method and a commitment to open inquiry, intellectual rigor, integrity, and collaboration. AI tools have the potential to unlock new areas of scientific research and knowledge in important areas such as biology, chemistry, medicine, and environmental sciences. We need to strive for high standards of scientific excellence for advanced AI development. Building trustworthy AI systems is critical, because only when technology is trustworthy, including the processes and people behind it, can humans safely and fully benefit from it. Trustworthy AI was therefore a fundamental goal when creating these guidelines and principles. These principles need not remain esoteric and abstract. As we all seek refuge, we have an opportunity to stop and think about the future we want to create. Whether this AI aligns with good values or not depends on the choices made as a business today.

Conclusion

In conclusion, AI has the potential to revolutionize our world and drive innovation and growth across various industries. However, it is important to recognize that with this potential comes responsibility, and we must take steps to ensure that AI is developed and used in a way that is ethical, fair, and beneficial to society.

To achieve this, we need to promote responsible AI, which involves designing and using AI systems that are transparent, explainable, and configurable. This means ensuring that AI systems are designed with principles such as transparency, accountability, fairness, privacy, and security in mind. It also involves collaboration between developers, users, and other stakeholders to ensure that the technology is used in a way that aligns with human values and priorities. There are several benefits to promoting responsible AI, including improved accuracy, increased trust, reduced risk, improved efficiency, enhanced decision-making, and increased innovation. By promoting responsible and ethical use of AI, we can ensure that the technology is used to promote social and economic development in a way that is fair and equitable. However, promoting responsible AI is not without its challenges. It requires an understanding of the ethical implications of AI and a commitment to address these issues through collaborative efforts. It also requires ongoing monitoring and evaluation of AI systems to ensure that they remain aligned with human values and priorities.

Key facts

- As we are entering the age of AI revolution, now is the time when we need to think about making AI more human compatible.
- AI needs to be more responsible and trustworthy as well.
- Responsible AI refers to the development and use of AI systems that are transparent, explainable, and configurable.
- The main principles of responsible AI are fairness, transparency, accountability, safety and security, privacy, and robustness.

Key terms

- Responsible AI
- Trust AI
- Transparent AI
- Explainability
- Sustainability

Questions

1. Why is there a need for AI to be responsible?
2. What are the important principles of Responsible AI?
3. What is Trust AI and its main principles?
4. State in brief, how to make AI trustworthy.
5. What are the main ethical issues associated with AI?

CHAPTER 8

Impact of Machine Learning with Hyperautomation

*"A baby learns to crawl, walk, and then run. We are in the crawling
stage when it comes to applying Machine learning"*

— *Dave Waters*

Introduction

Machine Learning is a popular technology that makes computers learn automatically from past data. ML uses many different algorithms for making predictions and mathematical models using information or historical data. Nowadays, it is being used for various tasks such as recommender systems, speech recognition, Facebook auto-tagging, image recognition, and many more. ML can be trained in many ways. Based on ways of learning, ML is broadly divided into different categories:

- Supervised learning
- Un-supervised learning

There are many other categories as well, such as semi-supervised learning and semi-unsupervised learning. This differentiation is based on the treatment of data (how data can be used under these techniques). Moreover, there are other types of Machine Learning which are based on the method of implementation, such as reinforcement learning and deep learning. We will learn more about these techniques and technologies in this chapter.

Structure

In this chapter, we will cover the following topics:

- Machine Learning
- Deep learning and its fundamentals
- Types of Neural Networks
- Machine Learning Operation (MLOps)
- ModelOps
- Role of Machine learning in Hyperautomation

Objectives

The objective of this chapter is to discuss Machine Learning, its different types, and it's working. This chapter discusses the role and involvement of Machine learning in Hyperautomation. Machine Learning plays an important role in the implementation of Hyperautomation, as it can be used to sort the decision-making process if needed in Hyperautomation.

Machine Learning

Machine Learning is a part of Artificial Intelligence. ML models learn from experiences the same way humans do without direct programming. When defined to new data, these ML models learn, grow, change by themselves, and develop. In other words, ML involves finding useful information without being told. Here are the steps of the ML process:

- The ML process involves giving training to the selected algorithm.
- We can already know the training data to create the final ML algorithm or data can be unknown.
- Then the step comes where the new data is given to the ML algorithm to test whether the ML algorithm gives the correct results or not.
- Then to check whether the ML algorithm worked finely or not, the next step is to check the prediction and results against each other. If the results and forecast do not match, then the ML algorithm is trained repeatedly until the Data scientist gets the correct output.

This helps the ML algorithm to learn continuously and to produce an excellent answer, constantly increasing the accuracy over time. *Figure 8.1* demonstrates the lifecycle of Machine Learning:

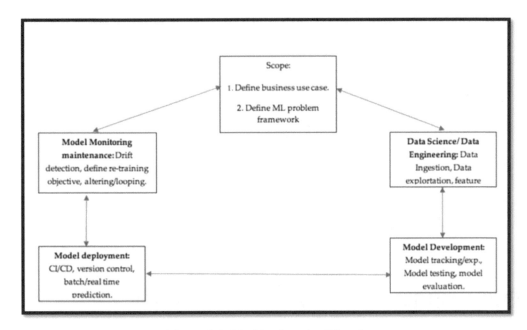

Figure 8.1: Machine learning lifecycle

This figure describes the ML lifecycle process, which explains that the business stakeholder and subject matter are involved through different parts of the process. It is important to know that the ML lifecycle is an interactive process.

Working of Machine Learning

The ML process begins with dividing data into training and testing data which is then put into the selected algorithm. The training data can be known or unknown for developing the final ML algorithm.

Then the New input data is given into the ML algorithm to check whether the algorithm works correctly or not. Then the prediction given by the model is checked with the results.

If the results and prediction do not match, then the algorithm should be re-trained multiple times until the results are not correct. This makes the ML algorithm learn on its own and provide optimal answers. *Figure 8.2* demonstrate how ML works:

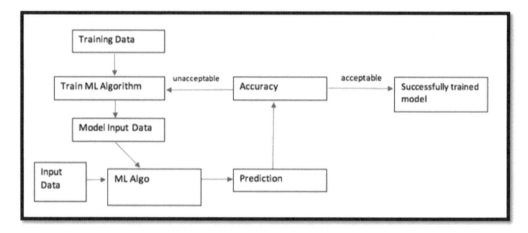

Figure 8.2: How ML works

Different types of Machine Learning

ML can be implemented using numerous ways and algorithm. Accordingly, ML has been divided into two areas, which are Supervised and unsupervised learning. Approximately, 70 percent of current ML implementation is supervised learning and the other 30 percent is unsupervised and reinforcement learning.

Supervised learning

In supervised learning, one uses labeled and known data for the training data. As the data is known, the learning is directed into the successful execution. The labeled data goes through the ML algorithm and is used to train the model. Once the model is trained on the known data, it can also use unknown data to get a new response.

The algorithms used for supervised learning are as follows:

- Polynomial regression
- Random Forest
- linear regression
- logistic regression
- Decision trees
- K-nearest neighbors
- Naive Bayes

Unsupervised learning

In unsupervised learning, the data used to train the model is unlabeled, meaning that no one has looked at the data before. This data is then given to the ML algorithm and is used to train the model. Then the trained model finds the pattern and accordingly gives the desired response.

Here are the algorithms used for unsupervised learning:

- Partial least square
- Fuzzy means
- singular value decomposition
- K-means clustering
- Apriori
- Hierarchical clustering
- Principal component analysis.

Advantages of Machine Learning

The advantages of ML are as follows:

- **Easily identify patterns and trends:** ML can examine large amounts of data to discover specific trends and patterns that humans cannot detect. For e-commerce sites such as Amazon, for example, it helps us understand our users' browsing behavior and purchase history to provide them with relevant products, offers, and reminders. We use the results to show you relevant ads.

- **No human intervention is needed:** With ML, you do not have to babysit every step of your project. This means giving machines the ability to learn, so that they can make predictions and even improve the algorithms themselves. A common example of this is antivirus software. Learn how to filter new threats as soon as they are detected. ML is also good at detecting spam.

- **Continuous improvement:** Accuracy and efficiency improvements as the ML algorithm gains experience. This helps them make better decisions. Suppose we need to create a weather forecast model. As the number of data increases, the algorithm learns to make more accurate predictions faster.

- **Handling multi-dimensional and multivariate data:** Machine learning algorithms excel at handling multidimensional and diverse data and can operate in dynamic or uncertain environments.

Point to look out for while implementing ML

Here are some points that you need to look put for, while implementing Machine Learning:

- **Data acquisition:** ML requires huge datasets for training, and these must be comprehensive, unbiased, and of high quality. Moreover, you may have to wait for new data to be generated.

- **Time and resources:** ML requires enough time for algorithms to learn and evolve with sufficient accuracy and relevance to achieve their goals. Moreover, the work requires a huge number of resources. This may imply additional computing power requirements.

- **High error susceptibility:** ML is autonomous but highly error prone. Suppose you want to train your algorithm on a dataset small enough to be non-inclusive. You end up with skewed predictions that come from a skewed training set. This results in irrelevant ads being shown to customers. For ML, bugs like this can lead to a long series of undetected bugs. Moreover, when you notice a problem, it takes longer to determine what caused it, and even longer to fix it.

Challenges in Machine Learning

The challenges in Machine Learning are as follows:

- **Not enough training data:** Suppose a small boy can learn what an apple is, just by pointing to it and saying it repeatedly. Now, the boy will be easily able to recognize all kinds of apples. Well, machine learning is not at that level yet. Most algorithms require large amounts of data to function properly. Thousands of examples are required to create a simple task, while advanced tasks such as image and speech recognition may require millions of examples.

- **Poor quality of data:** Of course, if the training data contains many errors, outliers, and noise, then the machine learning model will fail to identify the correct underlying pattern. So, it does not work. Therefore, make every effort to clean up their training data. No matter how good a person is at model selection and tuning, this part plays an important role in creating accurate machine-learning models. Most data scientists spend a significant amount of time cleaning data.

- **Irrelevant features:** Training data should be increasingly relevant and contain few or no irrelevant features. The benefit of a successful machine learning project lies in developing a good set of features with which to train (often called feature engineering). This includes feature selection, extraction, and creating new features that are interesting to others.

- **Non-representative training data:** For the model to generalize well, we need to ensure that our training data represents the new cases we want to generalize. Training a model on a non-representative training set will result in inaccurate predictions and bias towards classes or groups. For example, suppose you are trying to build a model that recognizes genres of music. One way to create a training set is to search on YouTube and use the resulting data. We are assuming here that YouTube's search engine provides representative data, but searches are targeting popular artists or popular artists in your area. Therefore, use representative data during training to avoid biasing the model to one or two classes when testing data.

ML is a powerful tool for making predictions from data. However, it is important to remember that machine learning is only as good as the data used to train the algorithms. To make accurate predictions, it is important to use high-quality data that is representative of the real-world data to which the algorithm is applied.

Deep learning and its fundamentals

Artificial Intelligence (AI) is the ability of computers or machines to mimic the human brain without being explicitly programmed. Just as human kids learn by example, AI also follows the same path. Machine learning is the subset of Artificial Intelligence that uses traditional algorithms to predict the outcome. Deep learning can be considered the subset of machine learning, and it is based on learning and improving on its own. Deep learning works with artificial neural networks, which are designed to imitate how humans think and learn.

The architecture of artificial neural networks is designed following the structure of the human brain, which possesses neurons connected to one another for the purpose of transmitting and analyzing information. We can accomplish a variety of tasks using neural networks, including clustering, classification, and regression. Without involving humans, these activities can be used to resolve any pattern recognition problem. Artificial neural networks, comprising many layers, drive deep learning. **Deep neural networks (DNNs)** are such types of networks where each layer can perform complex operations such as representation and abstraction that make sense of images, sound, and text.

Many AI apps and services are powered by deep learning, which enhances automation by performing physical and analytical tasks without the need for human intervention. Deep learning is the technology that powers many common products and services, including digital assistants, voice-activated gadgets, fraud detection, and cutting-edge innovations like self-driving cars.

Working of deep learning

Deep learning has the concept of neural networks. Neural networks are layers of nodes also called neurons. Neurons within individual layers are connected to adjacent layers.

Layers are categorized into three different categories:

- Input layer
- Hidden layer
- Output layer

Input layer

This is the first layer in the neural network architecture. It receives the input data. There are various kinds of input that can be fed to input layers such as 2-D images, 3-D images, sequence data, and so on. The input layer might perform certain functions which enable smoother functioning of the neural network such as normalization.

Hidden layer

Hidden layers are the ones that come after input layers; there may be one or more layers. On input data, hidden layers perform mathematical operations. It can be difficult to determine how many hidden layers there will be. It performs the feature extraction and transformation of non-linear processing units. Each layer uses the outcomes of the layers before it as an input. It forms the hierarchical concept of learning. Each level of the hierarchy aims to transform the input data into a composite representation that is more and more abstract.

Hidden layers can consist of several types of layers, which are as follows:

- **Convolutional layer**: This layer applied filters to the input such that the features may be detected along with their locations.

- **Pooling layer:** This layer decreases the sensitivity of features, creating more generalized data for better test results.

- **Activation layer:** This applies a mathematical function to the input layer such that the ability to learn something complex and interesting is developed.

- **Dropout layer:** This layer nullifies certain random input values to generate a more general dataset and prevent the problem of overfitting.

Output layer

The output layer is the final layer in the neural network where desired predictions are obtained. There is only one output layer in the network. *Figure 8.3* represents the different layers of Deep Learning Architecture:

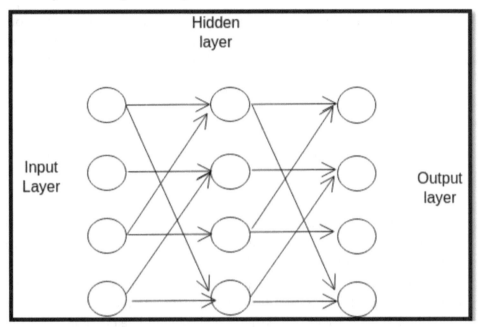

Figure 8.3: Representation of different layers in Deep Learning Architectures

Key concepts in deep learning

To understand how deep learning works, you need to understand the key terms and concepts of deep learning. A few of them are as follows:

- **Perceptron:** Perceptron is a simple linear binary classifier. It takes input and associate weights, and combines them to produce an output, which is then used for classification.

- **Multilayer perceptron:** A multilayer perceptron is the implementation of several fully adjacent connected layers of perceptron, forming a simple feedforward neural network. It has the additional benefits of nonlinear function which a single perceptron does not process.

- **Feedforward neural network:** Feedforward is the simplest form of neural network architecture in which connections are non-cyclical.

- **Weights:** Represents the relative importance of neural networks, and it indicates how much input X will have an impact on the output.
- **Bias:** Bias is an additional input to each layer starting from the input layer. It is not dependent on, nor impacted by the preceding layer. It is an intercept term and constant.
- **Activation function:** As we discussed previously, weight control of the transmission of the neurons, and adding bias, makes the nodes a linear combination of weight and bias, but it does not work well with complex data.

$Y = \sum(input^*weights)+bias$

To prepare the model for complexity, it needs transformation to make it non-linear activation function, that brings non-linearity to the neural networks.

$Y = Actiuvation(\sum(input^*weights)+bias))$

- **Backpropagation:** The essence of neural network training is Backpropagation. It is a technique for adjusting a neural network's weights based on the error rate preceding the epoch (iteration). It enables you to reduce the error rate and increase the model's reliability.
- **Cost function:** The cost function measures the difference between actual output and predicted output from the model. A zero-cost difference would signify that the network has been trained as would be possible.
- **Gradient descent:** To minimize the difference between actual and expected output, deep learning uses gradient descent. It is an optimization algorithm used for finding the local minima of a function.

Types of Neural Networks

There are several types of neural networks in deep learning. As this technology grows, scientists are developing more kinds of neural networks for different purposes. We will be discussing which are widely used, such as:

- **Artificial Neural Networks (ANN)**
- **Convolutional Neural Networks (CNN)**
- **Recurrent Neural Networks (RNN)**

Artificial Neural Networks

Artificial Neural Networks, often known as feed-forward neural networks since inputs are only processed in the forward direction, they are groupings of multiple perceptrons/neurons at each layer. It consists of an input layer, a hidden layer, and an output layer. After the input layer processes the data, it sends the processed data to the hidden layer, which then uses the data to perform more complex mathematical operations and extract more information. The output layer then gets the info from the hidden layer and produces the results.

ANN can be used to solve problems related to

- Tabular data
- Image data
- Text data

Convolutional Neural Networks

Currently, Convolutional Neural Networks are widely applied in the AI industry. Different applications and domains use CNN models to resolve real word problems. They are especially common in projects involving image and video processing. Multiple convolutional layers of CNN are responsible for extracting relevant features from the input image.

The convolutional operation uses a custom matrix, also called filters, to convolute over the input image and produce maps. These filters are initialized randomly and then updated via backpropagation. Then pooling layer is applied which is responsible for aggregating the maps produced by the convolutional layer. CNNs can also include a dropout layer which can be applied to reduce overfitting.

CNNs were introduced to solve problems related to image data; they perform impressively on sequential data as well.

Recurrent Neural Networks

Recurrent Neural Networks come into the picture when there is a need for predictions using sequential data. Sequential data can be sequences of text, images and so on. RNN has the same architecture as feed-forward networks, except that the layers also receive a time-delayed input of the previous instance prediction. This instance prediction input is stored in the RNN cell which is a second input for every prediction. RNN has the vanishing gradient problem which makes it very difficult to remember previous layers of information.

Long short-term memory networks

LSTM Neural Networks overcome the issue of vanishing gradient that recurrent neural networks face, by adding a special memory cell that can store information for long periods of time. LSTM uses gates to define which output should be used or forgotten. It used 3 gates:

- The input gate controls what data should be kept in memory,
- The output gate controls the data given to the next layer.
- The forget gate controls when to dump/forget the data that is not required.

Machine Learning Operation

Organizations need a framework that can automate the whole process of ML models or AI solutions that can reduce manual efforts. Despite the growing number of organizations investing in AI, data science and machine learning, many organizations still struggle to transform their investment into real business value. In big enterprises, AI solutions must be implemented in hundreds of use cases, and so it becomes difficult to manage them manually. **Machine Learning Operations (MLOps)** is the framework which can be used for the same purpose. MLOps focus mainly on ML models from model building to model deployment and managing them.

MLOps is an emerging field, it is rapidly gaining momentum amongst Data Scientist, ML Engineer and AI enthusiasts. It is inspired by DevOps. The DevOps movement defined a new, agile **Software Development Life Cycle (SDLC)**, which encouraged frequent innovation. Developers work on small, frequent releases, each of which undergoes automated testing and is automatically deployed to production.

Similarly, MLOPs defines a new lifecycle for AI technology that allows rapid experimentations, in response to business need or live model performance, and seamless deployment of new models as a predictive service.

What is MLOps

MLOps is the practice of creating new machine learning and deep learning models and running them through a repeatable, automated workflow that deploys them to production. MLOps pipeline provides a variety of services to data science teams, including model version control, **continuous integration,** and **continuous delivery (CI/CD)**, model service catalogs for models in production, infrastructure management, monitoring of live model performance, security and governance.

MLOps aims to scale from a **Proof of Concept (POC)** more efficiently to a machine learning workload in production.

Implementing MLOps helps you to make machine learning workloads robust and reproducible. For instance, you will be able to monitor, retrain, and deploy a ML model whenever needed while always keeping a model in production.

The purpose of MLOps is to make the machine learning lifecycle scalable:

- Train model
- Package model
- Validate model
- Deploy model
- Monitor model
- Retrain model

Challenges with MLOps

There are many challenges an organization faces when MLOps comes into play, as this technology sounds exciting. One of the primary challenges is addressing how to combine code and data to get predictions. <ore challenges are discussed as follows:

- Deployment and automation'
- Reproducibility of models and predictions
- Diagnostics
- Scalability
- Collaboration
- Governance and regulatory compliance
- Monitoring and management

Benefits of MLOps

MLOps technology and practices provides a scalable and governed means to deploy and manage machine learning models in production environments. Some of the benefits are as follows:

- Reduce the time and complexity of moving models into production.
- Enhance communication and collaboration across teams that are often siloed: data science, development, operations.
- Operationalizes models issues critical to long-term applications health, such as versioning, tracking, and monitoring.

- Makes it easier to monitor and understand ML infrastructure and compute costs at all stages, from development to production.
- Standardizes the ML process and makes it more auditable for regulation and governance purposes.
- MLOPs reduce technical debt across machine learning models.

Working of MLOps

There are three ways you can go about implementing MLOps:

- MLOps level 0 (Manual Process)
- MLOps level 1 (ML pipeline automation)
- MLOps level 2 (CI/CD pipeline automation)

MLOps level 0

This level is for when starting out with ML. An entirely manual process workflow and the data scientist-driven process might be enough if your models are rarely changed or trained.

Characteristics:

The characteristics are as follows:

- Manual, script-driven, and interactive process
- Disconnect between ML and operations
- Infrequent release iterations
- No Continuous Integration (CI)
- No Continuous Delivery (CD)
- Deployment refers to the prediction service
- Lack of active performance monitoring

Challenges:

In practice, models often break when they are deployed in the real world. Models fail to adapt to change in the dynamics of the environment or changes in the data that describes the environment.

To address the challenges of this manual process, it is good to use MLOps practice for CI/CD and CT. By deploying an ML training pipeline, you can enable CT, and you can set up a CI/CD system to rapidly test, build, and deploy new implementations of the ML pipeline.

MLOps level 1

The goal of MLOps level 1 is to perform **Continuous Training (CT)** of the model by automating the ML pipeline. This way, you can achieve continuous delivery of model predictions service.

It can be helpful for solutions that operate in a changing environment and need to proactively address shifts in data and other indicators.

Characteristics:

The characteristics are as follows:

- Rapid experiment
- **Continuous Training (CT)** of the model in production
- Experiment: Operational symmetry
- Modularized code for components and pipelines
- Continuous delivery of models
- Pipeline deployment
- Data and model validation
- Feature store
- Metadata management
- ML pipeline triggers

Challenges:

This setup is suitable when you deploy new models based on new data, rather than based on new ML ideas.

However, you need to try new ML ideas and rapidly deploy new implementations of the ML components. If you manage many ML pipelines in production, you need a CI/CD setup to automate the build, test, and deployment of ML pipelines.

MLOps level 2

For a rapid and reliable update of pipelines in production, you need a robust automated CI/CD system. With this automated CI/CD system, your data scientist rapidly explores new ideas around feature engineering, model architecture, and hyperparameters.

This level of automation fits tech-driven companies that must retrain their models daily. If not hourly, update them in minutes, and redeploy on thousands of servers simultaneously. Without an end-to-end MLOps cycle, such organizations will just not survive.

This level includes the following components:

- Source control
- Test and build services
- Deployment services
- Model registry
- Feature store
- ML metadata store
- ML pipeline orchestrator

Characteristics:

The characteristics are as follows:

- Development and experimentation
- Pipeline continuous integration
- Pipeline continuous delivery
- Automated triggering
- Model continuous delivery
- Monitoring

It is possible to achieve a smooth MLOps goal with the implementation of standard practice. MLOps attempt to combine the machine learning and software applications release cycles. It enables ML artifacts to be tested automatically, for instance, data validation, machine learning models testing, and machine learning model integration testing. Machine learning operation helps machine learning models reduce technical debt.

ModelOps and its applications

ModelOps is a framework that is designed to reduce manual operations and streamline model deployment and maintenance to the production environment, so that it can be used to solve real-world problems.

ModelOps can be defined as the framework for the governance and operations of ML models at the enterprise level. It primarily focuses on governance, automation, and lifecycle management for the operationalization of ML models at scale.

According to Forbes, almost 80% of the enterprises are investing in AI technology to get business values, though most stakeholders are struggling to find the ROI for their investments. This is because of a general lack of capabilities at the enterprise level to measure the returns and exposure of business values that AI models are generating. In recent years, more than 50% of enterprises have invested in ModelOps which is the key to model deployment and governance at scale. With the growing demand for implementing AI-based solutions, AI governance is needed for maintaining and observing these solutions. This is where the need for ModelOps has emerged, with most enterprises investing in ModelOps capabilities.

In today's market, AI and ML are the buzzwords in every industry, that wants to or is leveraging the potential it holds. Applying ML models to a software suite or application is only the first step toward this goal. The implementation and deployment of AI models are only the beginning. Somewhere around 90% of all the models created, never make it to the production stage. This is because of the challenges and complexities that arise during the deployment and then the maintenance of the ML model.

ModelOps lifecycle management

ModelOps enables the model lifecycle to be automated. It automates the process of model building, deployment, validation, and monitoring of the model in a production environment. ModelOps lifecycle management is highly based on DevOps concepts but has changed to adapt to the need for AI model deployment and monitoring. The key capabilities include:

- **Data collection/ updation/ validation:** This ensures the Data scientist gets validated data and up-to-date data.
- **Model building and versioning/ model scoring:** To compare and ensure only better models are deployed.
- **Model evaluation:** Test the model for accuracy, biasedness, and so on.
- **CI/CD:** Continuous Integration and Continuous Deployment of models to the environment.
- **Model monitoring/management:** Monitor the model for drift, biasedness, and accuracy to ensure the model is relevant and delivers results.

Figure 8.4 demonstrates the life cycle of ModelOps:

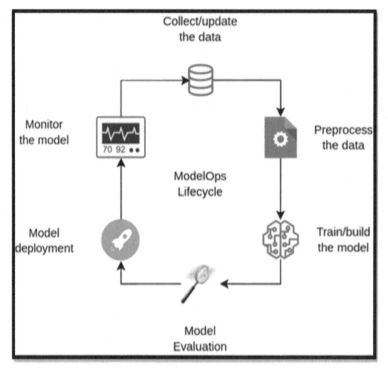

Figure 8.4: *Lifecycle of ModelOps*

ModelOps vs MLOps vs DevOps

The differences between the three can be seen in the following *Table 8.1:*

	MLOps	DevOps	ModelOps
Aim	MLOps create a collaborative environment that lets enterprises develop AI-based solutions.	DevOps integrates development with IT infrastructure such as the cloud, to improve efficiency, reliability, and security.	Complete governance and operations of models in production.
Lifecycle	Focuses on model building, monitoring, and deployment	Continuous development, Integration, and deployment of applications.	Model governance and complete lifecycle management from data validation to model evaluation and monitoring.

Tools, Framework and platforms	AWS Sagemaker, MLFlow, Weights & Biases.	GIt, JIRA,TFS.	ModelOp, Datatron, Sperwise.ai.
Primary Users	Data Scientists and MLOps Engineers.	Software engineers and DevOps Engineer.	Data scientist, IT and Operations team.

Table 8.1: Differences between ModelOps vs MLOps vs DevOps

Why is ModelOps important

ModelOps is the solution to implementing ML models, to solve real-life problems at the enterprise level. ModelOps can provide some key values, such as:

- **Observability and monitoring:** ModelOps can provide model evaluation, validation, and continuous monitoring for ML models being developed, and deployed in any production environment.

- **Accelerated deployment:** Enterprises in recent years have struggled with delivering AI solutions at scale and on time. With a shortage of skilled data scientists, model deployment and monitoring, ModelOps enables enterprises to deploy at speed and scale.

- **Mitigate model drift:** Drift in the model is a major cause of any model being useless; this can render the application or platform ineffective at best and dangerous at worst. ModelOps helps enterprises to detect model drift and avoid such a scenario.

- **Improved efficiency and collaboration with various stakeholders:** ML model building and deployment need multidisciplinary teams working together. ModelOps makes this process more efficient by defining goals, processes, and outlines for each team, increasing collaboration.

- **AI-driven outcome:** ModelOps can bring AI-driven KPIs for better-informed business decisions for stakeholders by generating key insights and patterns.

- **Simple onboarding:** ModelOps provides data scientists with a unified environment to build, deploy and monitor models in a single platform reducing time to market by streamlining model onboarding to the production environment.

- **Cost optimization:** ModelOps greatly reduces time, effort, and resources by automating model monitoring and deployment. It also reduces resources by detecting bias, drift, and performance in the model.

- **Risk management:** ModelOps perform the much-needed role of model governance and risk management, which becomes very important as multiple models are deployed in production. ModelOps enables the monitoring and identification of early risks.

- **Increased revenue:** ModelOps can enable analytics for AI models deployed and provide insights for business investments, as well as stopping the unnecessary waste of resources, therefore increasing revenue.

Use cases of ModelOps

Some of the use cases of ModelOps are as follows:

- **Bias detection:** ModelOps is employed to detect biasedness in ML models in industries such as finance and insurance. It validates if the dataset is skewed towards one class.

- **Drift detection:** ModelOps enables users to detect drift in datasets, thus maintaining the quality and integrity of data.

- **Robustness of AI/ML models:** With ML, models are being used for a multitude of different use cases, which are based on similar types of problems. ModelOps are being used to check the robustness of these models in the production environment.

- **Compliance:** ModelOps take care of compliance with continuous monitoring, governance, and deployment of models.

- **Analytics-based business KPI:** Delivers business value with analytics-based insights and KPIs for better business performance.

Applications of ModelOps

Some applications of ModelOps are as follows:

- **Finance:** Financial institutions are using ML models for credit approval, which has reduced both cases of biased rejection and minimized manual efforts and resources for this. ModelOps are being used to monitor and govern the models for biasedness and are deployed for this.

- **Healthcare:** AI models in healthcare are increasing efficiency and decreasing cost. ModelOps are being used to validate these models' performance, as they are being used in an industry sensitive to errors.

- **Retail:** With the consumer and retail markets moving online, ML models are used in a variety of use cases in the retail industry. ModelOps helps in detecting drift in consumer behavior patterns.

- **Fraud detection:** ML models are used in the Insurance sectors which can help in faster claim management and fraud detection. ModelOps are being used to validate model accuracy as well as detect biasedness in the model at scale.

- **Risk management:** With continuous model validation and monitoring early detection of model, drift can be detected, and models can be retrained or rebuilt, mitigating the risk of damages.

ModelOps platforms in the market

Here is how the ModelOps platform has been performing in the market:

- **ModelOp:** Started in 2016, it has addressed the gap between deployment and model maintenance at the enterprise level. ModelOp lets the user register the model from several development platforms such as Jupyter notebook with predefined information and lets the user monitor model scoring, accuracy, and training. It provides users with a list of metrics for detailed and comprehensive model monitoring such as F1 score, ROC, AUC, and so on.

- **Datatron:** Datatron is another ModelOPs platform that provides a platform for automating, optimizing, and accelerating the building and deployment of ML models. Supporting a range of frameworks such as TensorFlow, PyTorch, H2O, SAS, Python, R, Scala, and so on, it also provides users with features suhc as model catalog, deployment, monitoring, governance, management, and workflows.

- **SAS:** SAS model management software provides ModelOps capabilities to the users excelling in analytical model management, project management, model assessment, and support.

- **Superwise.ai:** Supports incident management and model monitoring. Superwise.ai provides users with model monitoring and insights about model performance.

- **Modzy:** Launched in 2019, it can integrate a lot of tools, frameworks, and data pipelines and CI/CD as well as a multitude of predefined models. It supports Python, JavaScript, and Java SDK.

Challenges in ModelOps implementation

With enterprises in almost every industry keen on adopting AI/ML solutions to solve their real-life problems, most find it difficult to deploy the said solution even after its development. Deployment, management, and governance of ML models at the enterprise level are very difficult. The challenges are:

- **Data management and data quality assurance:** Most enterprises have a mix of data management and storing systems which make it difficult for data scientists to acquire accurate data for model building.

- **Collaborating among multidisciplinary teams:** Model building and deployment needs several multidisciplinary teams to collaborate like data scientists, data engineers, IT infrastructure experts, and business experts among themselves. Poor workflow management makes it difficult to have an efficient model-building and deployment process.

- **Scalability of model:** ML models need to be lightweight and scalable and must have the ability to seamlessly integrate with existing cloud or edge infrastructure.

- **Model monitoring tools:** Once deployed, the models tend to drift and show poor performance over time. ML models need to be monitored and evaluated continuously.

- **Retraining of models:** Once drift or bias is detected in models; they are required to retrain which starts the entire process from data acquisition to model evaluation and validation. Retraining can be difficult, expensive, and time-consuming if there is a lack of automated processes.

Future scope for ModelOps

With more and more organizations adopting ModelOps for themselves, it has been noted that most develop their own framework of ModelOps with a lack of uniformity, as well as there is a lack of consensus as to whom, responsibilities should be delegated for ModelOps. Awareness of the need for ModelOps and investment in the field has significantly risen from the past. Future enterprises' organizational structures demand a robust and dedicated team for ModelOps, to achieve a higher level of AI maturity in the industry as well as for greater visibility and higher ROI from their AI investments.

ModelOps in recent years has satisfied the need of enterprises for a framework to deliver meaningful AI-based solutions to their customers. The challenge with using ML models to solve real-life problems is not about building a better model, it is the steps after one build one. ModelOps provide enterprise-level ML solutions to be built, deployed, monitored, and governed at scale, so that they can be used in actual production. With more and more industries opting for AI-enabled solutions, companies across this industry will try to adopt and incorporate ModelOps in their process to empower their products, platforms, and applications with AI.

Role of Machine Learning in Hyperautomation

ML is one part of the AI sub technologies. AI and ML play an important role in Hyperautomation. It uses advanced technologies, including AI and Machine Learning, to automate tasks that humans previously performed. ML algorithms continuously analyze data inputs and identify patterns that are used to make more accurate predictions. Computers can use this information to make better decisions and perform complex tasks with little human input.

ML is a branch of computational algorithms that are designed to emulate human intelligence by learning from the surrounding environment. Currently, many IT industries are continuously putting software engineering requirement analysis, designing, coding, developing, and testing new packages for business applications. The beauty of this technology is that the machines will get intelligence by learning from data sets with the help of algorithms written by programmers along with subject experts.

ML applies AI capabilities to lend business context to tasks executed by RPA systems, enabling the latter to make better decisions and be more productive. AI and Machine Learning can automate various tasks, from simple tasks such as data entry to more complex tasks such as customer service, Attendance Calculation, Image classification, fraud detection, and financial analysis. As businesses continue to look for ways to improve efficiency and cut costs, hyperautomation will likely increase shortly.

Benefits of Machine Learning in Hyperautomation

Benefits of using AI and ML in hyperautomation are as follows:

- **Improved accuracy:** Machine Learning can be used to *learn* from data, identify patterns, and make predictions. It can help to reduce errors and improve the quality of output. It can help to improve the accuracy of automation processes.

- **Speeding up the processes:** AI and Machine Learning can help to speed up processes by saving time. Automated processes that use advanced technology such as AI and Machine Learning can often be completed more quickly than those that rely on human input. It is because machines can work faster than humans and do not need breaks in between.

- **Better decision making:** AI and Machine Learning can improve decision-making capability. Automated systems that cognitive technologies such as AI and ML can often make better decisions than humans because they have access to more data and can process it more quickly.
- Other benefits worth mentioning:
  o Fast (automated) identification of automatable processes.
  o Efficient automation using Machine Learning and artificial intelligence components.
  o Enabling the entire organization to automate.
  o End-to-end automation of complex processes, as completely as possible.
  o Management of the complete lifecycle of automation.
  o Performed by multiple machine learning, packaged software (No code/ low code platforms, analytics) and automation tools.
  o AI based process automation with cognitive ability and can loop humans into the processes.
  o Smart and efficient operations.
  o Performed by multiple machine learning, packaged software (No code/ low code platforms, analytics) and automation tools.
  o AI based process automation with cognitive ability and can loop humans into the processes.
  o Smart and efficient operations.
  o Everything that can be automated will be automated.

Conclusion

Machine learning is pivotal in Hyperautomation, merging AI, RPA, and analytics to enhance business processes. It enables smart systems to predict, pattern-spot, and decide. MLOps, vital in machine learning workflows, bridges data science and operations teams, deploying models efficiently. It entails data management, model development, deployment, monitoring, and retraining. MLOps maximizes machine learning's potential, aligning models with systems, benefiting Hyperautomation. It automates manual tasks via ML algorithms, boosting efficiency and reducing errors. ML also enhances hyper-automated systems, learning and improving over time. This iterative learning enhances processes, informs decisions, and optimizes performance, underpinning Hyperautomation's effectiveness.

Overall, machine learning is a critical component of Hyperautomation, enabling organizations to automate complex processes, improve efficiency and accuracy, and continuously optimize performance.

Key facts

- Machine Learning is a part of AI. ML models learn from experiences the same way humans do without direct programming.

- In supervised learning, one uses labeled and known data for the training data. As the data is known, so the learning is directed into the successful execution.

- In unsupervised learning, the data used to train the model is unlabeled, meaning no one has looked at the data before.

- Deep learning can be considered the subset of machine learning; it is based on learning and improving on its own. Deep learning works with artificial neural networks, which are designed to imitate how human thinks and learn.

- Artificial neural networks, often known as feed-forward neural networks since inputs are only processed in the forward direction, are groupings of multiple perceptrons/neurons at each layer.

- **Machine learning operation** (**MLOps**) is an emerging field, and it is rapidly gaining momentum amongst Data Scientist, ML Engineer and AI enthusiasts.

- MLOps is the practice of creating new machine learning and deep learning models and running them through a repeatable, automated workflow that deploys them to production.

- ModelOps is a framework that is designed to reduce manual operations and streamline model deployment and maintenance to the production environment so that it can be used to solve real-world problems.

Key terms

- Machine Learning
- Deep Learning
- Machine Learning Operations (MLOps)
- Model Operations (ModelOps)
- Artificial Neural Networks (ANNs)
- Convolutional Neural Networks (CNNs)
- Recurrent Neural Networks (RNNs)
- Long Short-term Memory Networks (LSTM)

Questions

1. What are the different types of Machine Learning techniques?

2. What are the different steps in the Machine Learning Life cycle?

3. Describe MLOps and its process of implementation.

4. What are the different levels of MLOps?

5. What is ModelOps and what is its importance?

6. Describe differences between MLOps, DevOps and ModelOps.

Join our book's Discord space

Join the book's Discord Workspace for Latest updates, Offers, Tech happenings around the world, New Release and Sessions with the Authors:

https://discord.bpbonline.com

CHAPTER 9

Operationalizing Hyperautomation

"The automation of automation, the automation of intelligence,
is such an incredible idea that if we could continue to improve
this capability, the applications are really quite boundless."

— *Jensen Huang*

Introduction

Hyperautomation is a framework for automating enterprise workload using advanced technologies such as artificial intelligence, natural language processing, computer vision, **Robotic Process Automation (RPA)**, and other digital tools, to automate and streamline business processes across an organization. It goes beyond traditional automation by combining multiple technologies and intelligent capabilities to enhance productivity, efficiency, and agility at scale. Hyperautomation has been conceived to tackle the drawbacks of enterprise level process automation in terms of scalability, as implementing such solutions can be challenging to scale at the enterprise level as well as it can be bounded in terms of capabilities with limited types of automation it is able to provide. Hyperautomation entails recognizing and automating routine, rule-based tasks as well as more intricate procedures, including analysis and decision-making. It allows systems to learn and adapt, boosting accuracy and decision-making over time by utilizing AI and ML algorithms. Hyperautomation aims to take advantage of the data gathered and produced by digitized operations to reduce costs, increase productivity, and improve efficiency. Businesses can use that data to make more accurate and timely business choices. It can play a vital role in so many ways in modern day businesses, and a few of them are:

Enhanced customer experience: Organizations can simplify customer-facing activities like onboarding, support, and service delivery by using Hyperautomation. organizations can offer self-service alternatives, personalized experiences, and quicker response times by automating these operations. Customer loyalty and satisfaction increase as a result.

- **Cost reduction**: By reducing the need for manual intervention, automation lowers labor costs. It decreases the possibility of costly mistakes and does away with the need for additional people to handle repeated activities. organizations can reduce costs in areas like resource allocation, inventory management, and supply chain operations by streamlining procedures and getting rid of inefficiencies.

- **Improved accuracy and compliance**: Hyperautomation lessens the possibility of human mistake and process irregularities, which improves accuracy and compliance. Automation technologies can do jobs with a high degree of accuracy and compliance, lowering the danger of breaking laws or internal rules. This is crucial in sectors with stringent regulatory standards.

- **Agility and scalability**: Automation makes it possible for businesses to scale up processes as needed and quickly respond to shifting business needs. It offers the adaptability needed to handle rising volumes, shifting market conditions, and fresh opportunities. organizations can respond to market demands more quickly and gain a competitive advantage by implementing Hyperautomation.

- **Data-driven decision making**: Hyperautomation creates enormous amounts of data from automated operations, which is used to drive decision-making. To obtain insights, spot patterns, and make data-driven decisions, this data can be examined. organizations may find untapped possibilities, forecast trends, and streamline operations based on real-time data with the use of AI and ML capabilities.

- **Innovation and transformation**: Hyperautomation is a crucial facilitator of initiatives for digital transformation. organizations may create the framework for future innovation and the adoption of cutting-edge technologies by automating procedures. It makes it possible to combine technologies like AI, ML, IoT, and analytics, resulting in the creation of a connected and intelligent ecosystem.

- **Employee empowerment**: Automation frees up workers to concentrate on more important and difficult jobs by getting rid of boring and repetitive chores. It can improve workers' job satisfaction, engagement, and skill growth. Automation may supplement human abilities, empowering workers to use technology and carry out higher-value jobs that call for creativity, critical thought, and problem-solving.

Structure

In this chapter, we will cover the following topics:

- Hyperautomation as a solution to the busyness of business processes
- Scaling Hyperautomation solutions
- Developing a scalable Hyperautomation strategy
- Architecture of Hyperautomation

Objectives

This chapter not only focuses on the theoretical but on the practical aspect of Hyperautomation, what will be the architecture and framework while implementing the Hyperautomation, and what could be tools which can help the implementation of Hyperautomation. These kinds of questions have been entrained during this chapter. Before beginning, be advised that the reader must go through previous chapters, or at least the reader should have a fair idea of all the theoretical aspects of Hyperautomation.

Hyperautomation as a solution to the busyness of business processes

The Ford Motor Company coined the word **automation** in 1946, at the start of the third Industrial Revolution. Today, a concept born in the automotive industry is revolutionizing other companies around the world. On the road paved by artificial intelligence, businesses are beginning to unlock the full potential of automation through Hyperautomation.

Hyperautomation, a term coined by *Gartner* in 2020, is a business-centric strategy for discovering, evaluating, and automating various IT and business processes using multiple technologies, platforms, and/or tools. Interestingly, in 1910 Forrester proposed the idea of using various automation techniques. He called it **Intelligent Business Process Automation (iBPM)**. iBPM is different from Hyperautomation. In iBPM, AI replicates human intelligence to perform sophisticated operations that require a certain level of cognition and judgment.

Hyperautomation is like a toolbox. It takes on higher-level functions, starting with coordination, intelligence, predictive insight, informed suggestions, and ending with decision-making. This gives him two main advantages. Business-oriented from the start so you can be confident in your ROI. It is also much more powerful than traditional **Robotic Process Automation (RPA)**.

The need for businesses to scale to Hyperautomation

Hyperautomation is a technological solution that allows complete automation of operating processes in an enterprise. This advanced technology can tackle more complex tasks and processes that cannot be eliminated using one automation technology.

The concept of Hyperautomation is not only an option but a prerequisite for businesses to break through and create a competitive advantage in the fierce **digitalization** race. According to Gartner, 90% of large enterprises globally will **adopt RPA by 2022**. Meanwhile, 50% of enterprises surveyed have already started implementing AI solutions, according to McKinsey.

According to a survey from Deloitte, Hyperautomation brings impressive operational efficiency for businesses:

- Improve 90% of data quality and accuracy
- Boost 86% of productivity
- Reduce 59% of operating costs

Assiduity in different business sectors and its solution with Hyperautomation

Hyperautomation is an increasing industry that can automate most of the business processes for businesses, by implementing the solution using Hyperautomation. There are different industries where Hyperautomation can help in the assiduity associated with these business processes.

Manufacturing sector

When we think about automation in the manufacturing industry, the first thing that comes to mind is the robots are in assembly lines. However, the advent of **Robotic Process Automation (RPA)**, **Artificial Intelligence (AI)**, **Machine Learning (ML)**, and so on, have also led to software **Robots (bots)** being adopted by the manufacturing sector.

There are some manufacturing industries use cases of Hyperautomation, such as the following:

- **Inventory management**: With Hyperautomation, manufacturing industries can monitor, manage, and track inventory at various stages of production, including near real-time **work in process**, and inventory updates in the ERP system. It can help manufacturing companies to streamline their inventory management processes by automating tasks such as data collection, analysis, and forecasting. AI and ML algorithms can be used to analyze historical sales data, production schedules, and market trends to predict demand accurately. This can help companies optimize their inventory levels, reduce waste, and prevent stockouts, resulting in better cost management.

- **Stamping die process costing:** Read the die process sheet for the stamping part. Cross-reference with financial information from PLM. Calculate the cost and load it back into the PLM system against the part.

- **Inventory shortage reporting:** Pull open ticket information from systems related to inventory shortages for all plants. Analyze and sort it based on plant and part. Determine the target supply plant and create a supply notification.

- **Supply and demand planning:** Forecast inventory needs to examine complex records and market indicators and use complicated techniques. Bots can do this faster and more efficiently than humans.

- **Vendor selection and procurement:** RPA can be used in the preliminary analysis of vendor documents evaluating the vendor and running a credit check, as well as finalizing the vendor selection.

- **Sales analytics:** RPA can be used for gathering data from multiple sources daily and presenting comprehensive reports to decision-makers regarding the market performance of their product lines.

- **Direct store delivery:** RPA can enhance sales behavior to increase revenue, reduce the number of hours, and reduce the turnover rate by bypassing the Distribution Center.

Banking and finance industry

The banking and financial services industry has been one of the fastest-growing industries in the world. With this growth, it has become obligatory for banks to deliver these services efficiently, reducing the loss or risk, or delays over time.

The role of Hyperautomation is to increase the speed at which banks can manage their assets, process transactions, and provide products and services to customers. In addition, it helps to achieve their goals by providing increased accuracy and visibility into the processes they need to run.

Here are some benefits of using Hyperautomation in the banking and financial sector:

- **Ensuring compliance:** Banks and finance firms set a high priority on compliance to prevent the risks, penalties, and financial fraud. Hyperautomation of management processes allows banks to meet complex regulatory reporting requirements, improve reporting accuracy, and ensure transparency to improve compliance.

- **Gaining operational efficiency:** Hyperautomation allows banks to accelerate processing, improve accuracy, streamline operations, and improve overall experience. This in turn leads to higher ROI and profitability. This technology reduces operational expenses and shifting banking staff to other core financial tasks, while leaving the mundane tasks to machines or other software systems.

- **Saving time:** The most valuable resource that organizations have at their disposal is Time. Automating the data entry process with auto-document generation software, Hyperautomation can help banking sectors save time by eliminating tedious manual operations such as typing data into databases manually or copying information from one place to another.

- **Increase productivity:** Another advantage of Hyperautomation is that it can save both time and money. With a system like IBM Watson, businesses can generate new revenue streams by offering big data analytics services. For example, a bank can provide an AI solution for customers who want to make more informed decisions about their finance or investments. The bank could then use this data to generate revenue from selling these insights to other customers - a win-win situation for everyone involved!

Insurance industry

Hyperautomation in insurance industry is a disciplined approach to rapidly identifying and automating as many as possible. It can used to make the decisions about risks, fraud, and policyholder behavior. For example, Hyperautomation can be used to detect fraudulent claims or identify policyholders who are at risk of lapse or churn.

Hyperautomation combines multiple technologies to automate business process end-to-end and to make decisions that would traditionally be made by humans. It has the potential to transform the insurance sector by making it more customer-centric, and operationally efficient.

Any technology is only as useful as its applicability. Here are some use cases:

- **Claims processing:** Claim processing is singularly the heavyweight champion of all insurance processes. Claim processing includes the review of claims related details from different sources, data formats standardization, sorting through lots of information, verifying the same, and working with it. Such a series of activities typically takes about week – if everything is in order. Depending on data availability, associated tasks and claims complexity, this timeline could stretch up to 30 days. However, Hyperautomation can completely transform claims processing by reducing manual effort through software bots. These intelligent bots can accept, review, and verify data to approve claims automatically. As such, insurance agencies would be saving a bulk of time and resources.

- **Policy management:** In a policy of insurance, a lot of documentation is involved. At this stage, the broker or insurance agent will accept all the documents, compare them, and communicate any discrepancies with the customer. At the same time, they will save, upload, and organize the documents on the internal databases systems and platforms. While managing the collected data manually, it is complicated by itself, the problem will occur when the customer makes a minor change in the policy details. This change would have to reflect across all channels, it will rise to possible errors. With involving Hyperautomation in insurance, Machine can leverage **Intelligent Document Processing (IDP)** to seamlessly collect data from various touchpoints – such as emails, call transcripts and so on – while the bots implement the requisite changes uniformly.

- **Fraud detection and prevention:** As per data, Insurance fraud costs American consumers to the tune of USD 80 billion per annum. Not just in America, being such a pressing issue worldwide, insurance fraud is difficult to crack. Internal fraud, False claims, and so on, have been on the rise, especially since the pandemic and the sheer volume of claims has made it nearly impossible to handle them all manually. Against this backdrop, Hyperautomation could offer considerable relief through smart data processing. For a start, it can automatically screen all claims and verify them against their respective insurance policies. At the same time, it can profile the claimant and check their history and activities to note any anomalies. This proactive assessment allows insurance agencies to carry out a major crackdown on potential insurance fraud. Additionally, the automation of internal processes shields it from internal manipulation and puts an end to fraudulent practices. As such, Hyperautomation serves as a breath of fresh air for carriers drowning in claims.

- **Compliance and regulatory requirements:** Hyperautomation is being used to help insurers comply with regulatory requirements. This includes the use of automated reporting tools that can generate regulatory reports, monitor compliance with regulatory requirements, and manage regulatory risk. Overall, Hyperautomation is helping insurers to operate more efficiently, reduce costs, and provide better services to their customers. It is enabling insurers to improve underwriting accuracy, reduce claims processing times, prevent fraud, and comply with regulatory requirements.

BPO and customer service center industry

Customer service Hyperautomation is a customer support process that can help to reduce the human need for respond the customer inquiries. Self-service resources, simulated chat conversion, and proactive messaging are used by the businesses to achieve automated customer service.

Here are some of the ways that Hyperautomation is being used in this industry:

- **Quicker support:** When we consider the customer service issue, it is best to put yourself in the shoes of the customers. When the customer gets a late response, they are generally not going to the support team again. But with the help of Hyperautomation involvement, customer can get 24X7 support without involving or minimum involving of human resource.

- **Chatbots and virtual assistants:** Hyperautomation is being used to develop virtual assistants and chatbots that can provide customers with personalized support and assistance. These automated systems can handle routine inquiries and requests, freeing up human agents to focus on more complex issues. Chatbots can also be used for customer engagement, such as promoting products and services, and conducting customer satisfaction surveys.

- **Customer data management:** Hyperautomation is being used to automate customer data management, including data entry, verification, and updating. This helps to reduce manual errors, improve data accuracy, and enable faster access to customer information.

- **Workflow management:** Hyperautomation is being used to automate workflow management, including task assignment, routing, and prioritization. This helps to improve efficiency, reduce turnaround times, and ensure that tasks are handled by the right person with the right skills.

- **Quality assurance:** Hyperautomation is being used to automate quality assurance processes, including call monitoring, evaluation, and feedback. This helps to improve the quality of customer interactions, identify areas for improvement, and provide coaching and training to agents.

- **Fraud detection and prevention:** Hyperautomation is being used to identify and prevent fraudulent activities, including identity theft, credit card fraud, and phishing attacks. This involves the use of advanced analytics tools that can detect patterns and anomalies in customer behavior, enabling fraud prevention teams to take proactive action.

Overall, Hyperautomation is helping BPO and Customer Service Center companies to operate more efficiently, reduce costs, and provide better services to their customers. It is enabling them to automate routine tasks, improve data accuracy, streamline workflow management, improve quality assurance, and prevent fraud.

Healthcare industry

Hyperautomation has the potential to transform healthcare through multiple use cases, such as the following:

- **AI-led diagnostics:** Hyperautomation with Artificial Intelligent, Machine Learning and Computer vision with intelligent workflows can give exact outcomes quicker than expected. Doctors can quickly diagnose medical condition with the help of computer vision and Machine Learning. The system will automatically prioritize secondary readings and assigns cases by functional area, specialty and so on. After validation, diagnostic reports are directly delivered to doctors and integrated with **Electronic Medical Records (EMR)**.

- **Revenue cycle management:** In healthcare, Hyperautomation also means to improve front-end sales cycle management using process mining, conventional AI, RPA, and data analytics. For example, an NLP-enabled voice agent can contact the insurance company to gather missing details, and AI-enabled virtual agents can schedule or reschedule appointments. So, data analytics and process mining can make it easier for patients to sign up and verify their insurance.

- **Personalized health screening:** Remote monitoring is gaining traction. **Internet of Things (IoT)**, data analytics, wearables, digital health assistants are all becoming important parts of overall health. For instance, sensors and wearables monitor high-risk patients' blood pressure and glucose levels, while digital health assistants increase adherence to treatment guidelines. Moreover, data analytics can suggest plan for getting patients involved, and predictive analytics can use the data they already have to predict the future illnesses. Together all these components help to revolutionize patient care.

- **Lab automation:** Robotics and advanced software systems also help to speed up lab tasks that take a lot of time, save money, reduce manual work, and improve efficiency.

Scaling Hyperautomation solutions

Hyperautomation is an advanced approach to automation that optimizes and streamlines business operations by combining several technologies including RPA, AI, ML, and intelligent automation. By incorporating human duties and decision-making abilities, it goes beyond typical automation and enables enterprises to automate complicated operations, boost operational effectiveness, and reach unprecedented levels of scalability. Hyperautomation can handle unstructured data and adapt to changing conditions since it uses AI and ML algorithms to assess and learn from data. Hyperautomation helps firms accomplish quicker, more precise, more agile business processes, which ultimately increases productivity and improves overall business performance. Hyperautomation, which seamlessly combines human and machine skills, has the potential to completely change how businesses function in the digital age.

The key components of Hyperautomation are:

- **Robotic Process Automation (RPA):** It is a technology that automates routine, rule-based processes that are usually done by people. RPA bots may replicate human behavior, making a wide range of tasks ideal for automation.

- **Artificial Intelligence (AI)** and **Machine Learning (ML):** These are crucial elements of Hyperautomation because they allow systems to learn from data, spot patterns, and make predictions or suggestions. AI and ML algorithms can automate complex decision-making procedures by analyzing unstructured data, including text, videos, and photos.

- **Intelligent automation:** The automation of more complex processes using AI, ML, and other cutting-edge technologies like computer vision and **Natural Language Processing (NLP).** By removing errors and lowering manual interventions, intelligent automation can increase process efficiency and accuracy.

- **Process discovery and mining:** To find processes that can be automated, process discovery and mining refer to the use of data mining and process mining approaches. Organizations can find automation opportunities, improve processes, and cut costs with the use of process discovery and mining.

- **Collaboration between humans and machines:** Hyperautomation blends human and machine abilities to provide the best results. The first step in human-machine collaboration is to determine which jobs are best completed by humans and which are best automated by computers. By handling repetitive and rule-based jobs, computers free up human workers to focus on high-value tasks that call for creativity, judgment, and decision-making.

- **Scalability and flexibility:** These two attributes are crucial to Hyperautomation. Solutions for Hyperautomation must be able to perform intricate workflows and handle vast amounts of data. Additionally, they must be adaptable enough to change with the demands of the business and effortlessly integrate new technology.

Solutions for Hyperautomation have been used in the real world across numerous sectors, transforming operations and increasing productivity. For instance, Hyperautomation is used in the banking industry to automate fraud detection, loan approval, and customer onboarding operations. Hyperautomation is used by healthcare organizations to speed up claim processing, appointment scheduling, and patient data management. Retailers employ Hyperautomation to improve customer service with chatbots, automate e-commerce order fulfilment, and manage inventory more effectively. Hyperautomation is also used by industrial businesses to streamline production lines, automate quality control procedures, and enable predictive maintenance. These real-world examples show how Hyperautomation solutions have revolutionized conventional business processes, allowing businesses to save money and time, increase accuracy, and enhance customer experiences.

Need to scale Hyperautomation solutions

Scaling Hyperautomation systems is crucial for several reasons such as:

- **Efficiency gains:** By automating more processes and jobs, scaling automation solutions enables businesses to operate more effectively. As automation is expanded across numerous departments and operations, it speeds up and improves the accuracy of task execution, lowers error rates, and decreases the need for manual intervention. Scaling enables businesses to handle heavier workloads, boost throughput, and produce outcomes more quickly and efficiently.

- **Cost savings:** Businesses can save a lot of money by automating at scale. Organizations can decrease the demand for manual labor and boost productivity by automating repetitive and time-consuming processes. This lowers labor expenses. As automation spreads across a wider range of processes and services thanks to economies of scale, it becomes more affordable.

- **Enhanced scalability:** Scaling Hyperautomation allows businesses to handle larger workloads without sacrificing efficiency or quality. The organization may simply scale its operations to meet increasing demands and commercial expansion because automation is simple to reproduce and deploy to new processes, departments, or even entire business units.

- **Enhanced precision and compliance:** When scaled properly, Hyperautomation technologies offer more consistency and accuracy in task execution. Automation lowers the possibility of human error and guarantees adherence to laws and regulations. Scaling automation reduces the possibility of expensive errors or non-compliance while maintaining a high degree of accuracy and compliance over a wider range of operations.

- **Innovation and agility:** Scaling Hyperautomation solutions increases organizational agility and encourages an innovative culture. Employees can concentrate on more strategic and creative work, which promotes innovation and problem-solving, by automating repetitive and routine processes. Additionally, scaled automation systems are simple to adapt and modify to include new technology, enabling businesses to stay ahead of the curve and take advantage of openings in the market.

- **Competitive advantage:** In today's fast-paced corporate environment, implementing and growing Hyperautomation systems might give an advantage. Businesses that adopt automation on a large scale can streamline processes, provide better customer experiences, and react swiftly to market changes. Businesses can stand out from rivals and establish themselves as industry leaders by streamlining operations, cutting expenses, and increasing efficiency.

Assessing readiness for scaling

Analyzing the level of automation in your business right now and looking for scaling opportunities are two steps in determining your readiness for scaling Hyperautomation solutions. The best way to tackle these two factors is as follows:

Analysing the automation's current state

To assess the current state of automation in your organization, consider the following steps:

- **Inventory of automated processes:** Take stock of the automated processes that are currently in use at your organization. Decide which procedures or tasks have already been automated and note these places where it is already being used.

- **Performance analysis:** Analyze how well current automation initiatives are performing. Analyze important performance indicators such as process cycle time, Manual AHT, bot AHT, cost savings, error rates, and customer satisfaction. Determine how automation affects process productivity, accuracy, and efficiency.

- **Automation maturity assessment:** Evaluate the organization's level of automation maturity. Analyze the degree to which automation is incorporated into various business operations, the degree to which automation methods are standardized, and the presence of governance and support frameworks for automation. It can also include establishing a **Center of Excellence (COE)** for automation with appropriate stakeholders and clearly defined roles for everyone involved.

- **Technology assessment:** Examine the platforms, tools, and technologies that are currently used in your firm for automation. Examine their potential for integration, scalability, and capability. Determine any gaps or restrictions that might obstruct scaling efforts.

Finding opportunities for Hyperautomation scale-up

Consider the following methods to find chances for scaling Hyperautomation:

- **Process assessment**: Examine your organization's procedures to determine which ones can be automated and which have the potential to have a big impact. Look for repetitive, rule-based, and prone to human error procedures. Give top priority to operations that handle large quantities, need human handoffs, or have a big influence on the bottom line. Employing process mining and task mining tools to detect obstructive, concealed, and automatable processes and tasks.

- **Business impact analysis:** Evaluate how scaling automation may affect important business indicators like operational effectiveness, cost savings, customer satisfaction, and revenue creation. Determine the areas where increasing automation can add the most value and be in line with long-term business goals. Employing process mining and task mining tools to detect obstructive, concealed, and automatable processes and tasks.

- **Automation roadmap:** Create an automation roadmap that lists the procedures that should be scaled in priority. Establish the objectives, schedule, and resources needed to scale automation programs. When creating your plan, consider elements like dependencies, complexity, and integration needs.

- **Stakeholder engagement:** Talk to people from various business functions to get their opinions and find chances for automation. To identify pain spots, bottlenecks, and places where automation can be beneficial, consult process owners, subject matter experts, and end users.

- **Collaboration and knowledge sharing:** Collaboration and knowledge sharing should be encouraged among the teams working on automation projects. Share successful case studies, lessons learned, and best practices to encourage and accelerate the implementation of automation. To make it easier to identify and capitalize on automation possibilities, create a platform for cross-functional communication and cooperation.

Organizations can build a solid base for their scaling efforts by assessing the level of automation they now have and looking for ways to scale Hyperautomation. This evaluation offers insightful information about how prepared your company is for growth and aids in prioritizing automation projects that can have the most impact.

Developing a scalable Hyperautomation strategy

For firms looking to exploit the advantages of automation across their operations, developing a scalable Hyperautomation strategy is crucial. Clearly, establishing objectives and goals is the first stage in developing such a plan. This entails figuring out which procedures and jobs may be automated, deciding what results are needed, and coordinating them with the overarching business plan. Setting priorities for automation initiatives is essential once the objectives have been identified. To establish the best order for deployment, organizations should evaluate the potential impact, viability, and complexity of each automation project. The timing, available resources, and key milestones for growing automation are then laid out clearly in a roadmap. Choosing the appropriate automation tools and technologies that facilitate scalability and interface with current systems is crucial.

To guarantee a seamless adoption and implementation of automation, firms must also build appropriate governance and change management systems. The ability for organizations to pinpoint areas for improvement and optimize automation systems as they scale depends on continuous assessment and monitoring of automation performance. Organizations can efficiently simplify processes, increase productivity, and realize the full potential of automation throughout their operations by implementing a scalable Hyperautomation plan.

Scaling Robotic Process Automation

Expanding the use of RPA across a variety of organizational procedures, divisions, or business units is referred to as scaling RPA. By increasing the number of automated operations and processes, it seeks to optimize the advantages of automation. Here is how the procedure is explained:

- **Assess automation potential**: Evaluate the organization's procedures to find areas with a high potential for automation. Look for jobs that are repetitive, rule-based, and high volume and that can be automated. Think about elements like likelihood of occurrence, degree of difficulty, and potential effect on effectiveness and production.

- **Organize automation projects by priority:** Set priorities for automation projects based on their viability and possible impact. Identify the processes that will be automated in what order, considering dependencies, resource availability, and strategic goals. To generate momentum and show the value of RPA, start with processes that deliver immediate wins and large returns on investment.

- **Process standardization and improvement:** To enhance efficiency and effectiveness, standardize and optimize the processes before growing RPA. To get rid of inefficiencies, variances, and unnecessary stages, streamline and reengineer processes as needed. Standardized procedures offer a strong framework for effective RPA installations.

- **The Best RPA tools and platforms to use:** Choose an RPA platform or piece of software that fits the needs and scalability objectives of the firm. Examine the functionalities, scalability, compatibility, and security of various RPA tools. Select a tool that can integrate with current systems and applications and offers the appropriate level of scalability.

- **Create a Center of Excellence (CoE) for RPA governance:** To manage and oversee the scalability of RPA, create a governance framework and a **Center of Excellence (CoE)**. The CoE offers direction, recommendations, and assistance with the deployment of RPA. It guarantees uniform standards, information exchange, and collaboration amongst various teams and departments.

- **Automate gradually:** Instead of aiming to automate all procedures at once, introduce RPA gradually. Start with proof-of-concept or pilot projects to confirm the viability and advantages of RPA. Once the automation is working, gradually broaden the scope to include more procedures while addressing any difficulties or lessons discovered.

- **Track and improve RPA performance:** Always keep an eye on how RPA bots and automated procedures are performing. To determine the efficacy, efficiency, and return on investment of RPA implementations, gather, and evaluate data. Find any faults or places that need improvement and make the necessary adjustments to the automated procedures.

- **Employee upskilling and training:** Employees who will be impacted by RPA implementations should have access to training and upskilling opportunities.

Help people embrace automation, adjust to the changes, and concentrate on higher-value jobs that call for human judgment and creativity. Encourage cooperation between humans and robots to take advantage of each group's advantages.

- **Expand and continuously evaluate RPA:** Analyze the results and advantages of RPA implementations on a regular basis. Expand the application of RPA to new processes or departments by finding new automation opportunities. To stay ahead of the curve, keep up with RPA technology improvements and industry best practices.

Scaling process discovery and mining

Expanding the application of process discovery and mining methodologies to find and evaluate processes across a greater scope inside an organization is known as scaling process discovery and mining. It seeks to find opportunities effectively and efficiently for automation, enhance process visibility, and enhance operations. Here is how the procedure is explained:

1. **Establish the scope:** Establish the size of the mining and discovery effort for the scaling process. The sectors, divisions, or business units that will be involved in the process discovery and mining operations should be identified. Establish precise scaling goals and objectives, such as the quantity of processes to be examined or the desired effect on productivity and efficiency.

2. **Standardize procedure writing:** Establish uniform techniques and instruments for recording processes. Make sure that process documentation is formatted consistently and includes important details like decision points, inputs and outputs, and stakeholders. The scalability and comparability of process discovery and mining operations are made possible by this standardization.

3. **Collect data:** Gather pertinent information from a variety of sources, such as process documentation, workflow diagrams, system logs, transactional data, and other process-related data. Make sure the data is thorough, precise, and indicative of the processes under consideration. The data forms the basis for tasks like process discovery and mining.

4. **Applying process discovery techniques:** To identify and comprehend the processes within the specified scope, use process discovery tools including workshops, surveys, interviews, and other methods of observation. Engage stakeholders, process owners, and subject matter experts to learn more about the processes as they are now, their variations, and their pain areas. Utilize

process mining techniques to examine system data and event logs to find hidden process flows and deviations.

5. **Analyze process performance:** Examine the gathered data using process mining techniques to discover insights into process performance. Find the weaknesses, inefficiencies, variations, and possible areas for improvement in the process. To evaluate the efficacy and efficiency of the process, analyze indicators including cycle time, throughput, error rates, and resource consumption.

6. **Find opportunities for automation:** Find opportunities for automation within the processes that were found using the performance analysis of the processes. Look for activities or subprocesses that can be automated because they are routine, governed by rules, time-consuming, or prone to mistakes. Decide which automation options are most important, practical, and in line with company objectives.

7. **Improve process discovery constantly:** Continuously develop the process discovery strategies and procedures as the scale process discovery and mining activities advance. To improve the efficacy and efficiency of the process discovery strategy, consider stakeholder comments, learn from prior discoveries, and iterate.

8. **Leverage technology:** To simplify and scale the process discovery and mining activities, make use of process mining tools, data analytics platforms, and automation technologies. These tools can speed up process analysis, automate data collecting, and offer insightful information that can help with decision-making. The journey from process discovery to automation implementation can be made simple through integration with automation platforms or intelligent process automation technologies.

9. **Work together and exchange knowledge:** Encourage cooperation and knowledge exchange between the various parties engaged in the process of discovery and mining. To find hidden process insights and spot automation opportunities, encourage cross-functional teams to cooperate, share thoughts, and draw on collective experience. Create a central knowledge base or repository to collect and exchange information about processes.

Integrating intelligent automation technologies

Integrating intelligent automation technology is referred to as *incorporating artificial intelligence and machine learning capabilities*, and it improves automation capabilities.

Organizations can develop superior cognitive skills by integrating automation with AI and ML. Large-scale data analysis, pattern recognition, and prediction or recommendation making are all capabilities of AI systems. The performance of ML algorithms can be improved over time by learning from data.

The potential of intelligent automation is further increased by using computer vision and **Natural Language Processing (NLP)**. NLP gives computers the ability to comprehend and interpret human language, enabling the automated processing of unstructured text data like emails or customer support requests. Automation opportunities in fields like image identification or quality control are made possible by computer vision, which enables machines to study and comprehend visual content, such as photographs or videos.

The cycle of intelligent automation is finished by integrating cognitive automation and decision-making abilities. Combining AI, ML, NLP, and computer vision allows for the cognitive automation process, which simulates human-like decision-making processes. Without human assistance, it enables systems to manage difficult situations, reach educated choices, and take the necessary measures.

Organizations may improve their automation solutions with sophisticated data analysis and prediction capabilities by integrating AI and ML capabilities. Automation in situations requiring visual perception or human-language understanding is made possible by combining NLP and computer vision. By combining cognitive automation and decision-making abilities, systems may manage complicated tasks on their own, improving accuracy and efficiency while requiring less manual interaction. Organizations can achieve higher degrees of automation and get more value out of their automated operations thanks to these integrated intelligent automation solutions.

Measuring and monitoring automation performance

A crucial component of successful automation implementation and continuing management is measuring and monitoring automation performance. It entails creating a solid framework to monitor, assess, and improve the effect of automation on business processes. Organizations can obtain important insights into the efficacy, efficiency, and return on investment of their automation initiatives by efficiently measuring and monitoring automation performance.

Start by defining pertinent **Key Performance Indicators (KPIs)** that are in line with the aims and purposes of automation. Process cycle time, cost savings, mistake rates, throughput, customer happiness, or any other indicators that are significant to the organization might be included in these KPIs. Organizations can assess the practical advantages and results of automation by identifying and monitoring certain KPIs.

For gathering and analyzing data on automation performance, it is essential to implement reliable tracking and reporting tools. This could entail creating unique reporting systems or combining automation platforms with analytics tools. Organizations can learn how automation affects business operations and spot areas for improvement by routinely monitoring and analyzing the acquired data.

Baseline evaluations are used as a starting point to gauge the effectiveness of automation. Organizations can successfully quantify the advantages brought about by automation by setting baseline measurements prior to applying it. These evaluations offer a standard by which the effect of automation can be quantified, proving the worth and success of automation activities. The effectiveness of automated processes must be tracked by ongoing monitoring of process KPIs. Key metrics such as process cycle time, throughput, mistake rates, and resource usage should be regularly measured by organizations. Continuous monitoring makes it possible to quickly take remedial action and optimize automated operations by identifying any deviations or problems.

Evaluations made after installation are essential for determining the overall impact of automation. Organizations can quantify the gains made and verify the efficacy of automation by contrasting post-automation performance indicators with baseline measurements. These evaluations offer information on the effectiveness of automation programs and aid in locating potential improvement areas. For assessing automation performance, feedback from users and stakeholders is important in addition to quantitative data. Participating with folks who use automated procedures can assist find chances for improvement, user experience issues, and potential bottlenecks. The rich insights that qualitative feedback offers, can guide decision-making, and encourage further automation workflow optimization.

The value and impact of automation must be communicated through regular reporting on its performance. Sharing performance reports with important stakeholders' aids in promoting openness inside the firm, securing continued support, and fostering a culture of data-driven automation. These reports should highlight realized achievements, cost reductions, efficiency improvements, and other pertinent KPIs while presenting data in a simple and comprehensible manner.

In conclusion, organizations can evaluate the efficacy and efficiency of their automation initiatives through the constant and iterative process of measuring and monitoring automation performance. Organizations can improve automation workflows, promote continuous improvement, and make sure alignment with business goals by defining pertinent KPIs, putting in place reliable tracking mechanisms, conducting baseline and post-implementation assessments, continuously monitoring process metrics, gathering feedback, and regularly reporting on automation performance. Organizations can utilize the advantages of automation and achieve long-term operational excellence by measuring and monitoring automation performance effectively.

Benefits and challenges of scaling Hyperautomation solutions

Scaling Hyperautomation systems provides businesses with a wide range of advantages and prospects. However, it also has some difficulties that must be resolved. Let us investigate the advantages and difficulties of scaling Hyperautomation.

The benefits of scaling Hyperautomation solutions are as follows:

- **Enhanced efficiency:** Organizations may automate a greater number of activities, thanks to scaling Hyperautomation, which boosts operational effectiveness. Organizations can boost productivity by getting rid of manual chores and optimizing workflows to achieve faster and more accurate processing.

- **Cost savings:** By eliminating the need for manual labor and reducing human error, scaled-up automation can result in significant cost savings. Through economies of scale, businesses can reduce labor costs, remove repetitive processes, and allocate resources more efficiently.

- **Improved scalability:** Businesses may manage heavier workloads and meet rising demand by scaling Hyperautomation technologies. To maintain smooth operations, it offers the flexibility to adjust to shifting business requirements, seasonal swings, or unexpected increases in demand.

- **Better accuracy and quality:** Automation removes the possibility of human errors and inconsistent behavior, thus providing improved process accuracy and quality. Organizations may consistently produce high-quality results by growing automation, increasing customer satisfaction, and lowering the need for rework.

- **Accelerated digital transformation:** Scaling Hyperautomation is a key factor in the acceleration of digital transformation. It lets businesses adopt cutting-edge technology, combine various systems, and take advantage of powerful analytics and machine learning capabilities, which boosts innovation and competitiveness.

The challenges of scaling Hyperautomation solutions are as follows:

- **Complex implementation:** Organizations must make sure that automation across many departments and systems is properly planned, integrated, and coordinated. A thoughtful planning process and strategic implementation are both necessary to manage the complexities of a large-scale automation deployment.

- **Change management:** Implementing automation at scale frequently necessitates a change in corporate culture and philosophy. Because they are worried about losing their jobs or changing positions, employees could encounter resistance or dread. To meet these problems, it is crucial to manage the shift and promote a cooperative and accepting culture of automation.

- **Integration with legacy systems**: Legacy systems from a variety of companies must be integrated with automation solutions. It can be difficult to ensure smooth integration and compatibility with current systems; it calls for careful planning, data migration, and system changes.

- **Data privacy and security:** As automation scales, more data is being processed and managed. Organizations must make sure that sensitive data is handled securely, that privacy laws are followed, and that strong data security procedures are in place. As automation grows, maintaining data integrity and protection becomes essential.

- **Talent and skill gap:** Experts that can design, build, and manage sophisticated automation workflows are needed to scale Hyperautomation. However, it is frequently difficult to find talent with the required knowledge. To close the skills gap, organizations must either engage with automation service providers or invest in staff training and upskilling.

A systematic approach is needed to address these issues and reap the rewards of increasing Hyperautomation. Investments in change management, data security as a top priority, a culture of automation, and a thorough personnel strategy should all be made by organizations. Organizations may successfully grow their Hyperautomation solutions and realize the full potential of automation in their operations by proactively tackling these problems.

Overcoming scalability issues

Hyperautomation scalability difficulties must be resolved with careful planning and execution. Here are some methods for overcoming scaling difficulties:

- Businesses need to build scalability into the design of their Hyperautomation solutions. Taking future expansion into account and ensuring that the architecture, infrastructure, and processes can handle growing workloads and data volumes are necessary for this. Utilizing cloud-based platforms and infrastructure, which allow for flexible resource allocation and simple demand-based scaling, may be a part of a scalable solution.

- Scaling and replicating complex processes are made easier by decomposing them into smaller, modular components. Organizations can add or remove components using this modular method as necessary, giving them flexibility and adaptability to changing requirements.

- For centralized management and coordination of numerous automation activities, automation orchestration tools or platforms are essential. Scalability is made possible by automation orchestration, which controls the execution of automation tasks, maximizes resource use, and efficiently distributes workloads.

- To sustain scalability, regular monitoring and optimization are essential. Organizations should regularly assess the effectiveness of their systems, spot any bottlenecks or inefficiencies, and then optimize the solution. This iterative method guarantees that the solution will always be effective and scalable.

- Additionally, it is crucial to keep up with the most recent developments in Hyperautomation technology. Improved scalability features and capabilities may be provided through new tools, platforms, and frameworks. Organizations can use the most recent tools and approaches to improve scalability and cater to unique business demands by staying abreast of technological developments.

These strategies help businesses solve scaling problems with their Hyperautomation technologies. A scalable solution makes it possible to manage growing user demands, data quantities, and workloads effectively, which ultimately boosts productivity and agility in corporate operations. To maximize the advantages of automation and promote operational excellence, enterprises must scale Hyperautomation solutions. Businesses may overcome scalability issues and guarantee that their automation programs can successfully handle growing workloads, data volumes, and user demands by putting the correct measures into place.

Careful planning, modular design, cloud adoption, automation orchestration, continuous monitoring, optimization, and keeping up with technological advances are all essential components of a scalable Hyperautomation approach. It necessitates that businesses take scalability into account from the beginning, deconstruct operations into manageable parts, use cloud computing for flexibility, centrally manage automated processes, and continuously assess and improve performance. Scaling Hyperautomation technologies has many advantages, including greater production, cost savings, efficiency, and accuracy.

It lets businesses to automate routine processes, improve workflows, and free up staff to work on higher-value jobs. Scaling automation also ensures that companies can respond to shifting customer needs, grasp fresh possibilities, and maintain a competitive edge in a quickly changing digital environment.

Organizations must embrace scalability as a key component of their automation plans as Hyperautomation develops and matures. Businesses can unleash the full potential of automation, spur innovation, and achieve sustainable success in the digital era by expanding their automation solutions effectively. Scaling Hyperautomation can be an effective accelerator for success in today's cutthroat corporate environment with careful planning, meticulous implementation, and continual improvement.

Architecture of Hyperautomation

There is not a single standardized framework for Hyperautomation although, organizations can adopt a structured approach to implement Hyperautomation initiatives effectively. Although most frameworks work with a three layer of architecture, an integrated system of intelligence with Artificial Intelligence, Machine Learning, and Natural Language Processing with task automation and orchestration. There are various perspectives on the components of Hyperautomation, and the three main components are automation, orchestration, and optimization which provide a useful framework to understand its key elements.

Key elements of architecture of Hyperautomation

The key elements of the architecture of Hyperautomation are as follows:

- **Automation**: Hyperautomation is built on automation. It entails the automation of manual, repetitive, and rule-based processes through the application of technologies like RPA, AI and ML. Automation minimizes errors, speeds up procedures, and lessens the need for human involvement. Data entry, form processing, report production, and other activities may be included.

- **Orchestration**: The coordination and integration of multiple automated processes and tasks across systems, applications, and divisions is referred to as orchestration. To achieve end-to-end process automation, it entails building workflows and connecting various automation tools and technologies. Using orchestration, the many automated components are made to operate in unison, exchanging information and launching appropriate actions.

- **Optimization:** The constant development and enhancement of automated processes is known as optimization. To find bottlenecks, inefficiencies, and places for improvement, it requires utilizing data analytics, machine learning, and process monitoring. The goal of optimization is to increase the functionality, effectiveness, and performance of automated processes. To get better results, it can be necessary to tweak automation algorithms, improve business rules, and take feedback into account. The elements 's placement can be seen in *Figure 9.1*:

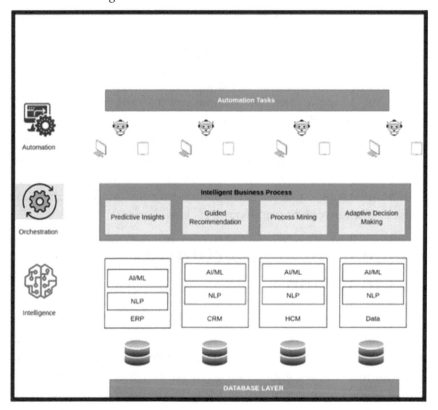

Figure 9.1: Placement of key elements of Hyperautomation architecture

Hyperautomation uses a vast array of technology and focuses on integrating several of them, including:

- **Robotic Process Automation (RPA):** Software robots that replicate human actions and interact with a variety of systems and applications are used to automate routine, rule-based processes.

- **Artificial Intelligence (AI) and Machine Learning (ML):** Artificial intelligence and machine learning allow systems to learn from data, recognize patterns, predict outcomes, and carry out cognitive tasks like sentiment analysis, image recognition, and natural language processing.

- **Process mining:** It involves analyzing event logs and data from various systems to identify process inefficiencies, bottlenecks, and improvement opportunities. It offers knowledge for process automation and improvement.

- **Intelligent Business Process Management (iBPM):** To develop intelligent workflows and enhance decision-making, iBPM platforms integrate process automation, monitoring, and optimization capabilities with AI and ML.

- **Chatbots and virtual assistants:** AI-powered chatbots and virtual assistants are used to automate consumer interactions, offer self-service choices, and help employees with clerical tasks and general queries.

- **Advanced analytics:** Hyperautomation leverages data analytics to extract insights, generate reports, and make data-driven decisions. It may involve analytical methods that are descriptive, diagnostic, predictive, and prescriptive.

In a modern enterprise IT stack, which is a collection of software and hardware technologies, all the components of Hyperautomation come together. The components of the IT stack are created so that they may support your organization in accomplishing its objectives for the digital transformation. Depending on an organization's unique goals and requirements as well as your adoption maturity level, the specific elements and technologies that make up a contemporary business IT stack will change. Implementation of Hyperautomation in a modern complex IT environment is a lengthy process. This entails reviewing your enterprise environment and your present business processes as well as creating a roadmap outlining the actions your company can take to deploy Hyperautomation. To gain a rapid victory and demonstrate value, it is always advisable to start small with a tactical initiative like the implementation of RPA, BPM, or process mining. *Figure 9.2* demonstrates high level view of Hyperautomation architecture:

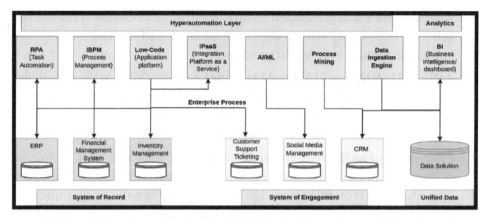

Figure 9.2: *High level of Hyperautomation Architecture*

Even though there is not a concrete path to Hyperautomation, these technologies do provide a structured approach to Hyperautomation which has several components working in tandem with human augmentation and cutting-edge technology. The architecture of Hyperautomation solutions typically involves identifying and prioritizing processes, analyzing, and optimizing them, selecting appropriate technologies, building automation capabilities, and continuously monitoring and optimizing the implemented automation. It also encompasses change management, training, and scaling initiatives to drive long-term success. The architecture of Hyperautomation is further explained as follows:

- **Identify and prioritize processes**: Begin by determining which business processes can be automated. Analyze the potential advantages and effects of automating each process, taking complexity, volume, and potential ROI into account. Determine which processes are most important based on their strategic importance and room for growth.

- **Process analysis and optimization:** Conduct a detailed examination of the identified processes, then optimize them. Utilize process mining techniques to collect information and insights on process variances, inefficiencies, and bottlenecks. Determine the areas where automation can have the biggest influence. Prior to automating operations, optimize and standardize them to cut out extra stages and boost effectiveness.

- **Define automation goals and metrics:** Set objectives and metrics for automation. For endeavors including automation, set up clear goals and objectives. Establish metrics and KPIs to gauge the accomplishment of automation programs. Process cycle time reduction, cost savings, mistake reduction, and increases in customer satisfaction are a few examples of measurements. Ensure compliance with the overarching company goals.

- **Technology selection:** Consider and choose the best tools and technology for Hyperautomation. As you choose RPA platforms, AI/ML frameworks, process mining tools, and analytics platforms, keep in mind the requirements of your processes. Pick technologies that are flexible and scalable, and that integrate effectively with current systems.

- **Build automation capabilities:** Create automation capabilities. Create or set up the chosen tools and technologies to create the required automation capabilities. RPA should be used for routine, rule-based operations. Utilise AI/ML skills for activities requiring analytical thinking, natural language processing, and data processing. For customer support and employee assistance, create chatbots and virtual assistants.

- **Pilot and iterate:** To test the automation solution, start with a pilot project or a small-scale implementation, and then adjust based on feedback and lessons learned. Utilise user feedback to iterate and enhance the automation, filling in any gaps or problems that appear during the trial phase. To ensure adaptability and continual improvement, use agile approaches.

- **Change management and training:** Automation programs frequently call for adjustments to roles, responsibilities, and workflows. By integrating stakeholders, explaining the advantages of automation, and teaching staff how to use and adapt to automated procedures, you can ensure effective change management. Actively address worries and reluctance to change.

- **Monitor and optimize:** Track the established KPIs and continuously monitor the efficiency of automated procedures. Tools for real-time monitoring and process analytics can be used to pinpoint areas that could want more tweaking and enhancing. Improve decision-making and automation algorithms by using machine learning approaches. Evaluate the results of your automation efforts on a regular basis.

- **Scale and expand:** Scale up the implementation across the organization once successful automation initiatives have been created. Find more procedures that can be automated, and then use the knowledge gained from earlier efforts. To establish a comprehensive automation ecosystem, investigate ways to integrate automation with other digital projects like cloud computing, IoT, and data analytics.

Hyperautomation frameworks

In utmost simplicity, Hyperautomation can be divided into three critical stages: Input (data that needs to be processed), processing (the technology or process that is to be implemented), and output (the result).

Information could enter a business process in a variety of ways. To name a few, we have:

- Sales orders, invoices, and service requests may be delivered through email or email attachment.
- **Document**: It could be a text, image, or PDF, Word, or Excel document.
- **Web sources**: Data present in web pages.
- **3rd Party application**: You might need to get information from another application. This could appear as an API, a database, or even just the app's user interface.

The following can be used with each of the input sources to bring in the data:

- **Email reader**: This scans for new emails, recognizes the different sorts of content they include, and forwards the data.
- **File reader:** It pulls data from the file based on the file type.
- **OCR:** OCR is a tool for finding text on images. It arranges it for processing after that.
- **Web scraper:** This device directly reads information from a website and feeds it to a processor.
- **Automation tools:** RPA is essentially a bot posing as a user. For instance, it imitates keyboard strokes and mouse operations to retrieve data from another application.
- **Connectors:** With the help of numerous third-party connectors, it is simple to connect to data from numerous sources without the need for programming. This covers everything, from email to calendars to databases to weather reports.

The introduction of a different set of tools follows the data enters the system:

- **Workflow:** This entails information routing, calculations, and decision trees, the majority of which do not require programming. For specifying the intended process, many systems provide a **Graphical User Interface (GUI)**.
- **User interface:** A human touch is occasionally required during an automated procedure. We need a means for someone to signify their approval for an invoice or a time off request. For instance, customers might utilize a smartphone app or get an email with a link.

The final outcomes need to go somewhere once the procedure is complete:

- **File system:** The file is kept in a network disc or an online document archive using this system.

- **Database**: Finalized data may need to be pushed into a database.
- **Notification:** A notification lets you know how far along a process is, whether it has been completed, approved, or rejected.

Challenges for Hyperautomation

The challenges for Hyperautomation solutions are as follows:

- **Selecting an organization's CoE (center of excellence) strategy:** When it comes to managing large-scale initiatives, some organizations may perform better with a more centralized approach, while others will achieve greater outcomes with a federated or distributed approach.
- **Tools:** Software for Hyperautomation is not a panacea. Enterprises will struggle to secure interoperability and integration among various solutions, even though top automation providers are growing their Hyperautomation capabilities.
- **Governing and security:** In-depth monitoring and analysis of business processes that cross several departments, services, and even national boundaries can be beneficial for any Hyperautomation activities. Numerous new security and privacy risks may arise as a result. Additionally, businesses must create the right safeguards for assessing the security flaws of automatically created apps.
- **Immature metrics:** The methods for figuring out how much automation will cost and what it might be worth are still in their infancy.
- **Requires manual augmentation:** According to a Forrester study, only 40% to 60% of the code for automations could be written automatically using current tools. When creating robust automations at scale, a significant amount of manual work is still necessary and must be budgeted.
- **Getting human buy-in:** Although most automation suppliers promote the idea that Hyperautomation would complement rather than replace people, the truth is that automation eliminates occupations that were previously performed by people. To succeed, these initiatives need to persuade workers that robots will not take their jobs. Additionally, knowledge workers concerned about possible data exploitation may react negatively to the different monitoring technologies employed in Hyperautomation initiatives.

Tools for Hyperautomation

There are many Hyperautomation software solutions available. Here is a list some of the most popular Hyperautomation software tools in the market:

- **Automation Anywhere:** Automation Anywhere is a leading RPA platform. It enables organizations to automate repetitive and rule-based tasks by using software robots. Automation Anywhere offers a user-friendly interface, drag-and-drop functionality, and supports integration with various systems and applications.

- **Alteryx:** Alteryx is a comprehensive data analytics and process automation platform. It combines AI and machine learning capabilities to enable data preparation, blending, and advanced analytics. Alteryx empowers users to perform complex data analysis tasks without the need for extensive coding.

- **Zendesk support suite:** Zendesk Support Suite provides customer support and engagement solutions, including chatbots. With the help of AI and NLP, Zendesk's chatbots can handle customer inquiries, provide self-service options, and assist human agents in resolving complex issues.

- **Celonis:** Celonis is a process discovery and mining tool that allows organizations to analyze and optimize their business processes. It uses event data to visualize end-to-end processes, identify bottlenecks, and uncover inefficiencies. Celonis provides insights to improve process performance and supports process automation initiatives.

- **ProcessMaker:** ProcessMaker is an **intelligent Business Process Management Software (iBPMS)** that combines process automation, workflow management, and decision-making capabilities. It allows organizations to design, automate, and optimize complex business processes, integrating data, systems, and stakeholders in a unified platform.

Vendors for Hyperautomation

Some possible vendors for Hyperautomation are as follows:

- To expand its process mining capabilities, UiPath purchased Process Gold and StepShot.

- For autonomously creating bots, Automation Anywhere has been developing its own task and process mining tools.

- Blue Prism has established a cooperation with Celonis and has been developing its own internal process mining capabilities.

- The top process mining vendor, Celonis, has acquired Integromat to increase its automation capabilities.

- With the help of its Process Advisor for process mining and Power Automate series of RPA tools, Microsoft has been continuously enhancing its Hyperautomation capabilities.

- One of the first manufacturers of intelligent automation solutions, **Kryon** built process discovery right into their products.
- Leading provider of OCR, ABBYY has steadily increased the number of tools in its toolkit to offer a range of IPA capabilities. To increase the equipment available for Hyperautomation, it recently provided a variety of process mining capabilities.

Conclusion

Organizations can benefit greatly from Hyperautomation. By automating time-consuming and repetitive operations, it improves operational efficiency and productivity and frees up staff time for more strategic endeavors. By reducing manual labor and eliminating mistakes, it lowers costs. Hyperautomation also gives organizations a competitive edge by enhancing accuracy, compliance, and customer experiences. Organizations are also given the ability to use data-driven decision-making thanks to the architecture of Hyperautomation technologies. Using real-time data and analytics, businesses may identify trends, forecast outcomes, and streamline operations. Additionally, Hyperautomation acts as a spur for innovation and digital transformation, enabling businesses to adopt cutting-edge technology and build intelligent ecosystems. Organizations must take a disciplined approach to the solutions' architecture for Hyperautomation. Organizations may choose the necessary processes to automate, choose the proper technology, and iteratively deploy and optimize automation initiatives by adhering to a well-defined framework. For the deployment of Hyperautomation to be successful, change management, employee empowerment, and continual monitoring are crucial elements.

Key facts

Some of the roles in which Hyperautomation can play an active role are enhanced customer experience, cost reduction and improved accuracy and compliance, agility and scalability, data-driven decision making, innovation and transformation and employee empowerment.

Hyperautomation is like a toolbox. It takes on higher-level functions, starting with coordination, intelligence, predictive insight, informed suggestions, and ending with decision-making.

Scaling Hyperautomation systems provides businesses with a wide range of advantages and prospects. However, it also has some difficulties that must be resolved.

Hyperautomation is a technological solution that allows complete automation of operating processes in an enterprise. This advanced technology can tackle more complex tasks and processes that cannot be eliminated using one automation technology.

Although most automation suppliers promote the idea that Hyperautomation would complement rather than replace people, the truth is that automation eliminates occupations that were previously performed by people.

Key terms

- Automation
- Optimization
- Orchestration
- Integration with legacy systems
- Talent and skill gap
- Web Scrapper
- Centre of Excellence

Questions

1. Describe Hyperautomation framework.
2. What are the main challenges of scaling a Hyperautomation solution?
3. What are the key elements of the architecture of Hyperautomation?
4. What can be the different steps to overcome scalability issue of Hyperautomation?

Join our book's Discord space

Join the book's Discord Workspace for Latest updates, Offers, Tech happenings around the world, New Release and Sessions with the Authors:

https://discord.bpbonline.com

CHAPTER 10

Successful Use Cases of Hyperautomation

"Automation platforms that employ artificial intelligence and machine learning, coupled with guiding expertise from industry veterans, are the best answer to help us create the premier revenue cycle management department of the future."

—*Varun Ganapathi*

Introduction

In a fast-evolving tech landscape, organizations seek innovative ways to optimize processes and fuel growth. Robotic Process Automation (RPA) emerged in the late 1950s as a standalone concept, offering a virtual workforce to automate specific tasks within predefined capabilities. Yet, it fell short in meeting complex digital demands. Enter Hyperautomation – combining RPA with AI and ML. This holistic approach transforms processes using advanced analytics, AI, ML, and RPA. Hyperautomation revolutionizes business processes, going beyond traditional automation by integrating tools like process mining and analytics. It emphasizes human-technology collaboration, recognizing decision-makers' role. For instance, in social media, Hyperautomation tools analyse customer sentiment, requiring marketing teams to craft strategies for retention.

We explore a comprehensive overview of Hyperautomation, covering its history, definition, key components, comparisons with other automation technologies, market value, and future forecasts. It includes insights, quotations, statistics, and summaries from various global platforms and experts in the field. By exploring several aspects of Hyperautomation, this chapter aims to provide readers with a deeper understanding of this emerging technology and its advantages and limitations.

Structure

In this chapter, we will cover the following three topics:

- Case study 1
- Case study 2
- Case study 3

Objectives

Following the previous chapters, this chapter completely focuses on case studies related to Hyperautomation, and three different case studies explore the practical and real-life implications of implementing Hyperautomation as a solution to different business problems. Till this chapter, the theoretical knowledge has been explained around what and how of Hyperautomation. This chapter discusses Hyperautomation not as theory but as solution of problems and advantages also.

Case study 1

Hyperautomation goes beyond traditional automation by involving both people and processes to optimize and eliminate low-value tasks. It does not aim to replace humans but rather empower them to focus on higher-level responsibilities. While RPA is a good starting point for process automation, Hyperautomation offers even greater benefits, including reduced human error, streamlined operations, and improved adaptability. Informatica has successfully implemented Hyperautomation in various industries, such as automating loan processes for nCino, enhancing customer order visibility for Reitmans, driving digital transformation for the Austin Community College District, and improving data access for Metropolitan Thames Valley Housing to address England's housing crisis. These case studies demonstrate the tangible advantages of Hyperautomation in terms of efficiency, transparency, and improved services. To fully leverage these benefits, organizations must address the barriers to Hyperautomation adoption and embrace an integrated approach that involves change management and an end-to-end perspective.

Challenge or problem statement

All IT services company encountered significant hurdles stemming from the intricacy of its IT infrastructure. With a staggering number of enterprise applications (over

200) spread across more than 4,500 servers hosted on various public clouds and on-premises data centers, managing the entire landscape posed a complex challenge. Complicating matters further, we had to cater to the needs of its vast employee base, exceeding 160,000 individuals, who relied heavily on critical applications such as Helpline and their day-to-day tasks. The complexity of the IT environment gave rise to efficiency issues and intensified security concerns. Monitoring and managing disparate applications and infrastructure silos necessitated the involvement of multiple monitoring teams, causing delays in identifying the root causes of failures. This fragmented approach to monitoring also resulted in some servers and devices being left unmonitored, creating blind spots. Additionally, tracking, and reverting configuration changes proved to be a cumbersome process, and the availability of historical change tracking was limited. Recognizing the pressing need to address these challenges, we found a solution that would provide real-time monitoring, efficient incident and change management, and automation capabilities to deliver a seamless user experience. Their objective was to shift from a reactive approach to a proactive one, where the entire IT infrastructure could be continuously monitored, issues identified and resolved in real-time, and routine tasks automated to enhance operational efficiency. We managed an overly complex IT landscape encompassing many applications and servers. Fragmented monitoring and incident management processes hindered their ability to promptly address failures, while the security and compliance aspects demanded more robust measures. We sought a comprehensive solution that would enable real-time monitoring, efficient incident and change management, automation, and self-healing capabilities to ensure a seamless user experience and overcome the challenges at hand.

Solution

To tackle the infrastructure, critical application, and data center monitoring and management challenges, the team adopted a systematic steps approach as part of their Hyperautomation drive. Let us now explore each step-in detail.

Diagnostics and monitoring

To establish a robust monitoring framework for their heterogeneous infrastructure and applications across physical, cloud, and virtual environments, we implemented a combination of network node manager, operations manager insight, system center operations manager, SiteScope, storage essentials, and AppDynamics. This comprehensive suite of tools allowed effective diagnostics and monitoring. Let us now go over them in detail:

- **Network node manager, operations manager insight, and system center operations manager:** These tools provided network and infrastructure monitoring capabilities. Network Node Manager enabled monitoring and management of network devices, while Operations Manager Insight and System Center Operations Manager facilitated end-to-end monitoring of the entire IT infrastructure. This included servers, networks, and storage systems, allowing for proactive identification of issues and faster troubleshooting.

- **SiteScope:** SiteScope is a monitoring tool that helps monitor the performance and availability of web applications and servers. By implementing SiteScope, we gained visibility into the health and performance of critical applications, allowing them to detect any potential bottlenecks or anomalies and take proactive measures to address them.

- **Storage Essentials:** Storage Essentials is a storage resource management tool that enables monitoring, analysis, and reporting on storage devices and their utilization. By utilizing Storage Essentials, we could monitor storage systems in real-time, identify potential capacity or performance issues, and take necessary actions to optimize storage utilization.

- **AppDynamics:** AppDynamics is an application performance monitoring and management tool that provides insights into the performance and user experience of applications. By leveraging AppDynamics, we gained visibility into application performance, transaction traces, and end-user experience, allowing them to identify and resolve performance issues quickly, ensuring a seamless user experience.

This combination of monitoring tools provided with a unified view of their entire IT landscape. It allowed IT support teams to troubleshoot effectively by filtering events and alerts through de-duplication and event suppression techniques. The single pane of glass view enabled the teams to focus on critical events and prioritize their efforts for efficient problem resolution.

Configuration, change and auto remediation

We implemented configuration, change, and auto remediation capabilities within their IT infrastructure by leveraging network automation, server automation, and operations orchestration. This allowed them to automate routine tasks such as repetitive maintenance, change provisioning, and incident resolution. Explore each component and its benefits:

- **Configuration and change automation**: Configuration automation refers to the automated management of device configurations across the network infrastructure. Employed network automation tools to streamline the process of configuring and managing network devices, reducing manual effort and the likelihood of human errors. Change automation, on the other hand, enabled the automated execution of configuration changes in a controlled and auditable manner. By automating configuration and change management, we ensured consistency, accuracy, and efficiency in their IT operations.

- **Server automation:** Server automation involved automating various tasks related to server management, including provisioning, patching, and configuration updates. By implementing server automation tools, we eliminated manual interventions and reduced the time and effort required to manage server infrastructure. Automated provisioning ensured rapid and consistent deployment of servers, while automated patching and configuration updates helped maintain server security and compliance.

- **Operations orchestration:** Operations orchestration involved the automation and coordination of various IT processes and workflows. We utilized operations orchestration tools to create workflows that automated routine tasks and standardized IT operations. This included tasks such as repetitive maintenance activities, change provisioning, and incident resolution. By orchestrating these processes, we reduced the dependency on manual efforts, improved operational efficiency, and minimized the risk of errors. By implementing configuration, change, and auto remediation capabilities through network automation, server automation, and operations orchestration, we achieved several benefits. They experienced improved efficiency and accuracy in configuration management and change execution, reduced manual effort and human errors, and accelerated provisioning and maintenance processes. Additionally, automating incident resolution enhanced the speed and accuracy of problem identification and remediation.

Integration of incident management with e-helpline

We integrated incident management with their e-helpline system to establish a closed-loop incident process. This integration involved intricately linking the e-helpline system with monitoring tools to enable auto-ticketing and closure of incidents. As a result, the status of tickets in the operations manager and e-helpline systems remained synchronized in real-time. delve into the details of this integration and its benefits:

- **E-helpline integration:** The e-helpline system is a digital platform utilized by employees to log tickets and seek assistance for their IT-related issues. By integrating incident management with the e-helpline system, we established a seamless flow of information between users reporting incidents and the IT support team responsible for resolving them. This integration allowed for the efficient capture and tracking of incidents from the initial report to their closure.

- **Auto-ticketing and closure:** Through the integration with monitoring tools, incidents and alerts generated by the monitoring system were automatically captured and converted into tickets within the incident management system. This eliminated the need for manual ticket creation, saving time and reducing the chances of errors. Once an incident was resolved, the closure status was also automatically updated in real-time, reflecting the accurate and up-to-date status of the ticket.

- **Real-time synchronization:** By integrating the operations manager and e-helpline systems, the status of tickets remained synchronized on a real-time basis. This synchronization ensured that all stakeholders, including users and IT support teams, had access to the most up-to-date information about the incidents. Real-time updates improved communication, collaboration, and decision-making, enabling faster incident resolution, and reducing the time taken to provide feedback to users. The integration of incident management with the e-helpline system brought several benefits. It streamlined the incident reporting process by automating ticket creation, reducing manual effort and potential errors. Real-time synchronization of ticket statuses improved transparency and facilitated efficient tracking and monitoring of incidents. This integration also enhanced the overall user experience by providing prompt updates and timely resolution of issues.

Collaboration and ChatOps for critical incident management

The implemented collaboration and ChatOps for critical incident management, enabling their infrastructure and applications monitoring teams to effectively handle all critical incidents on a global scale. This approach not only facilitated efficient incident resolution but also ensured compliance with **Service Level Agreements (SLA)** for both customers and employees. Let us explore the details of this implementation:

- **Collaboration and ChatOps**: Collaboration and ChatOps involve leveraging collaboration platforms and chat-based communication tools to facilitate real-time collaboration and information sharing among team members during incident management. We implemented these practices to create a collaborative environment where monitoring teams could work together, share knowledge, and communicate seamlessly to resolve critical incidents promptly.

- **Global incident management:** Our infrastructure and applications monitoring teams utilized collaboration and ChatOps techniques to manage critical incidents globally. With teams operating across various locations and time zones, the ability to collaborate in real-time through chat-based platforms allowed for faster incident response and efficient allocation of resources. This approach ensured that incidents were addressed promptly, regardless of their geographical location.

- **SLA compliance:** By implementing collaboration and ChatOps for critical incident management, we were able to ensure compliance with SLAs for both customers and employees. SLAs define the expected response and resolution times for incidents. Through effective collaboration and communication, the monitoring teams could coordinate their efforts, share updates, and work together towards meeting the SLA commitments. This resulted in improved customer satisfaction and enhanced employee experience.

The implementation of collaboration and ChatOps for critical incident management brought several benefits. It enabled real-time collaboration, knowledge sharing, and efficient communication among the monitoring teams, leading to quicker incident resolution. By managing incidents globally, we could ensure consistent and standardized incident management practices across separate locations. Additionally, the adherence to SLAs improved service delivery and customer satisfaction.

Business impact

The implementation of a single pane of glass, integration with other tools, enhanced coverage, improved service management, greater monitoring efficiency, and increased customer confidence had significant business impacts for our organization. Let us examine each of these impacts in detail:

- **Single pane of glass:** Integration with other tools and the availability of a single window for end-user diagnostics, event consolidation, and topology synchronization provided a unified view of the IT environment. This integration reduced response time by 15% and critical incident response time by 20%. Mean time to resolution, a key metric for IT support, improved by 8%. This streamlined and consolidated view enabled faster decision-making and incident resolution.

- **Enhanced coverage:** We achieved maximum device coverage under the monitoring tools. Advanced level monitoring **Key Performance Indicators (KPI)** are now being tracked, allowing for a comprehensive understanding of the IT infrastructure. The monitoring of close to 5,000 network devices provided broader visibility into the network, enabling proactive identification and resolution of potential issues.

- **Improved service management:** The transition from event-based monitoring to service-based monitoring allowed for a clearer tracing of the impact of infrastructure issues on applications and user experiences. This shift enabled the measurement of service availability with greater accuracy. Overall system availability improved by 5%, ensuring a more reliable and stable IT environment.

- **Greater monitoring efficiency:** The automation of closure for a high percentage of alerts/events using advanced analytics reduced the workload for the monitoring team. With automatic closure of non-critical alerts, the team could focus their efforts on addressing the few vital alerts that required immediate attention. This increased monitoring efficiency and allowed for more effective resource allocation.

- **Increased customer confidence:** With improved monitoring and compliance measures, we enhanced its ability to manage customer infrastructure within SLAs. Meeting SLAs instills customer confidence in the company's services. By delivering reliable and responsive infrastructure management, strengthened its relationships with customers and enhanced their overall satisfaction.

In summary, the adoption of a single pane of glass, integration with other tools, enhanced coverage, improved service management, greater monitoring efficiency, and increased customer confidence had a positive business impact. It resulted in faster incident response, improved service availability, streamlined operations, and enhanced customer satisfaction.

Hyperautomation ecosystems

Hyperautomation involves combining automation tools, machine learning applications, and packaged software to carry out work efficiently. While RPA is a significant component of Hyperautomation, it is not the only technology driving this approach. Other technologies such as **Intelligent Business Process Management Suites (iBPMSs)**, **Integration Platform as a Service (iPaaS)** platform, and decision management systems contribute to the robust toolkit of Hyperautomation. The RPA market is experiencing disruptions with increased research and development investments, leading to the emergence of new offerings, vendors, and commercial models that go beyond traditional task-based RPA.

Figure 10.1 describes the flow of different tasks in Hyperautomation:

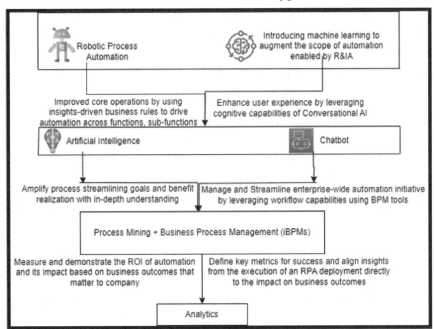

***Figure 10.1:** Hyperautomation ecosystem*

Let us go over the different tasks in Hyperautomation:

- **RPA:** RPA automates repetitive tasks and offers benefits for organizations undergoing digital transformation. It improves customer service, ensures regulatory compliance, speeds up processes, increases efficiency, saves costs, and enhances employee productivity.

- **Process mining:** Process mining uncovers insights from event logs to monitor and improve real processes. It helps in improving process models, identifying inefficiencies, generating simulation models, and conducting conformance checking.

- **AI:** AI enhances process automation by utilizing technologies like **Optical Character Recognition (OCR)**, **Natural Language Processing (NLP)**, Chatbots, and ML. OCR extracts text from images, NLP analyzes and structures data from documents, Chatbots interact with users, and ML enables decision-making capabilities.

- **IBPMS:** IBPMS provides a comprehensive platform for orchestrating processes and automating tasks. It brings together integration services, decision management, process orchestration, and advanced analytics.

- **Advanced analytics:** Advanced analytics combined with RPA allows organizations to extract valuable insights from RPA program performance, enabling informed decisions and optimization of automation initiatives.

Delivery approach for Hyperautomation

The impact of COVID-19 prompted a reevaluation of technology solution delivery, leading to an evolved approach. Thriving in this challenging time required navigating three key phases. **Firstly**, the *Imaging* phase involved identifying suitable automation opportunities, redesigning processes for optimal execution, and conducting a comprehensive assessment to establish an automation pipeline.

Secondly, in the Deliver phase, an automation solution was devised, developed, and deployed in the production environment.

Lastly, the *Run* phase focused on realizing the anticipated benefits outlined in the business case and planning subsequent steps for the automation program.

Figure 10.2 describes the journey of solution considering Hyperautomation:

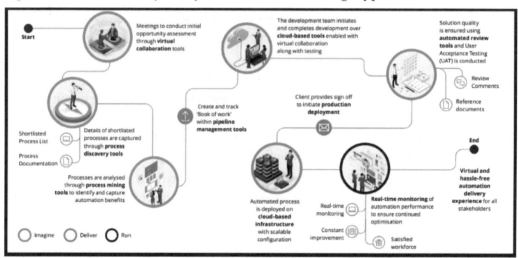

Figure 10.2: High-level delivery journey enabled with Hyperautomation

Case study 2

This case study focuses on a Bank, a leading financial institution that implemented Hyperautomation to address various challenges in their operations. The bank faced problems such as manual and time-consuming processes, compliance and regulatory requirements, data fragmentation, cost and resource inefficiencies, and customer experience expectations.

To overcome these challenges, the Bank embarked on a Hyperautomation journey. They implemented automation technologies, including RPA, to streamline processes, automate manual tasks, ensure regulatory compliance, integrate data sources, and optimize resources. The Hyperautomation solution aimed to improve operational efficiency, enhance compliance management, enable better data analysis, achieve cost savings, and elevate the customer experience.

Through the implementation of Hyperautomation, the Bank achieved several positive outcomes. They experienced improved operational efficiency, reduced processing times, and minimized errors in their manual processes. Automation of compliance checks ensured adherence to regulatory requirements and reduced the risk of penalties. Integration of data sources provided a holistic view of customer information and enabled data-driven decision-making. The optimized resource allocation and cost savings contributed to improved financial performance.

Furthermore, the implementation of Hyperautomation enhanced the customer experience by providing faster and more personalized services. The bank leveraged automation technologies such as chatbots to provide efficient customer support and meet evolving customer expectations. Overall, the successful implementation of Hyperautomation transformed Bank's operations, enabling them to stay competitive in the finance and banking industry.

This case study showcases the potential of Hyperautomation in addressing operational challenges, enhancing compliance management, improving data analysis, and elevating the customer experience in the finance and banking domain. It highlights the importance of leveraging automation technologies to optimize processes, drive efficiency, and achieve business objectives in a rapidly evolving industry.

Organizational overview

The Bank has a strong presence in the finance and banking industry, offering a wide range of banking services, including retail banking, corporate banking, investment banking, and wealth management. With a large customer base and a complex network of operations. The Bank faced significant challenges that prompted them to adopt Hyperautomation.

The problem

The bank faced several challenges that prompted the need for improvement and optimization in their operations.

Manual and time-consuming processes

In the context of the finance and banking domain, manual and time-consuming processes can include:

- **Loan applications:** The manual processing of loan applications involves collecting customer data, verifying documents, conducting credit checks, and assessing eligibility. This process is time-consuming and prone to errors, leading to delays in loan approvals and customer dissatisfaction.

- **Account opening:** Opening new bank accounts for customers typically involves filling out forms, collecting necessary documentation, performing identity verification, and inputting customer details into the system.

- **Transaction monitoring:** The bank monitors transactions for potential fraud, money laundering, and other suspicious activities. Manual monitoring involves reviewing transaction data, investigating anomalies, and reporting any suspicious transactions.

- **Customer onboarding:** The process of onboarding new customers involves collecting and verifying customer information, setting up accounts, and providing necessary documentation.

- **Data entry and reconciliation:** Manual data entry tasks, such as inputting transaction details, updating customer information, and reconciling accounts, are time-consuming and prone to errors.

The impact includes:

- Slower service delivery
- Increased errors
- Higher operational costs
- Inefficient resource utilization

Compliance and regulatory requirements

The bank faced several issues related to compliance and regulatory requirements in the finance and banking domain, such as:

- **Know Your Customer (KYC) and Anti-Money Laundering (AML) Compliance:** KYC an AML regulations require bank to identify and verify the identity of their customers, monitor transactions for suspicious activities, and report any suspicious transactions to relevant authorities.

- **Data privacy and security regulations:** The Bank handles sensitive customer information, and protecting this data is of utmost importance. Compliance with data privacy and security regulations, such as the **General Data Protection Regulation (GDPR)** and data breach notification laws, is critical.

- **Reporting and documentation requirements:** The Bank require to generate various reports and maintain extensive documentation to demonstrate compliance with regulatory standards.

- **Audits and internal controls:** Regular audits are conducted to assess a financial institution's compliance with regulations, internal controls, and risk management practices.

The impact includes:

- Increased compliance costs
- Reputational risk
- Legal consequences

Customer experience and expectations

These are the key points related to customer experience and expectations the bank is trying to focus on:

- **Rise of digital banking:** Manual and paper-based processes no longer meet these expectations, requiring the bank to adopt digital solutions to enhance customer experience.

- **Personalized and relevant services:** Manual processes often lack the ability to gather and utilize customer data effectively, making it challenging to deliver personalized experiences.

- **Speed and efficiency:** Customers value speed and efficiency in their interactions with financial institutions. They expect quick response times, fast account opening processes, and efficient transaction processing. Manual processes can be time-consuming, resulting in delays and frustrations for customers.

- **24/7 availability:** Customers want to access their accounts, make transactions, and seek assistance at any time, from anywhere. Manual processes may have limited availability or require manual intervention, hindering the seamless 24/7 customer experience.

- **Seamless multichannel experience:** Customers interact with financial institutions through multiple channels, including in-person, online, mobile, and telephone.

The impact of customer experience and expectations on the bank includes:

- Customer satisfaction and retention
- Competitive advantage
- Brand image and reputation
- Revenue growth

Data fragmentation and Silos

Data fragmentation and silos in the finance and banking industry refer to the scattered and isolated storage of data across different systems, departments, and applications within an organization. Here are key points related to data fragmentation and silos, that the bank is facing:

- **Multiple systems and applications:** The bank is having multiple systems and applications that store and manage various types of data, such as customer information, transaction data, risk data, and compliance data.

- **Departmental data silos:** Different departments within the bank maintain their own databases or systems to store and manage data relevant to their specific functions. This departmental segregation of data creates silos, making it difficult to access and integrate data across departments.

- **Data redundancy and inconsistencies:** Data fragmentation and silos often result in data duplication and inconsistencies. When the same data is stored in multiple systems or departments, it increases the risk of data redundancy, which consumes storage resources and makes it difficult to maintain data integrity and consistency.

- **Limited data accessibility and analysis:** Data fragmentation and silos restrict the accessibility and usability of data. It becomes challenging to access, combine, and analyze data holistically to gain insights and make informed decisions.

The impact of data fragmentation and silos on the bank includes:

- Incomplete customer view
- Inefficient reporting and analysis
- Increased operational costs
- Compliance and risk management challenges

The solution

To address the challenge of manual and time-consuming processes, the organization implemented a Hyperautomation solution. Here is how they solved this problem:

- **Robotic Process Automation (RPA)**: The organization implemented RPA bots to automate repetitive and manual tasks such as loan application processing, account opening, transaction monitoring, customer onboarding, and data entry.

- **Intelligent document processing**: The organization leveraged intelligent document processing capabilities to automate the extraction and processing of information from documents.

- **Integration of systems and data**: The organization integrated various systems and data sources to ensure seamless data flow and eliminate data silos. Integration enabled real-time access to customer information, transaction data, and other relevant data points, reducing the need for manual data retrieval and reconciliation.

- **Analytics and reporting**: The organization implemented data analytics and reporting tools to gain insights into process performance and identify areas for improvement. These tools provided dashboards, reports, and visualizations that highlighted process bottlenecks, inefficiencies, and potential areas of automation.

- **Chatbots and virtual assistants:** The organization deployed chatbots and virtual assistants to automate customer interactions and support self-service options. Chatbots could handle common customer inquiries, provide account information, and assist with basic transactions, reducing the need for manual customer support and improving response times.

To address the compliance and regulatory issues faced by the bank, the following solutions were implemented:

- **Know Your Customer (KYC) and Anti-Money Laundering (AML) Compliance**: The bank deployed advanced technology solutions that automate the identification and verification of customer identities, monitor transactions for suspicious activities, and generate alerts for potential money laundering or fraud cases. The bank integrated with external data sources, such as government databases and credit bureaus, to streamline the verification process and ensure accurate customer identification.

- **Data privacy and security regulations**: The bank enhanced its data security infrastructure, including encryption techniques, access controls, and intrusion detection systems, to protect sensitive customer information from unauthorized access or breaches.

- **Reporting and documentation requirements:** The bank adopted automated reporting tools that gather data from various sources and generate regulatory reports in a standardized format. This reduces manual effort and ensures timely and accurate reporting.

- **Audits and internal controls:** The bank implemented robust internal control frameworks to ensure adherence to regulations, risk management practices, and compliance standards. This includes regular internal audits, segregation of duties, and defined approval processes.

To address the challenges related to customer experience and expectations, the bank implemented a Hyperautomation solution. Here is how they solved this problem:

- **Digital transformation:** The bank embraced digital solutions to replace manual and paper-based processes. This involved the implementation of online and mobile banking platforms, allowing customers to access their accounts, make transactions, and seek assistance digitally.

- **Customer data utilization:** The bank utilized advanced analytics and **Customer Relationship Management (CRM)** systems to gather and analyze customer data. This data-driven approach enabled the bank to understand individual customer preferences, behavior, and needs.

- **Process automation:** The bank automated various processes to improve speed and efficiency. For instance, account opening processes were streamlined by implementing automated workflows and digital document submission.

- **24/7 availability:** The bank implemented self-service options, such as online and mobile banking, that provided customers with 24/7 access to their accounts and services.

- **Multichannel integration:** The bank integrated its various channels, including in-person, online, mobile, and telephone, to deliver a seamless multichannel experience. Customers could initiate transactions on one channel and seamlessly continue another, without the need to start over.

To address the issue of data fragmentation and silos in the finance and banking industry, the following solution can be implemented:

- **Data integration and centralization:** The bank can adopt a centralized data integration platform that connects and integrates data from various systems and applications across different departments. This platform should support data transformation, data mapping, and data synchronization capabilities.

- **Data governance and collaboration**: The bank can formulate data governance teams with representatives from different departments to oversee data management, define data standards, and resolve data-related issues.

Figure 10.3 represents the flow of developing continuous path for automation:

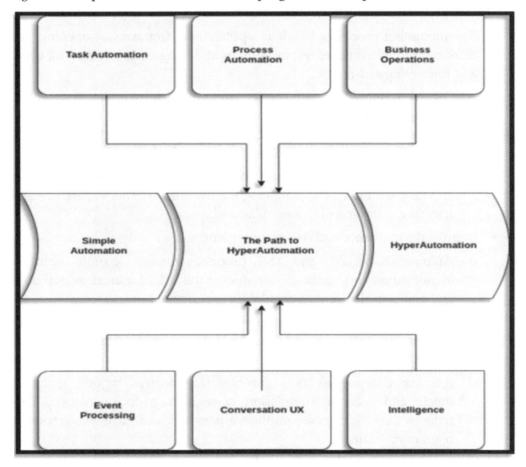

Figure 10.3: *The flow of building continuous path for Automation*

Results and benefits

The implementation of Hyperautomation at the bank resulted in several significant results and benefits across their operations. Here are some key outcomes:

- **Increased efficiency and productivity**:

  Automation of manual processes, such as loan applications and data entry, significantly reduces processing time and minimizes the risk of human errors. This results in faster turnaround times, increased throughput, and improved operational efficiency. Streamlined workflows and integrated systems enable seamless data flow and collaboration across departments. This eliminates redundancies, reduces duplication of efforts, and optimizes resource utilization, leading to improved productivity.

- Enhanced customer experience:

  By automating processes like loan applications and account opening, the bank can provide quicker response times, reducing customer waiting times and improving satisfaction.

  o Digital solutions and self-service options, such as online and mobile banking, empower customers to perform transactions, access account information, and seek assistance conveniently and at any time. This 24/7 availability meets customer expectations for flexibility and convenience.

  o Leveraging customer data and analytics enables personalized services and targeted offerings, enhancing the overall customer experience and fostering long-term customer relationships.

- Improved compliance and risk management:

  o Automation of KYC and AML processes ensures accurate customer identification and verification, reducing the risk of fraudulent activities and non-compliance with regulatory requirements.

  o Robust data privacy and security measures protect sensitive customer information, instilling customer trust and demonstrating compliance with data protection regulations.

  o Automated reporting tools generate standardized reports, ensuring timely and accurate submission of regulatory documentation. This reduces the risk of non-compliance penalties and facilitates smoother regulatory audits.

- Better data quality and decision-making:

  o Integration of systems and data sources eliminates data silos and fragmentation, ensuring a single source of truth and consistent data across the organization. This leads to improved data quality, accuracy, and integrity.

  o Advanced analytics and reporting tools provide insights into process performance, customer behavior, and market trends. This enables data-driven decision-making, strategic planning, and the identification of areas for optimization and improvement.

- Cost reduction and resource optimization: Under this, we have:
  - o By automating manual processes and reducing reliance on manual resources, the bank can achieve cost savings through increased operational efficiency and optimized resource allocation.
  - o Eliminating redundant tasks and minimizing human errors reduces the need for costly rework and improves resource productivity.
- Strengthened internal controls and audits: Under this, we have:
  - o Implementation of internal control frameworks, segregation of duties, and defined approval processes strengthen compliance and risk management practices.
  - o Robust data governance and collaboration among different departments ensure data integrity, accountability, and transparency, facilitating smoother internal and external audits.

In conclusion, the finance and banking industry has faced various challenges related to manual and time-consuming processes, compliance and regulatory requirements, customer experience and expectations, and data fragmentation and silos. To address these challenges, the organization implemented a range of solutions.

By embracing Hyperautomation, which includes technologies like robotic process automation, intelligent document processing, and analytics, the organization was able to automate manual processes, improve operational efficiency, and enhance customer experience. These automation efforts resulted in increased efficiency, productivity, and cost savings, as well as improved compliance with regulatory requirements.

The implementation of advanced technology solutions enabled the organization to meet regulatory standards, such as KYC and AML compliance, data privacy and security regulations, and reporting and documentation requirements. Through these solutions, the organization achieved better risk management, data security, and streamlined reporting processes, contributing to overall compliance, and reduced regulatory risks.

Furthermore, the organization's focus on customer experience and expectations led to the adoption of digital solutions, personalized services, and multichannel integration. This resulted in improved customer satisfaction, 24/7 availability, and seamless customer interactions across various channels. By leveraging customer data and analytics, the organization was able to offer personalized services, anticipate customer needs, and enhance customer loyalty.

The organization also tackled the challenge of data fragmentation and silos by implementing data integration and centralization solutions. This allowed for better data accessibility, reduced redundancies, and improved collaboration across departments, leading to enhanced data quality and more informed decision-making.

Overall, the implementation of these solutions has driven positive results for the organization, including increased efficiency, enhanced customer experience, improved compliance, better data management, cost savings, and strengthened internal controls. These outcomes have positioned the organization for continued success in the finance and banking industry, enabling it to adapt to evolving customer expectations, regulatory requirements, and market dynamics.

Case study 3

In response to the rapid advancements in technology, business leaders are reshaping their organizational processes to prepare for the future of work. This includes leveraging Automation, AI technologies, and Analytics to revolutionize business functions and enhance overall performance. One notable example is the second-largest healthcare organization in the United States, which serves over 130 million customers and manages an annual underwritten direct premium exceeding US$100 billion.

To improve productivity, eliminate redundant tasks, enhance the customer experience, and reduce processing costs, the healthcare organization embarked on a journey to collaborate, co-develop, and implement Hyperautomation solutions. Within an impressive timeframe of less than 18 months, this ambitious initiative was successfully accomplished.

Hyperautomation involves the integration of various technologies such as RPA, ML, NLP and data analytics. By combining these technologies, businesses can automate repetitive and rule-based tasks, improve decision-making processes, and derive valuable insights from large amounts of data.

For the healthcare organization mentioned, the implementation of Hyperautomation brought numerous benefits. Firstly, it boosted productivity by automating manual and time-consuming tasks, enabling employees to focus on more strategic and value-added activities. This increased efficiency resulted in improved turnaround times and reduced processing costs.

Moreover, the utilization of AI technologies and analytics allowed the organization to gain actionable insights from the collected data. This facilitated better decision-making, enhanced customer experiences, and enabled personalized services tailored to individual needs.

The successful adoption of Hyperautomation by the healthcare organization exemplifies the transformative potential of automation, AI, and analytics. By embracing these technologies, businesses can optimize operations, improve performance, and adapt to the digital and data-driven landscape of the future of work.

Hyperautomation in healthcare processes

The large healthcare organization implemented automation strategies to streamline the back-end processes of their customer-facing operations. They categorized these processes into the following two main groups:

- Transactions
- Voice

Transactions

The healthcare organization successfully deployed Hyperautomation solutions for Claims, Appeals, and Grievances processes within its Transactions division. These processes consisted of clearly defined procedures, multiple rules engines, and structured data. Through the implementation of advanced automation technologies, the organization was able to streamline and automate the workflow for claims processing. With the help of software bots, manual clicks are now handled automatically, data is interpreted, and decisions are made based on predefined rules. This automation has led to several benefits, including improved productivity, accuracy, and overall quality of the claims process. By removing manual tasks and relying on automation, the organization has been able to reduce errors and ensure consistent adherence to predefined rules.

Figure 10.4 describes flow of transactions:

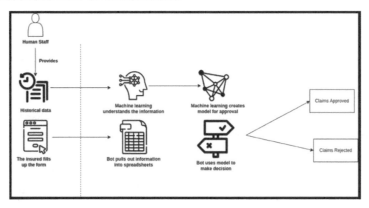

Figure 10.4: *Flow of transactions*

Moreover, the automation initiative has had a significant impact on the workforce. Thousands of full-time employees have been freed up from performing repetitive tasks, allowing them to shift their focus towards enhancing the customer experience. This reallocation of human resources has contributed to improved customer service and satisfaction.

The successful deployment of Hyperautomation in the claims, appeals, and grievances processes has resulted in a more efficient, accurate, and customer-centric approach. By leveraging automation technologies, the healthcare organization has optimized its operations, enhanced the quality of its services, and improved the overall experience for its customers.

Voice

The Voice segment of the enterprise implemented Hyperautomation techniques and technologies to support specific teams, including healthcare agencies, health advocates, and contact center operations. For healthcare agencies, which serve as medical care providers, Hyperautomation was utilized to enhance their operations. Automation technologies were employed to streamline administrative tasks, such as appointment scheduling and documentation management. By automating these processes, healthcare agencies were able to improve efficiency, reduce errors, and allocate more time and resources to patient care.

Figure 10.5 describes the flow of how-to user is interacting with system using chat or call mode:

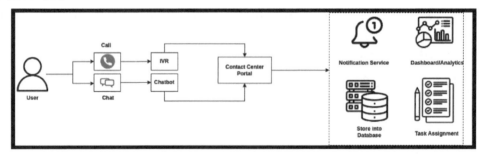

Figure 10.5: User interaction with System

Health advocates, acting as a centralized resource to assist and guide customers, also benefited from Hyperautomation. Automation tools were employed to automate the retrieval of relevant information, such as medical records or insurance coverage details, during customer interactions. This enabled Health Advocates to access accurate and up-to-date information quickly, leading to improved customer service and more effective support.

The adoption of Hyperautomation in the Contact Center operations had a significant impact as well. Automation technologies were utilized to handle routine customer inquiries and provide self-service options. This reduced the workload of contact center agents, allowing them to focus on more complex or specialized customer needs. The result was improved efficiency, reduced wait times, and enhanced customer satisfaction.

The implementation of Hyperautomation in the Voice segment of the enterprise provided tangible benefits for Healthcare Agencies, Health Advocates, and Contact Center operations. By automating repetitive tasks, improving access to information, and enabling self-service options, these teams were able to enhance their effectiveness, improve customer service, and allocate resources more efficiently.

Key steps for successful implementation of Hyperautomation

The organization's approach to Hyperautomation solutions involved several key steps to ensure long-term success, secure funding, and maximize the benefits of implementation, as they are explained as follows.

Vision

The organization developed a comprehensive vision focused on creating a rule-driven automation system using intelligent automation technology. This vision served as a guiding principle for the implementation process.

Plan

The organization identified the processes, functions, and business areas where automation could have a significant and valuable impact. This involved assessing existing workflows and determining which areas would benefit most from automation. Refer to *Figure 10.6:*

Figure 10.6: *Flow of the key steps of Planning of Hyperautomation*

Evaluate

Internal and external capabilities were evaluated to assess the organization's readiness and formulate a strategy for implementing the technology. This involved understanding the existing technology landscape, identifying potential partners or vendors, and determining the resources required for successful implementation.

Support

Strong support from top-level management was established to ensure the success of the Hyperautomation initiative. This support was crucial in securing funding, allocating resources, and providing the necessary leadership to drive the implementation process forward. A dedicated focus on a long-term roadmap ensured continued support and commitment.

Track

Key metrics were identified to track and measure the success of the Hyperautomation solutions. These metrics were essential for evaluating the effectiveness of the implemented automation, identifying areas for improvement, and ensuring sustained success in the long run. Regular tracking of these metrics allowed the organization to adjust strategies and optimize the benefits derived from Hyperautomation.

Results

The organization entered a partnership with UiPath, a leading provider of automation platforms that integrate RPA and AI technologies. This partnership allowed them to expand their automation capabilities over a period of six months. They leveraged the expertise of UiPath and their in-house team to achieve this.

As a result of their efforts, the organization successfully implemented over 50 Hyperautomation deployments, indicating significant progress. Based on their experience, they estimate that approximately 80-85% of their processed transactions have reached Stage 2 (advanced) or Stage 3 (intelligent) in terms of Hyperautomation maturity. They have even completed pilots and proof of concepts in certain areas that have reached Stage 4 (cognitive).

This progress highlights the organization's commitment to advancing their automation capabilities and adopting more sophisticated automation techniques. By partnering with UiPath and utilizing their own expertise, they have been able to implement a considerable number of successful Hyperautomation deployments. These deployments have enabled them to categorize a large percentage of their transactions as advanced or intelligent in terms of Hyperautomation maturity. Furthermore, they have gone a step further in specific areas by reaching the cognitive stage, indicating a high level of automation sophistication and cognitive capabilities.

Impact of automation on workforce

Contrary to what movies and popular opinion may suggest, the notion that software bots are superior to humans and will completely replace the workforce is not entirely accurate. The belief is that bots, being capable of working round the clock, should be at least three times more effective than humans who work only 8 hours a day, 5 days a week. However, the effectiveness ratio between bots and humans is more likely around 1.8:1 or perhaps 2:1, as observed by this organization.

One of the reasons for this difference in effectiveness is that software bots struggle with unstructured data and human interactions. These aspects require nuanced understanding and contextual interpretation, where humans excel. As a result, humans remain crucial in optimizing the customer experience and addressing complex or unstructured situations that bots may struggle with.

While bots can offer advantages in terms of their availability and consistency, they still have limitations. Humans possess unique qualities such as empathy, creativity, and critical thinking that are difficult to replicate in automation. These human qualities are particularly valuable in customer-centric industries where personalized experiences and emotional connections are essential.

Therefore, rather than perceiving a complete replacement of humans by bots, it is more accurate to recognize the value of a combined approach. By leveraging the strengths of both humans and automation, organizations can achieve optimal outcomes. Humans can focus on tasks that require human touch and cognitive abilities, while bots can handle repetitive and rule-based tasks, enhancing efficiency and productivity.

In the digital age, rethinking the workforce involves understanding the complementary nature of humans and automation. It is not about a binary choice between one or the other but rather finding the right balance to leverage the strengths of both and create a more effective and efficient workforce.

Benefits of leveraging Hyperautomation solutions

A marriage of human and automation is considered the best path forward in leveraging Hyperautomation solutions to enhance organizational processes. These solutions can play a crucial role by providing:

Conversational AI chatbots that can interact with customers and obtain relevant information. These chatbots utilize AI algorithms to understand and respond to customer queries, improving the efficiency of customer interactions.

AI-based analytics that can analyze unstructured customer information, such as voice recordings, text messages, or photos. By applying AI algorithms to these data types, organizations can derive valuable insights and make informed decisions based on the analyzed information. Let us go over a few more scenarios:

- Automation of financial reporting and other repetitive tasks that involve structured data: By automating these tasks, organizations can improve accuracy, reduce human error, and free up employees to focus on more strategic and value-added activities.

- Real-time access to customer data, enabling employees to retrieve up-to-date information quickly and efficiently: This real-time access to customer data improves responsiveness, enhances customer service, and enables personalized interactions.

- Automation of administrative and finance functions, such as managing calendars or generating reports: By automating these routine tasks, organizations can save time and resources, increase efficiency, and minimize manual errors.

- Reduction in the cycles employees go through to retrieve accurate customer data: Through automation, employees can access accurate customer data more efficiently, eliminating the need for multiple iterations or manual data gathering processes.

Conclusion

The presented case studies demonstrate how Hyperautomation can bring about transformative changes in organizations. By integrating RPA, AI and other advanced technologies, these organizations have successfully automated various tasks. This automation encompasses both rule-based processes and more intricate cognitive tasks.

The implementation of Hyperautomation has led to several significant benefits. Operational efficiency has been improved as repetitive tasks are automated, freeing up time for employees to focus on higher-value activities. This increased productivity has a positive impact on overall business performance.

Furthermore, Hyperautomation has facilitated enhanced customer experiences. By automating processes and utilizing AI, organizations can provide more personalized and efficient services to their customers. This results in improved satisfaction and loyalty.

The integration of RPA, AI, and other technologies enables organizations to automate a wide range of tasks. Rule-based processes that were previously performed manually can now be automated, reducing errors and increasing accuracy. Moreover, more complex cognitive tasks can be automated by leveraging AI algorithms and machine learning capabilities.

Overall, the case studies illustrate the transformative power of Hyperautomation. By harnessing the capabilities of RPA, AI, and other advanced technologies, organizations can drive operational efficiency, boost productivity, and deliver superior customer experiences.

Key facts

- Hyperautomation involves combining automation tools, machine learning applications, and packaged software to carry out work efficiently.

- Hyperautomation goes beyond traditional automation by involving both people and processes to optimize and eliminate low-value tasks.

- Data fragmentation and silos in the finance and banking industry refer to the scattered and isolated storage of data across different systems, departments, and applications within an organization.

- Automation of manual processes, such as loan applications and data entry, significantly reduces processing time and minimizes the risk of human errors.

- The organization's approach to Hyperautomation solutions involved several key steps to ensure long-term success, secure funding, and maximize the benefits of implementation: vision, plan, evaluate, support, track, and results.

Key terms

- AppDynamics
- Operation orchestration
- Data integration and centralization
- Data governance and collaboration
- Data fragmentation

Questions

1. Describe different parts of ecosystem of Hyperautomation.
2. Explain in brief the different benefits and results of Hyperautomation.
3. Describe the flow of transactions.
4. Describe the key steps of planning of Hyperautomation.

Join our book's Discord space

Join the book's Discord Workspace for Latest updates, Offers, Tech happenings around the world, New Release and Sessions with the Authors:

https://discord.bpbonline.com

SECTION III

Emergence of Generative AI and Its Collaboration with Hyperautomation

Highlighting the emergence of Generative AI and its transformative impact across industries and technologies, this section explores its interaction with Hyperautomation. This bonus chapter delves into the collaboration between Generative AI and Hyperautomation, discussing its potential applications through use cases and exploring its possibilities.

CHAPTER 11

Generative AI and Hyperautomation

"Generative AI, the brush of imagination wielded by machines, paints infinite possibilities on the canvas of our minds, blending the boundaries of what is, with the audacity of what could be."

—A quote generated by Generative AI (ChatGPT)

Introduction

The history of Generative AI goes back to the 1950s and 60s, when researchers first started exploring the potential of AI. This time, they focused on creating a system of control that could influence people's thoughts and decisions. Over the years, researchers have begun experimenting with emerging models in fields as diverse as speech recognition, image processing, and natural language processing. As the millennium approaches, models such as Bayesian networks and Markov models are finding application in robotics and computer systems. But the real breakthrough comes from the teaching and development of deep learning. This increases the ability to develop skills. In 2014, the release of **Generative Adversarial Networks (GAN)**, a machine learning algorithm, enabled manufacturers' artificial intelligence applications to generate realistic images, video and audio of real people.

Generative AI has gained significant attention with the rise of deep learning models. These models can generate new content by learning from raw data, such as text, images, or speech. **Variational Autoencoders (VAE)** were among the first deep-learning models used for generating realistic images and speech. VAEs enabled the scaling of generative models and paved the way for subsequent technologies like GANs and diffusion models.

Generative AI models, including VAEs and transformers, are built on the architecture of encoders and decoders. Transformers, introduced in 2017, revolutionized language models by combining the encoder-decoder architecture with attention mechanisms. Transformers can be pre-trained on vast amounts of raw text, allowing for efficient learning of powerful language representations. These models can later be fine-tuned for specific tasks with smaller amounts of labeled data. Transformers, also known as foundation models, have brought versatility to the field of natural language processing. They have applications in classification, entity extraction, translation, summarization, question answering, and even generating convincing dialogue and content. Language transformers can be categorized as encoder-only models (for example, BERT), decoder-only models (such as, GPT), or encoder-decoder models (for example, T5).

Structure

In this chapter, we will cover the following topics:

- Introduction to Generative AI
- Types of Generative AI Models
- Supervised learning strikes back
- Developing Generative AI Models
- Benefits of Generative AI
- Limitations of Generative AI
- Output produced by a Generative AI model
- Collaboration of Generative AI and Hyperautomation
- Challenges and Considerations
- Future Considerations
- Use case of Generative AI with Hyperautomation
- Considerations for Implementing Generative AI with Hyperautomation
- Business outcome of using Generative AI with Hyperautomation

Objectives

This is a bonus chapter that directly focuses on Generative AI and how it can help Hyperautomation. The first part focuses on the introduction of Generative AI, its types, and how it can be beneficial. The second part focuses on its collaboration with Hyperautomation. The third and last part is a case study considering Generative AI and Hyperautomation as the core technologies of the solution.

Introduction to Generative AI

Generative AI is a form of artificial intelligence technology that can produce various types of content, such as text, images, audio, and synthetic data. It has gained attention recently due to its ability to generate high-quality content quickly. While Generative AI has been around since the 1960s in the form of chatbots, significant advancements occurred in 2014 with the introduction of GANs, which allowed for the creation of realistic images, videos, and audio.

This technology has both positive and negative implications. On the positive side, it has led to improvements in movie dubbing and educational content creation. However, it has also raised concerns about deepfakes, which are manipulated and deceptive media, as well as potential cybersecurity threats, such as realistic impersonation attempts.

Two recent advances have contributed to the widespread adoption of Generative AI. Transformers, a type of machine learning algorithm, has made it possible to train larger models without the need for pre-labeling all the data. This enables models to be trained on massive amounts of text, resulting in more comprehensive and insightful responses. Transformers also introduced the concept of attention, which allows models to understand connections between words across different texts, not just within individual sentences. This ability to track connections has expanded the scope of Generative AI to analyze various types of data, including code, proteins, chemicals, and DNA. The development of **Large Language Models (LLM)** with billions or even trillions of parameters has further propelled Generative AI. These models can generate engaging text, photorealistic images, and even sitcoms in real-time. Additionally, advancements in multimodal AI have enabled the generation of content across multiple media types, such as text, graphics, and video. Tools like Dall-E can automatically create images based on text descriptions or generate text captions from images. Generative AI is still in its early stages. Early implementations have faced challenges with accuracy, bias, hallucinations, and nonsensical responses. Nonetheless, the progress made so far suggests that Generative AI has the potential to significantly impact various aspects of business, including coding, drug development, product design, process optimization, and supply chain transformation.

Difference between Generative AI and Traditional AI

Generative AI is focused on generating new content, such as chat responses, designs, synthetic data, or deepfakes. It utilizes techniques like transformers, GANs, and

Variational Autoencoders (VAE). On the other hand, traditional AI is more concerned with tasks like pattern detection, decision making, analytics, data classification, and fraud detection.

Generative AI typically involves using neural network techniques such as transformers, GANs, and VAEs to produce desired content. In contrast, other types of AI rely on different techniques like **Convolutional Neural Networks (CNN)**, **Recurrent Neural Networks (RNN)**, and reinforcement learning.

When using Generative AI, users or data sources provide a prompt or starting query to guide the content generation process. This allows for an iterative exploration of various content variations. Traditional AI algorithms, however, process new data and provide a straightforward result without the need for iterative input or exploration.

Traditional AI, also referred to as classic AI or conventional AI, relies on pre-programmed rules to accomplish specific tasks. Examples of traditional AI applications include web search engines like Google Search, YouTube, Amazon, Netflix, and **Search Engine Optimization (SEO)**.

Traditional AI is commonly used in various fields such as fraud detection, medical diagnosis, stock trading, video games, and automating expert knowledge in specific domains. It excels in tasks that involve making predictions based on available data.

In traditional AI, algorithms are designed with explicit rules and instructions to process information and produce desired outputs. These rules are carefully crafted by human experts to guide the AI system's decision-making process. This approach has been widely used for several years and has proven effective in many practical applications.

However, traditional AI has limitations in handling complex and unstructured data, as it heavily relies on predefined rules and lacks the ability to adapt and learn from new information without explicit programming. This is where newer approaches like Generative AI, which leverages deep learning techniques, have emerged to address these limitations, and enable AI systems to generate new content and make more advanced predictions based on large datasets.

What can Generative AI do

Generative AI offers several capabilities that can drive AI adoption and deliver value to organizations. These capabilities can be summarized into three categories:

- **Generating content and ideas:** Generative AI can create new and unique outputs across various modalities. For example, it can generate video advertisements or design new proteins with antimicrobial properties. This capability allows for the exploration of novel possibilities and creative solutions.

- **Improving efficiency:** Generative AI can accelerate manual or repetitive tasks, reducing the time and effort required. It can assist in tasks like writing emails, coding, or summarizing large documents. By automating these processes, it frees up human resources for more complex and strategic work.

- **Personalizing experiences:** Generative AI enables the creation of personalized content and information tailored to specific audiences. For instance, chatbots can provide personalized customer experiences, and targeted advertisements can be generated based on patterns in an individual customer's behavior. This capability enhances customer engagement and satisfaction. It is important to note that responsible AI practices are crucial in the context of Generative AI. Some Generative AI models have been trained on large amounts of data from the internet, including copyrighted materials. Organizations must ensure ethical considerations, data privacy, and compliance with relevant regulations when using Generative AI technologies.

Types of Generative AI models

Let us now explore the various types of Generative AI models:

Text models

The various types of text models are as follows:

- **GPT-3**, short for Generative Pretrained Transformer 3, is an advanced autoregressive model that has been trained on a vast amount of text data. Its primary purpose is to generate natural language text of exceptional quality. GPT-3 is highly versatile and can be customized for various language-related tasks, including but not limited to translation, summarization, and answering questions.

- **LaMDA**, also known as Language Model for Dialogue Applications, is a transformer-based language model that has been pre-trained to generate natural language text of excellent quality, like GPT. However, the key distinction of LaMDA is that it was specifically trained on dialogue data, aiming to capture the intricacies and nuances of open-ended conversations.

- **LLaMA** is a compact natural language processing model that is designed to be highly efficient, and performant compared to larger models like GPT-4 and LaMDA. Like GPT-4 and LaMDA, LLaMA is an autoregressive language model built on transformer architecture. However, what sets LLaMA apart is that it is trained on a larger number of tokens, which helps enhance its performance while keeping the number of parameters lower.

Multimodal models

The various types of multimodal models are as follows:

- **GPT-4** represents the most recent iteration of the GPT series of models. It is a state-of-the-art, multimodal model capable of handling both image and text inputs while generating text outputs. GPT-4 is built on the transformer architecture and undergoes pretraining where it learns to predict the next token in each document. The model also undergoes a post-training alignment process, which leads to enhanced performance in terms of factual accuracy and alignment with desired behavior.

- **DALL-E** is an advanced multimodal algorithm that could work with diverse types of data and generate unique images or artwork based on natural language text input. It combines text and image processing capabilities to create novel visual outputs.

- **Stable diffusion** is a text-to-image model that shares similarities with DALL-E. However, it employs a distinct approach known as "diffusion" to iteratively reduce noise in the generated image until it aligns with the provided text description. This gradual noise reduction process ensures a more stable and accurate image output.

- **Progen** is a multimodal model that has been trained on an extensive dataset of 280 million protein samples. Its purpose is to generate proteins based on specific properties that are described using natural language text input. By leveraging the training data and utilizing the power of natural language processing, Progen can generate proteins with desired characteristics and properties.

Supervised learning strikes back

The innovation of harnessing unlabeled data has been instrumental in advancing Generative AI. However, human supervision has made a comeback and is now playing a crucial role in shaping large language models. Supervised learning, particularly instruction-tuning, has enabled generative models to move beyond simple tasks and provide more interactive and human-like responses. By feeding the model instructions paired with responses across various topics, it can generate not just statistically probable text but accurate answers to questions or requests. This approach, known as zero-shot learning, allows the model to perform tasks even without explicit training for them. Additionally, few-shot learning, where one or a few examples are provided, further enhances the model's performance. Although zero- and few-shot learning significantly reduces the time required to build an AI solution, they come with limitations. The formatting of instructions can greatly impact the model's output, necessitating prompt-engineering techniques to achieve the desired results. Transferring prompts between models can be challenging. Another limitation is the difficulty of incorporating proprietary data into large generative models due to the cost of fine-tuning. To address these challenges, techniques like prompt-tuning and adaptors have emerged, allowing customization of models without extensively modifying their parameters. Furthermore, **Reinforcement Learning from Human Feedback (RLHF)** aligns generative models with human preferences by adjusting the model based on human-rated responses. This training method enhances the conversational abilities of AI systems like ChatGPT, resulting in high-quality conversational text outputs.

Developing Generative AI models

Generative models come in various types, and combining their strengths leads to the creation of more powerful models:

Diffusion models, also known as **Denoising Diffusion Probabilistic Models (DDPM)**, utilize a two-step process during training involving forward diffusion and reverse diffusion. This process involves gradually adding random noise to training data and then reversing the noise to reconstruct the data samples. By running the reverse denoising process starting from random noise, novel data can be generated. Diffusion models excel in generating high-quality output but may require longer training time compared to other models like VAEs. Let us learn more:

- **VAEs** consist of an encoder and decoder neural network. The encoder converts input into a compact representation, while the decoder reconstructs the original input using this representation. VAEs enable sampling of new representations to generate novel data. While VAEs can generate outputs faster, the level of detail in the generated images is typically lower than that of diffusion models.

- **GANs**, discovered in 2014, involve two neural networks competing against each other: a generator and a discriminator. The generator generates new examples, while the discriminator learns to distinguish between real and generated content. Through iterative training, both models improve, with the generator producing better content and the discriminator becoming better at detecting generated content. GANs can generate high-quality samples quickly, but they may lack diversity in the generated data, making them more suitable for domain-specific tasks.

- **Transformers**, the underlying architecture for many generative models, play a crucial role in Generative AI. Understanding how transformers work is essential in the context of generative models.

Transformer networks: Unlike recurrent neural networks, they are designed to process sequential input data in a non-sequential manner. They have become highly effective for text-based Generative AI applications due to two key mechanisms: self-attention and positional encodings. These mechanisms enable the model to capture the relationships between words over long distances and understand the sequential order of the input.

Self-attention allows the model to assign weights to different parts of the input, indicating their importance in the overall context. This helps the model focus on relevant information. Positional encoding, on the other hand, represents the order in which words appear in the input sequence.

A transformer consists of multiple transformer blocks or layers, which include self-attention layers, feed-forward layers, and normalization layers. These components work together to process tokenized data, such as text, protein sequences, or image patches, and make predictions based on the patterns and relationships within the data.

Evaluating Generative AI models

The three key requirements of a successful Generative AI model are:

- **Quality:** Especially for applications that interact directly with users, having high-quality generation outputs is key. For example, in speech generation, poor speech quality is difficult to understand. Similarly, in image generation, the desired outputs should be visually indistinguishable from natural images.

- **Diversity:** A good generative model captures the minority modes in its data distribution without sacrificing generation quality. This helps reduce undesired biases in the learned models.

- **Speed:** Many interactive applications require fast generation, such as real-time image editing to allow use in content creation workflows.

Working of text-based machine learning models

Text-based machine learning models, such as GPT-3 and BERT, have gained attention for their ability to process and generate text. Before these models, AI chatbots faced challenges and received mixed reviews. The initial text-based machine learning models were trained using supervised learning. Human trainers labeled inputs according to predefined categories, teaching the model to classify them. For instance, a model could be trained to classify social media posts as positive or negative.

The next generation of text-based models utilizes self-supervised learning. These models are trained by exposing them to a large volume of text data, allowing them to learn patterns and make predictions. For example, a model can be trained to predict the next word in a sentence based on the preceding words. By training on vast amounts of text, including internet data, these models achieve impressive accuracy. ChatGPT is one such example of a successful text-based model built using self-supervised learning.

Benefits of Generative AI

Generative AI has wide-ranging applications in various business domains, offering numerous advantages. It simplifies the interpretation and comprehension of existing content while also automating the generation of new content. Developers are actively exploring how Generative AI can enhance and optimize existing workflows and even transform them entirely to leverage the capabilities of this technology. Implementing Generative AI brings several potential benefits, including:

- Streamlining the manual content writing process.
- Reducing effort and time spent on email responses.
- Enhancing the handling of specific technical queries.
- Creating lifelike representations of individuals.
- Summarizing complex information into coherent narratives.
- Facilitating the creation of content in specific styles or formats.

By harnessing the power of Generative AI, businesses can unlock new possibilities, improve productivity, and achieve greater efficiency in various aspects of their operations.

Limitations of Generative AI

Early applications of Generative AI have highlighted several notable limitations that stem from the specific implementation approaches for different use cases. For instance, while a summary of a complex topic may offer better readability compared to an explanation backed by multiple sources, the source of information becomes less transparent in the summary.

Here are some of the limitations to consider when implementing or utilizing a Generative AI application:

- **Source identification:** Generative AI may not always provide clear indications of the content source, making it challenging to trace the origin of information.

- **Bias assessment:** Evaluating the bias present in original sources can be difficult when using Generative AI, posing potential challenges in ensuring a balanced and objective representation.

- **Accuracy identification:** Realistic-sounding generated content can make it more difficult to distinguish between accurate and inaccurate information, potentially leading to the dissemination of misinformation.

- **Adaptability to new circumstances:** Understanding how to fine-tune Generative AI models for new circumstances or specific contexts can be a complex task, requiring careful consideration and expertise.

- **Glossing over bias and prejudice:** Generative AI results may inadvertently overlook or reinforce biases, prejudices, or hateful content, necessitating robust mitigation strategies to address these concerns.

Output produced by a Generative AI model

Generative AI models have the capability to produce diverse types of output, ranging from text-based content to visual art, code, video, audio, and business simulations. The quality and realism of the outputs depend on the model's proficiency and its alignment with the specific use case or input. For instance, ChatGPT has demonstrated its ability to generate well-structured essays on complex topics within seconds and even mimic the writing style of different authors. AI-generated art models like DALL-E can create unique and intriguing images, such as a rendition of a Madonna and child enjoying pizza. Other Generative AI models specialize in producing code snippets, videos, audio compositions, or simulating business scenarios.

It is important to note that the outputs of Generative AI models are not always accurate or appropriate. There can be instances where the generated content deviates from expectations or exhibits biases. For example, DALL-E might generate images that include unusual or nonsensical elements in response to certain requests. ChatGPT, like other language models, can struggle with tasks involving counting, basic algebra, or addressing inherent biases present in the training data. The outputs of Generative AI models are a result of the vast amount of training data they have processed, which helps them produce seemingly creative and varied outputs.

Additionally, these models often incorporate random elements, enabling them to generate different outputs for the same input request, adding to their lifelike nature.

So, Generative AI has revolutionized the field of artificial intelligence by enabling models to interpret and create content in a remarkable way. The ability to harness unlabeled data and the incorporation of human supervision have propelled generative models to new heights of performance and versatility. From generating text, images, and code to assisting with complex tasks and interactions, Generative AI holds immense potential for various applications in businesses and beyond. While it showcases remarkable capabilities, there are still limitations to consider, such as the challenge of source identification, bias assessment, and potential inaccuracies. However, advancements in prompt-engineering, parameter-efficient tuning, and reinforcement learning from human feedback continue to push the boundaries of what generative models can achieve. As this field continues to evolve, the future of Generative AI promises exciting possibilities and further advancements in creating intelligent and creative AI systems.

Collaboration of Generative AI and Hyperautomation

Generative AI and Hyperautomation can collaborate in several ways to enhance various aspects of business processes. Here are some keyways in which these technologies can collaborate:

- Content generation and automation
- Design and prototyping
- Data analysis and decision-making
- Workflow optimization and automation
- Process automation and optimization
- Adaptive learning and continuous improvement

Content generation and automation

Generative AI algorithms can be integrated into the Hyperautomation system to automate content generation processes. For example, in marketing and advertising, Generative AI can create personalized marketing materials, such as targeted ads, social media posts, or email campaigns. Hyperautomation can then automate the distribution of these generated content pieces across various channels, optimizing reach and engagement.

- **Personalized content creation:** Imagine a retail company that wants to create personalized product recommendations for its customers. Generative AI algorithms can be integrated into the Hyperautomation system to analyze customer data, purchase history, and browsing behavior. Based on this information, Generative AI algorithms can generate personalized product recommendations for each individual customer. Hyperautomation can then automate the process of creating and delivering these recommendations, ensuring that each customer receives tailored suggestions through various channels such as email, website pop-ups, or mobile notifications.

- **Multichannel distribution:** Consider a marketing agency that wants to promote a new product launch across multiple channels. Generative AI algorithms can be employed to automatically generate engaging social media posts, blog articles, and even video content related to the product. The Hyperautomation system can then take over the distribution process by scheduling and publishing the generated content on various platforms like Facebook, Instagram, Twitter, and YouTube. By automating the content distribution, the agency can efficiently reach a wide audience and ensure consistent messaging across all channels.

- **Optimization and A/B testing:** Suppose an e-commerce company wants to optimize its email marketing campaigns. Generative AI algorithms can be utilized to generate multiple variations of email subject lines, body content, and visual elements. The Hyperautomation system can automate the A/B testing process by sending different email variants to a subset of the target audience and analyzing the engagement metrics. Based on the results, the Generative AI algorithms can learn which content combinations perform best and generate improved versions for subsequent campaigns. Hyperautomation ensures that the winning email variant is sent to the remaining audience, maximizing the effectiveness of the campaign.

- **Efficiency and scalability:** Consider a global fashion retailer that wants to create customized product catalogs for different regions and customer segments. Generative AI algorithms can be integrated into the Hyperautomation system to generate personalized catalogs based on customer preferences, purchasing history, and regional trends. The Hyperautomation system can automate the process of compiling and distributing these catalogs, ensuring that customers receive tailored catalogs through digital channels or direct mail. By automating the content generation and distribution, the fashion retailer can efficiently scale its marketing efforts and deliver personalized experiences to a wide customer base.

Design and prototyping

Generative AI can automate design processes and generate alternative design options based on predefined parameters. Hyperautomation enables the integration of Generative AI models into design tools, allowing for rapid prototyping and iterative design cycles. This collaboration accelerates the design process, automates repetitive design tasks, and provides designers with a broader range of options to choose from., as explained:

- **Automating design processes**: Consider a furniture design company that wants to create new chair designs. Generative AI algorithms can be trained on existing chair designs, customer preferences, and ergonomic principles. The Hyperautomation system can integrate these Generative AI models into design software, allowing designers to input parameters such as desired dimensions, style preferences, or material constraints. The Generative AI algorithms can then automatically generate multiple chair design options that meet the specified criteria. Designers can review and iterate on these generated designs, accelerating the overall design process.

- **Rapid prototyping:** Imagine an automotive manufacturer developing a new car model. Generative AI algorithms can be used to generate 3D design concepts for various car components, such as the exterior body, dashboard layout, or seating arrangements. The Hyperautomation system can automate the translation of these digital designs into physical prototypes using additive manufacturing technologies like 3D printing. By automating the prototyping process, the automotive manufacturer can quickly produce physical prototypes for evaluation and testing, reducing the time and cost associated with traditional prototyping methods.

- **Enhanced creativity and innovation:** Consider an architectural firm tasked with designing a new office building. Generative AI algorithms can generate design options for building layouts, facade designs, or interior configurations based on project specifications and user preferences. By integrating Generative AI with Hyperautomation, the architectural firm can explore unconventional design concepts that go beyond traditional architectural conventions. Generative AI algorithms can inspire designers by generating unique and innovative design alternatives, fostering creativity in the architectural design process.

- **Optimization and customization:** Imagine a consumer electronics company designing a new smartphone. Generative AI algorithms can analyze user feedback, market research, and competitor analysis to generate design variations that align with user preferences. The Hyperautomation system can integrate these Generative AI insights into the design software, enabling designers to optimize and customize the smartphone design. For example, Generative AI algorithms can generate alternative options for the placement of buttons, camera modules, or the shape of the device. Designers can then choose the most suitable design options based on user preferences, ergonomics, and branding considerations.

Data analysis and decision-making

Generative AI algorithms can analyze large volumes of data, identify patterns, and generate insights. Hyperautomation facilitates the automation of data collection, preprocessing, and analysis tasks. By collaborating, Generative AI can enhance the predictive modelling capabilities of Hyperautomation, enabling organizations to make data-driven decisions with increased accuracy and speed. This collaboration streamlines the entire data analysis pipeline and empowers organizations to optimize resource allocation, forecast trends, and improve decision-making processes, as further explained:

- **Data collection and preprocessing**: Consider an e-commerce company that wants to analyze customer behavior to improve its product recommendations. Hyperautomation can automatically collect data from various sources, such as website interactions, purchase history, customer feedback, and social media. This data can then be pre-processed using automated techniques facilitated by Hyperautomation, such as data cleaning, normalization, or feature extraction. By automating the data collection and preprocessing steps, the company can efficiently prepare the data for analysis by Generative AI algorithms.

- **Pattern identification and insights generation**: Imagine a financial institution that wants to analyze customer transactions to detect fraudulent activities. Generative AI algorithms can be integrated into the Hyperautomation system to analyze transaction data, identify patterns, and generate insights. For example, the Generative AI algorithms can detect unusual spending patterns, identify potentially fraudulent transactions, and provide real-time alerts to the fraud detection team. This collaboration enables the financial institution to proactively combat fraud and improve security measures.

- **Predictive modelling and forecasting**: Consider a manufacturing company that wants to forecast demand for its products to optimize production and inventory management. Generative AI algorithms, in collaboration with Hyperautomation, can analyze historical sales data, market trends, economic indicators, and customer demographics. The Generative AI algorithms can build predictive models that accurately forecast future demand, allowing the company to adjust production levels, allocate resources efficiently, and minimize inventory costs. Hyperautomation can automate the application of these predictive models to new data, enabling real-time forecasting and informed decision-making.

- **Decision support and automation**: Consider a healthcare organization that wants to automate the process of diagnosing medical images, such as X-rays or CT scans. Generative AI algorithms can be integrated with Hyperautomation to analyze a large volume of medical image data, identify patterns, and provide diagnostic insights. For example, Generative AI algorithms can detect abnormalities or anomalies indicative of specific medical conditions, supporting healthcare professionals in making accurate diagnoses. Hyperautomation can automate the integration of these diagnostic insights into the healthcare organization's imaging systems, improving diagnostic accuracy, reducing turnaround time, and enhancing patient care.

Workflow optimization and automation

Generative AI algorithms can be integrated into Hyperautomation workflows to automate cognitive and creative tasks. For instance, in customer service, Generative AI-powered chatbots can be used in combination with Hyperautomation to provide personalized and interactive customer support. This collaboration improves response times, reduces manual intervention, and enhances customer experiences, as described:

- **Customer service:** Consider the customer service department of an e-commerce company. Generative AI algorithms can be integrated into the Hyperautomation system to power chatbots or virtual assistants. These chatbots can handle customer queries, provide personalized recommendations, and assist in troubleshooting common issues. The Generative AI algorithms enable chatbots to understand and respond to customer enquiries in a conversational manner, simulating human-like interactions. Hyperautomation manages the deployment of chatbots across various customer communication channels, automating customer support and reducing the need for manual intervention. This collaboration improves response times, enhances customer experiences, and frees up customer service agents to focus on more complex or specialized tasks.

- **Workflow coordination and task assignment:** Imagine a project management team that needs to coordinate and assign tasks to team members across different projects. Generative AI algorithms, integrated with

Hyperautomation, can analyze project requirements, team member skills, and task dependencies to generate optimal task assignments and project schedules. Generative AI algorithms can consider factors such as workload balancing, skill matching, and project deadlines. Hyperautomation manages the coordination and assignment of tasks, automating the process of task allocation, progress tracking, and deadline reminders. This collaboration optimizes workflow coordination, improves task allocation efficiency, and enhances overall project management.

- **Creative content generation:** Consider a marketing department that needs to create engaging content for social media platforms. Generative AI algorithms, integrated with Hyperautomation, can automatically generate social media posts, including captions, hashtags, and visuals, based on predefined brand guidelines and target audience preferences. The Generative AI algorithms can analyze trending topics, customer sentiment, or previous successful campaigns to generate compelling content. Hyperautomation manages the scheduling and distribution of these generated social media posts, automating the content creation process and optimizing engagement. This collaboration enables the marketing team to streamline content generation, enhance brand presence, and drive customer engagement.

Process automation and optimization

Generative AI can assist Hyperautomation in automating complex business processes. For instance, in finance, Generative AI algorithms can analyze financial data, automate financial reporting, or even generate financial models for Hyperautomation systems to act upon. This collaboration streamlines financial processes, reduces errors, and enables organizations to achieve greater efficiency and accuracy, as described:

- **Financial reporting and analysis:** Consider a finance department that needs to generate periodic financial reports, such as balance sheets, income statements, or cash flow statements. Generative AI algorithms can be integrated into the Hyperautomation system to analyze financial data, identify patterns, and automate the generation of these reports. The Generative AI algorithms can extract relevant information from financial databases, perform calculations, and generate accurate and standardized financial reports. Hyperautomation manages the scheduling and distribution of these reports, automating the entire financial reporting process. This collaboration reduces manual effort, eliminates errors, and ensures timely and consistent financial reporting.

- **Fraud detection and risk management:** Imagine a banking institution that wants to automate the detection of fraudulent transactions and manage risks. Generative AI algorithms can analyze transaction data, customer behavior, and historical fraud patterns to identify suspicious activities. Generative AI algorithms can learn from past cases of fraud and proactively detect potential fraudulent transactions in real-time. Hyperautomation can integrate these Generative AI models into the transaction processing system, automating the detection, and alerting processes. This collaboration enhances fraud detection capabilities, reduces financial losses, and strengthens risk management practices.

- **Compliance and regulatory processes:** Consider a healthcare organization that needs to comply with various regulatory requirements, such as patient privacy regulations or medical coding standards. Generative AI algorithms can analyze compliance guidelines, organizational policies, and patient data to ensure adherence to regulations. The Generative AI algorithms can automate tasks such as data anonymization, consent management, or coding accuracy checks. Hyperautomation manages the integration of these Generative AI models into the organization's compliance processes, automating compliance checks and ensuring regulatory compliance. This collaboration streamlines compliance processes, reduces manual errors, and mitigates compliance risks.

- **Supply chain management:** Imagine a manufacturing company that wants to optimize its supply chain processes, from procurement to distribution. Generative AI algorithms can analyze historical demand data, supplier performance, inventory levels, and external factors such as market trends or transportation costs. The Generative AI algorithms can optimize supply chain parameters, such as order quantities, reorder points, or production schedules, to minimize costs and maximize efficiency. Hyperautomation can automate the execution of these optimized supply chain plans, managing procurement, inventory management, and logistics processes. This collaboration improves supply chain visibility, reduces inventory carrying costs, and enhances overall supply chain performance.

Adaptive learning and continuous improvement

Generative AI models can continuously learn and improve over time by leveraging the feedback and data from Hyperautomation systems. By integrating Generative AI into the Hyperautomation framework, organizations can create adaptive systems that optimize processes based on real-time data, user feedback, and changing business requirements. This collaboration fosters continuous improvement, ensuring that the generated outputs and automated processes remain up-to-date and aligned with evolving needs, as explained:

- **Customer experience enhancement**: Consider an e-commerce company that uses Generative AI algorithms integrated with Hyperautomation to personalize the customer experience. The Generative AI algorithms analyze customer behavior, preferences, and historical purchase data to generate personalized product recommendations. Hyperautomation manages the delivery of these recommendations through various channels such as email, website recommendations, or chatbots. As customers interact with the recommendations, their feedback and purchase behavior are collected and used to further refine the Generative AI models. This collaboration allows the system to adapt to individual customer preferences over time, continuously improving the accuracy and relevance of the recommendations, and enhancing the overall customer experience.

- **Dynamic pricing and revenue management**: Consider a travel agency that employs Generative AI algorithms and Hyperautomation to optimize pricing and revenue management. The Generative AI algorithms analyze historical booking data, market trends, competitor pricing, and customer demand patterns to generate dynamic pricing recommendations. Hyperautomation manages the pricing adjustments across different channels and markets, automatically updating prices based on the recommendations. As customers make bookings and the system collects data on pricing effectiveness and customer behavior, the Generative AI algorithms learn and refine their pricing strategies. This collaboration enables the system to adapt pricing in response to changing market conditions, optimize revenue, and improve profitability.

- **IT operations and service management**: Imagine an IT service provider that utilizes Generative AI algorithms and Hyperautomation to optimize IT operations and service management. The Generative AI algorithms analyze system logs, network performance data, and historical incident records to identify potential issues, predict failures, and recommend preventive measures. Hyperautomation manages the implementation of these recommendations, automatically triggering system maintenance, proactive repairs, or resource reallocation. As the system operates and incidents occur, data on system performance, response times, and incident resolution are collected and used to improve the Generative AI models. This collaboration enables the system to continuously learn from past incidents, adapt to changing IT environments, and enhance service reliability.

- **Predictive maintenance in manufacturing**: Consider a manufacturing company that leverages Generative AI algorithms and Hyperautomation to optimize equipment maintenance. The Generative AI algorithms analyze real-time sensor data, equipment performance metrics, and historical maintenance records to predict equipment failures and recommend maintenance actions. Hyperautomation manages the scheduling and execution of maintenance tasks based on the recommendations. As maintenance tasks are performed, data on equipment performance, maintenance effectiveness, and downtime are collected and used to refine the Generative AI models. This collaboration allows the system to continuously improve its predictive maintenance capabilities, reduce unplanned downtime, and optimize maintenance schedules.

Challenges and considerations

The collaboration of Generative AI and Hyperautomation brings about transformative benefits, but it also presents challenges and ethical considerations that need to be carefully addressed. Here are some of the key challenges and considerations:

- **Bias in AI models**: Generative AI models are trained on large datasets, and if those datasets contain biased or discriminatory information, the AI models can inherit those biases. This can result in unfair or discriminatory outcomes, such as biased decision-making or perpetuation of social inequalities. It is crucial to ensure that the training data is diverse, representative, and carefully curated to mitigate biases. Ongoing monitoring, evaluation, and bias correction techniques should be employed to reduce and eliminate biases in the AI models.

- **Data privacy and security**: Generative AI and Hyperautomation rely on vast amounts of data, often including personal and sensitive information. Organizations must prioritize data privacy and security to protect individuals' privacy rights and prevent unauthorized access or misuse of data. Strict data governance practices, including anonymization and encryption techniques, should be implemented. Compliance with relevant data protection regulations, such as the **General Data Protection Regulation (GDPR)**, is essential to safeguard individuals' data privacy.

- **Job displacement and workforce transition**: Automation through Generative AI and Hyperautomation may lead to job displacement or changes in job roles. While these technologies can streamline processes and enhance productivity, they can also impact employment in specific sectors. Organizations should consider workforce transition plans, reskilling initiatives, and efforts to create new job opportunities. It is crucial to balance automation and human labor, ensuring that workers are equipped with the skills required to collaborate effectively with technology.

- **Responsible AI development**: Developing and deploying Generative AI and Hyperautomation systems require a strong commitment to responsible AI development. This includes incorporating principles of fairness, transparency, accountability, and explainability into the AI models and automation processes. Organizations should have clear guidelines and policies in place to address ethical considerations, mitigate biases, and ensure compliance with legal and regulatory requirements. Transparency in AI decision-making and the ability to explain how decisions are made is crucial for building trust and understanding.

- **Human oversight and ethical decision-making**: Human oversight is essential to ensure ethical and fair outcomes in the collaboration of Generative AI and Hyperautomation. Human experts should be involved in the design, development, and deployment of these systems to provide critical judgment, assess the impact of decisions, and intervene when necessary. Human oversight is crucial in validating and monitoring the outputs of Generative AI models, ensuring they align with ethical standards and addressing any unintended consequences or errors.

- **Social and economic implications**: The widespread adoption of Generative AI and Hyperautomation can have broader social and economic implications. It may exacerbate existing inequalities if not carefully managed. Organizations and policymakers need to consider the broader impact of these technologies on society, such as accessibility, affordability, and equity. Collaboration between various stakeholders, including government bodies, industry experts, and civil society, is necessary to address these implications and ensure that the benefits of AI and automation are equitably distributed.

Future considerations

Let us now go over some future considerations:

- **Enhanced creativity and innovation**: As Generative AI algorithms continue to evolve; they will become more sophisticated in their ability to generate creative and innovative outputs. The integration of Generative AI with Hyperautomation will enable organizations to automate cognitive tasks, such as ideation, design, and content creation, with a higher degree of creativity. This will lead to the development of new products, services, and solutions that were previously unimaginable, driving innovation across industries.

- **Augmented decision-making**: Generative AI algorithms will become increasingly adept at analyzing complex datasets, identifying patterns, and generating insights. When integrated with Hyperautomation, these algorithms will provide enhanced decision-making support, enabling organizations to make more accurate and data-driven decisions in real-time. This will empower businesses to optimize operations, improve efficiency, and capitalize on emerging opportunities.

- **Transformation of job roles**: The collaboration between Generative AI and Hyperautomation will reshape job roles across various industries. While some repetitive and manual tasks may be automated, new roles will emerge that require human oversight, creativity, and critical thinking skills. Job roles will evolve to involve managing and collaborating with AI systems, interpreting, and validating outputs, and leveraging AI capabilities to drive innovation and value creation.

- **Upskilling and reskilling**: The integration of Generative AI and Hyperautomation will require a workforce that possesses the skills to collaborate effectively with these technologies. Organizations and educational institutions will need to focus on upskilling and reskilling initiatives to equip individuals with the necessary knowledge and abilities. This will involve training in data analysis, AI interpretation, ethics, and human-machine collaboration, fostering a workforce that can leverage the capabilities of AI to augment their own expertise.

- **Industry-specific applications**: Different industries will harness the collaboration of Generative AI and Hyperautomation in unique ways. For example, in healthcare, Generative AI can assist in diagnosing diseases and generating personalized treatment plans, while Hyperautomation can automate administrative tasks and streamline patient data management. In finance, Generative AI can analyze market data and generate investment strategies, while Hyperautomation can automate trading processes and risk management. The potential for industry-specific applications is vast and will continue to evolve as the technologies advance.

- **Ethical and regulatory considerations**: As the integration of Generative AI and Hyperautomation becomes more prevalent, there will be an increased focus on ethical and regulatory considerations. Governments and organizations will need to establish frameworks and guidelines to ensure the responsible and ethical use of these technologies. This includes addressing issues of bias, data privacy, transparency, and accountability to safeguard against potential risks and ensure the equitable and fair deployment of AI and automation.

Use case of Generative AI with Hyperautomation

Let us now go over a use case of Generative AI with Hyperautomation:

Problem statement

A Contact Center engages with many customers having a multitude of issues. These issues need to be resolved with maximum efficiency and minimum downtime. The entire process is intricate and requires repetitive tasks to be completed. The goal of this document is to address this problem and outline the solution approach to it that uses Generative AI alongside Hyperautomation framework to enhance productivity, save cost, and ultimately Improve customer experience.

Generative AI with Hyperautomation

Generative AI has propelled the capabilities of Hyperautomation to new horizons. With Generative AI, Hyperautomation is delivering better customer experience for various enterprises, enhancing marketing operations for enterprises, improving accuracy, and eliminating manual errors for banking sectors, and many more.

Why use Generative AI with Hyperautomation

Using Generative AI with Hyperautomation can provide a several advantages, including:

- **Enhanced efficiency:** Automating the generation of difficult and repetitive jobs using Generative AI can save time and effort. It can streamline operations and boost overall efficiency when combined with Hyperautomation, which is focused on automating end-to-end business processes.

- **Generating original and creative content:** Generative AI can produce unique and creative content, including text, photos, videos, and music. Businesses may speed up the production and personalization of content at scale by utilizing Hyperautomation to automate the processes involved in content development.

- **Personalization:** Hyperautomation and Generative AI work together to provide customized customer experiences. To help businesses produce specialized recommendations, offers, and adverts, it can analyze enormous volumes of data to determine individual preferences, behavioral trends, and purchase histories.

- **Support for decision-making:** Generative AI can help with decision-making by simulating various scenarios and producing recommendations. These AI-generated insights can be incorporated into company operations through Hyperautomation, providing decision-makers with useful data for improved strategic planning and problem-solving.

- **Improved customer service:** Better customer service is possible thanks to Generative AI, which enables companies to automate customer interactions through chatbots or virtual assistants that respond instantly and individually to questions from clients and support requests. By integrating chatbot systems with backend operations, Hyperautomation further optimizes this process and makes it possible to provide seamless customer service.

- **Data synthesis and analysis:** Generative AI methods, including GANs, may analyze and combine data to produce fresh insights and patterns. By automating the pipelines for data gathering, processing, and analysis, Hyperautomation enables quicker and more accurate decision-making based on real-time data.

- **Risk reduction:** Hyperautomation can automate procedures for risk assessment and prediction when paired with Generative AI. Hyperautomation may include these risk models into risk management systems after these models have been created using AI algorithms that analyze historical data. This enables proactive risk reduction techniques.

- **Streamlined operations:** Automating repetitive operations like data entry, data processing, report production, and administrative workflows is possible with Generative AI and Hyperautomation. Businesses can decrease errors, boost efficiency, and devote more human resources to activities that create value by automating these procedures.

Solution approach for using Generative AI with Hyperautomation for Contact centers

Both Hyperautomation and Generative AI are capturing the market by storm. With enterprises spending huge sums of money, resources, time, and expertise to develop solutions using Generative AI and Hyperautomation that can help solve their business problems. This trend is uniform across several domains including banking sector, marketing, contact centers, and so on.

The strategic application of Generative AI's many technologies, including machine learning, natural language processing and computer vision combined with the power of Hyperautomation can drive meaningful results for enterprises, from enhancing employee and customer experiences to improving back-office operations and business operations.

Both Generative AI and Hyperautomation are transforming the way contact centers work. Traditionally contact centers are associated with long wait times and inefficient solutions to the callers, with Generative AI and Hyperautomation contact centers can deliver efficient and improved responses to the queries and grievances of their callers.

The decision-making capabilities of algorithms that are used in Hyperautomation will be improved with the application of Generative AI. For instance, Generative AI can be used to develop predictive models, which can then assist bots in making more educated decisions based on the patterns and trends found in data. This in turn can make customer experience better within contact centers by providing intelligent recommendations, spot query resolutions with minimal downtime and maximum accuracy enhancing the capabilities of the contact center. *Figure 11.1* shows the flow of the contact center solution:

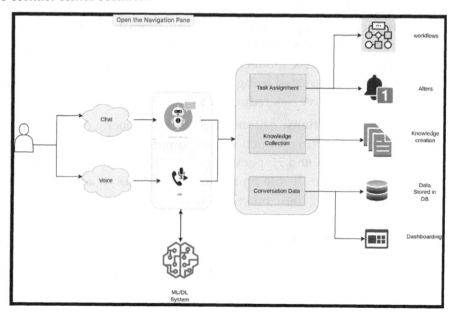

Figure 11.1: Flow of the contact center solution

Prerequisites

The prerequisites are as follows:

- **Clearly defined objectives:** Clearly define the objectives and goals of the Hyperautomation project. Identify the specific processes, tasks, or areas where Generative AI can bring value and automate effectively. This helps set the direction for the project and aligns stakeholders on the expected outcomes.

- **Outline AI models and Hyperautomation tools:** It is imperative to explore and experiment with different Generative AI models and find out which one suits best with the business requirements. The same applies to the Hyperautomation framework which will form the basis of automation in the business.

- **Data availability and quality:** Generative AI models require substantial amounts of data to learn and generate accurate outputs. Ensure that the required data is available and accessible for training the Generative AI models. Additionally, pay attention to data quality, ensuring it is reliable, representative, and properly labelled to achieve desired results.

- **Data security and privacy:** Consider the security and privacy implications of the data used in the project. Implement robust data security measures, adhere to data protection regulations, and ensure proper anonymization or pseudonymization techniques are applied when handling sensitive or personally identifiable information.

- **Expertise in AI and automation:** Acquire the necessary expertise in Generative AI and Hyperautomation techniques. This may involve hiring or upskilling team members with knowledge and experience in AI, machine learning, deep learning, and automation technologies. Having a team that understands the nuances and challenges of these technologies is critical for successful implementation.

- **Infrastructure and tools:** Evaluate and establish the required infrastructure and tools to support the Generative AI and Hyperautomation project. This may include powerful computing resources, storage capacity, and specialized software frameworks or libraries for training and deploying Generative AI models. Consider cloud-based solutions or dedicated hardware if necessary.

- **Stakeholder alignment:** Ensure alignment and involvement of key stakeholders across the organization. This includes business leaders, IT departments, legal and compliance teams, and end-users who will be impacted by the automation. Engage stakeholders early in the process to gather requirements, address concerns, and secure necessary support.

- **Scalability and future expansion:** Consider the scalability of the Hyperautomation solution and plan for future expansion. Anticipate potential growth in data volume, user demand, and complexity of automation tasks. Design the system with scalability in mind to accommodate future requirements and advancements in Generative AI technologies.

- **Continuous improvement and evaluation:** Establish mechanisms for continuous improvement and evaluation of the Hyperautomation project. Monitor performance, gather user feedback, and analyze outcomes to identify areas for enhancement and optimization. Iteratively refine the Generative AI models, automation workflows, and user experience based on insights gained from ongoing evaluation.

What a Generative AI and Hyperautomation are helping contact centers

Generation with collaboration with Hyperautomation can deliver better customer experience along with enhanced business process. Some key features this new technology provides are:

- **Chatbots:** Based on their interactions with customers, organizations may utilize Generative AI to give their chatbots additional features. As a result, the chatbots would eventually become more efficient and tailored, enhancing the user experience. The chatbots can then be automated, enabling them to reply to customer enquiries without requiring human intervention.

- **Empowering citizen developers:** Generative AI empowers citizen developers by allowing them to produce code more quickly and explore a range of choices, giving them a head start on the development of their applications. Additionally, it can make recommendations for streamlining and refining already-written code, which speeds up the development process.

- **Designing:** A company may utilize Generative AI to create new product designs to sell using client preferences and feedback. The designs can then be automated and incorporated into the manufacturing process, which will ultimately lead to a more productive and individualized production method.

- **Processing of images and videos:** The use of Generative AI enables the automatic processing and analysis of visual data, such as still photos and moving films, as well as the creation of new content based on that data. This can be useful in fields like advertising and entertainment where producing aesthetically appealing content is crucial, particularly for exhibited-on screens.

- **Marketing:** The application of Generative AI enables the development of individualized marketing plans for specific clients that are based on those clients' historical preferences and behaviors. This will enable the marketing process to be automated and the campaigns to be integrated into it, leading to marketing that is well-targeted.

- **AI-based task mining:** Organizations use tens of thousands of different procedures. They differ in terms of how long they take to complete, how complex they are, the systems they require, how crucial they are to customers and the business, how error-prone they are, and how much they change over time. Contact centers can fully automate job mining, data collection, and the identification of repetitive processes, app usage patterns, and bottlenecks with the help of Generative AI-based analytics paired with Hyperautomation capacity.

- **OCR:** Targeted applications of AI in Hyperautomation can give computers the ability to read and comprehend handwritten documents with accuracy. With Hyperautomation, the objective is to provide the best possible service to the client, provide employees with the support they require to meet their KPIs, and benefit the business in terms of both revenue and efficiency.

Contact centers using Generative AI with Hyperautomation

Contact Centers needs to deal with lots of calls inbound and outbound with limited human enabled workforce. Traditionally, this has created process bottlenecks, customers waiting for several minutes to resolve issues that require no human interventions, tedious repetitive tasks that can jam the business process, increased human error, and many more. Contact centers are using Generative AI and Hyperautomation to mitigate issues like these and many more, propelling the industry beyond traditional capabilities. Some of these capabilities achieved by this are:

- **Streamlines post-contact processing:** post-contact processing refers to all the activities that agents carry out after a customer encounter has concluded. The labelling of tickets, summarizing the contact, and sending follow-up emails are some of these duties. To automate more of these processes and shorten handling times, Contact Centers plan to deploy Hyperautomation and Generative AI models. This results in the solution automatically summarizing and categorizing customer chats.

- **Auto-generates knowledge articles:** Using generative models to analyze customer chat transcripts is one application case. Then it creates knowledge articles automatically for review. Then, a knowledgeable agent can assess, modify, and publish these within the knowledge base. Contact centers can thereby improve knowledge management procedures. In the meantime, these knowledge articles can be proactively served up during real-time client discussions by the agent-assist tools powered by Hyperautomation when appropriate.

- **Identifies opportunities and performs automation:** Generative AI models may group consumer conversations based on numerous characteristics, such as intent. It then scans these groups for patterns to identify opportunities for process automation and improvement. Contact centers can estimate the potential cost savings in resolving the issue by noting how frequently these opportunities come up in conversations.

- **Simplifies bot-building:** Bot development is made easier by Generative AI and Hyperautomation, which may be used to integrate chatbot technology into the Contact Centre AI Platform. With this, customer service centers may create a bot quickly. First, it must be fed content from the Contact Centre platform, such as FAQs, product manuals, and website information. Natural Language Processing jobs can be automated using Hyperautomation and generative artificial intelligence models, and a virtual agent can be created automatically that the company can test, tweak, and deploy.

- **Expands the application of conversational AI:** Generative AI and Hyperautomation can enhance the contact center platform in two important ways: they can respond to more inquiries and can recognize when a customer's intent changes. The solution first sorts through materials that are tailored to the business, such as the corporate website, product manuals, and knowledge articles. Conversational AI can therefore address customer queries that the company has not specifically designed a bot to address by highlighting pertinent findings and presenting them to the customer. The dialogue is brought back on course and containment rates are improved by the second feature, which recognizes when a customer's intent changes midway through an encounter.

- **Draws insights from consumer input:** Hyperautomation tolls may compile data from several sources of consumer input, remove tendencies, and then transform the data into clear, structured language. Transcripts from call centers, internet reviews, and polls are a few examples of these sources. Finally, a trends overview can be generated using Generative AI in a matter of minutes. The Smart Summary Generator can therefore be used by contact centers to keep track of new problems.

- **Alerts supervisors of agent problems:** With a collection AI models integrated into the contact center platform, it aims to provide insight to managers of contact centers and uses Generative AI to translate that information into action. Real-time customer satisfaction monitoring using Generative AI can produce responses, and when Hyperautomation alerts the supervisor, they can intervene to improve the experience. Additionally, it might notify the manager if an agent engages in a specific behavior and track complaints as they happen. The latter use case can help with reporting efforts for contact centers.

Considerations for implementing Generative AI with Hyperautomation

Implementing Generative AI with Hyperautomation requires careful consideration of several technical factors, such as:

- **Data management:** Training data for Generative AI models is frequently very huge. For producing accurate and dependable outputs, it is essential to ensure data quality, dependability, and relevance. For an implementation to be effective, it is crucial to execute sound data management procedures, including data collecting, cleaning, labelling, and storage.

- **Model selection and training:** It is crucial to pick the best Generative AI model architecture and training approach. Different models, such GANs, VAEs, or popular models like GPT or any other transformer-based model, have distinctive qualities and are appropriate for particular use cases. To get the desired performance, the models must be trained properly, which includes data pretreatment, hyperparameter adjustment, and regularization approaches.

- **Performance and scalability:** Generative AI models can be computationally demanding, particularly when working with huge datasets or challenging problems. The system's scalability and performance requirements, including its hardware setup, parallel processing capabilities, and optimization strategies, should be considered. It can be necessary to use distributed computing or cloud-based technologies to effectively manage the computational load.

- **Integration with existing systems:** Integrating Generative AI models into current business workflows and systems is a key component of Hyperautomation. Think about the needs for integration and compatibility with the IT infrastructure of the organization, including APIs, data formats, and security standards. Collaboration between Generative AI models and other elements of the automation ecosystem runs well due to seamless interaction.

- **Legal and ethical compliance:** Systems using Generative AI raise ethical issues such potential biases, data privacy, and intellectual property rights. It is essential to set precise rules and regulations for the ethical usage of

Generative AI. It should also guarantee compliance with **legal** and regulatory frameworks, such as data protection laws and industry-specific rules.

- **Interpretability and explainability of the model:** Generative AI models can be intricate and opaque, making it difficult to comprehend how they produce results. Consider the models' interpretability and explicability, especially in delicate areas or when making important choices. Interpretability can be improved by using methods like attention mechanisms, model distillation, or rule-based post-processing.

- **Continuous monitoring and maintenance:** To ensure the performance and dependability of Generative AI models over time, continuous monitoring and maintenance are required. It is crucial to keep an eye on the model's outputs, performance indicators, and feedback loops to quickly identify and address problems. As new data becomes available or the business context changes, regular retraining or fine-tuning may be necessary.

- **Security and privacy:** Generative AI systems must be designed with security and privacy considerations in mind. To safeguard sensitive data and stop unauthorized access, strong security measures including access limits, encryption, and secure data transmission should be put in place. It is important to handle privacy issues relating to data handling, anonymization, and compliance with data protection laws.

These technical factors help mitigate potential risks and problems while ensuring the effective deployment and operation of Generative AI with Hyperautomation systems. A thorough and successful implementation strategy requires cooperation between domain experts, data scientists, IT specialists, and legal teams.

Performance and scalability in using Generative AI with Hyperautomation

When incorporating Generative AI and Hyperautomation into contact centers and customer experience, scalability and performance are crucial factors to consider. It is crucial to make sure that both Generative AI and Hyperautomation systems can efficiently scale to meet user needs while retaining top performance as these experiences become more complex and dynamic.

One method for scaling Generative AI and Hyperautomation involves distributed computing. This method divides tasks into more manageable chunks that can be processed simultaneously across several nodes. Although this method can improve performance and reduce latency, it requires exact coordination and communication between nodes to ensure a reliable result. Use distributed computing frameworks when handling computationally demanding jobs or extensive automation. Spread the workload over several computers or clusters to boost processing power and decrease delay.

Utilizing cloud computing services, which provide nearly infinite resources that can be flexibly allocated to react to shifting demands, is another strategy. In terms of performance and scalability, this approach has a lot to offer. To avoid wasting money and maintain maximum effectiveness, it also necessitates careful resource management.

In Generative AI, aspects including algorithmic effectiveness, data pre-processing, and network design must be considered to improve performance and reduce latency for consumer interactions. Equally important is the ongoing monitoring and analysis of performance indicators to identify potential bottlenecks and areas for improvement.

The following are some best practices for Generative AI performance optimization and latency reduction:

- Investing in efficient algorithms and data pre-processing techniques.
- Modifying hyperparameters and network architecture.
- Using batch processing and caching to reduce duplicate computations.
- Monitoring and evaluating performance indicators to find and address potential issues.
- Utilizing cloud computing services to use dynamic resource allocation.

Optimizing Hyperautomation performance and minimizing latency is crucial to ensure efficient and responsive automation processes. Here are some best practices to achieve these goals:

- Automation workflows should be carefully designed to cut down on extra stages and expedite procedures. Decide which dependencies, redundant tasks, and bottlenecks could cause delays. Reduce latency and simplify and improve the process structure to ensure efficient operation.
- Determine which automation activities are most important, urgent, and dependent. High-priority projects should be given the proper resources and scheduling procedures to be finished as soon as possible. By doing this, latency for crucial processes is reduced.
- Use parallel processing and multithreading strategies to carry out several automation tasks at once. By utilizing the processing power of contemporary

hardware designs, this can greatly increase performance and decrease latency.

- Use caching techniques to store and reuse frequently accessed data or interim outcomes. Caching lowers latency and boosts overall performance by avoiding duplicate computations or data retrieval. Memorization, which includes saving the outcomes of pricey function calls for later use, might be especially helpful in some automated circumstances.

- To ensure effective use of hardware and software resources, optimize resource allocation. Watch how the system is using its CPU, memory, disk, and network resources, and change the allocation as necessary. By doing this, resource contention is avoided, and automated operations are carried out without interruption.

- To reduce latency, data handling must be efficient. Utilize strategies like data compression, indexing, and partitioning to cut down on processing and transmission costs. For better performance, use data structures and algorithms that provide quick access and retrieval times.

- Implement monitoring tools to keep an eye on the automation processes' performance in real time. Keep an eye on important data like resource usage, latency, and execution time. Analyze performance data to find bottlenecks, improve crucial areas, and make decisions that will increase performance.

- To evaluate the Hyperautomation system's effectiveness and reactivity, do periodical performance testing. To assess the behavior of the system under various circumstances, identify performance constraints and carry out load and stress testing. Utilize the outcomes to maximize performance by adjusting the system's settings.

- The improvement of Hyperautomation performance is a continuous process. To find areas for improvement, collect user insights, monitor system performance, and continuously gather feedback. To improve automation effectiveness, decrease latency, and solve new difficulties, use iterative refining strategies.

Businesses should prioritize scalability and performance when incorporating Generative AI and Hyperautomation into client interactions. Distributed or cloud computing can be used to do this, but careful resource management and coordination are necessary. Performance can be increased, and latency reduced through optimizing algorithmic efficiency, data pre-processing, network architecture, and monitoring and evaluating performance indicators. Businesses may deliver excellent digital experiences that meet customer expectations, promote satisfaction, and promote growth by following these best practices.

Collaboration between humans and machines

While Generative AI and Hyperautomation might boost productivity and efficiency, it is crucial to keep in mind that people are still essential to contact centers and the customer experience. As automation is employed to supplement human capabilities and enhance overall performance, it is projected that human-machine collaboration will expand.

This collaboration of Generative AI and Hyperautomation does not eliminate the need for human agents behind the desks manning the phone in a contact center, it surely empowers them with intelligent automation and generation of data and knowledge. This empowers human agents to help customers more efficiently. They also make human agents more productive by eliminating repetitive tasks and streamlining the process.

Business outcome of using Generative AI with Hyperautomation

Let us now go over the various business outcomes of using Generative AI with Hyperautomation:

- Generative AI with Hyperautomation increases efficiency and productivity.
- It improves the customer experience through personalized content and interactions.
- Decision-making is enhanced with data-driven insights and support.
- Organizations can achieve cost savings and optimize resource allocation.
- Scalability and agility are facilitated, enabling quick adaptation to changing demands.
- Compliance and risk mitigation efforts are strengthened.
- Generative AI with Hyperautomation provides a competitive advantage.
- Innovation and creativity are fostered through automated generation of new ideas and designs.

Conclusion

In this chapter, we were introduced to Generative AI, its types, as well as its benefits and limitations. Then we delved into the aspects of supervised learning, developing Generative AI models and the output produced by the model. We also discussed the collaboration of Generative AI and Hyperautomation, as well as the challenges and considerations for the same. We wrapped up the chapter by going over the use cases of Generative AI with Hyperautomation, considerations for implementing Generative AI with Hyperautomation and the business outcome of using Generative Ai with Hyperautomation.

Key facts

- In 2014, the release of **Generative Adversarial Networks (GAN)**, a machine learning algorithm, enabled manufacturers' artificial intelligence applications to generate realistic images, video and audio of real people.

- While Generative AI has been around since the 1960s in the form of chatbots, significant advancements occurred in 2014 with the introduction of GANs, which allowed for the creation of realistic images, videos, and audio.

- Generative AI is focused on generating new content, such as chat responses, designs, synthetic data, or deepfakes. It utilizes techniques like transformers, GANs, and **Variational Autoencoders (VAE)**.

- **Diffusion models**, also known as **Denoising Diffusion Probabilistic Models (DDPM)**, utilize a two-step process during training involving forward diffusion and reverse diffusion. This process involves gradually adding random noise to training data and then reversing the noise to reconstruct the data samples.

- Generative AI algorithms can be integrated into the Hyperautomation system to automate content generation processes. For example, in marketing and advertising, Generative AI can create personalized marketing materials, such as targeted ads, social media posts, or email campaigns.

Key terms

- Generative AI.
- **Generative Adversarial Networks (GAN)**.
- **Variational autoencoders (VAEs)**.
- **Large Language Models (LLMs)**.
- **Convolutional Neural Networks (CNNs)**.
- **Search Engine Optimization (SEO)**.
- Diffusion models.
- Transformer networks
- ChatGPT

- DALL-E
- Personalized content creation
- Multichannel distribution.
- Optimization and A/B testing

Questions

1. What is Generative AI?
2. How can collaboration of Generative AI help Hyperautomation?
3. Explain the difference between Generative AI and traditional AI.
4. What are the different types of Generative AI Models?
5. What are the prime benefits of Generative AI?
6. What are the limitations of Generative AI?

Join our book's Discord space

Join the book's Discord Workspace for Latest updates, Offers, Tech happenings around the world, New Release and Sessions with the Authors:

https://discord.bpbonline.com

Index

Made in United States
Troutdale, OR
01/25/2024

17160582R00184